AUSTRALIAN ARCHITECTURE NOW

DAVINA JACKSON CHRIS JOHNSON

AUSTRALIAN ARCHITECTURE NOW

With 494 illustrations, 392 in colour

Thames & Hudson

ACKNOWLEDGMENTS

Design Carl Martin
Design Production: Danielle Powell,
Michelina Evangelista

PAGE 2 Pee Wees at the Point, Darwin, by
Troppo, 1998. Photo Patrick Bingham-Hall.
PAGE 6 Bay of Fires Lodge, Mt William
National Park, Tasmania, by Ken Latona,
1999. Photo Simon Kenny.
PAGES 14–15, 38–39, 150–51
Photo images Arunas.

First published in the United Kingdom
in 2000 by Thames & Hudson Ltd,
181A High Holborn, London WC1V 7QX

www.thamesandhudson.com

British Library Cataloguing-in-Publication Data
A catalogue record for this book is available
from the British Library

ISBN 0-500-28388-5

Printed and bound in China by
Hong Kong Graphics & Printing Ltd

Australian Architecture Now could not have been produced without
the generosity of the photographers whose names are credited to the
images printed. We're grateful for their support in giving us rights to
publish their interpretations of the architecture documented here.

We're also indebted to the architects and designers who have trusted
us to explain their works in a context of local and international cultural
tensions and uncertainty about the profession's future.

Many scholarly friends, teachers and acquaintances have influenced
our understandings of contemporary Australian architecture. Our present
perceptions of the broad scene come from Peter Kohane, Ray Younis,
Leon van Schaik, Peter Droege, James Weirick, Philip Goad, Peter
Emmett, Michael Bogle, Paul Carter, Michael Bounds, Lawrence and
Andrea Nield, Alan and Anna Bowen-James, Janet Laurence, Ivan
Rijavec, Bill Mitchell, Philippe Robert, Neville Quarry, Ken Maher, Peter
Zellner and Paul-Alan Johnson.

Certain friends and colleagues have particularly helped us to produce
this book: Ian Close and Sue Harris, Lindsay, Kerry, Brendan, Alistair
and Mitchell Clare, Deborah Burdett, Stephen Varady, Alex Mazin, Cathy
Franko, John Gollings, Sue Shanahan, Samantha Biggs, Patrick and
Katrina Bingham-Hall, Simon Blackall, Nevill Drury and Anna Voigt, Ilsa
Konrads, Mick Bell, Duncan Gibbs, Dawn Leyland, Chris Hinge, David
Skillender and Cec Griffin of Graphic Skills, Caroline Colton and Lisa
Johnson of Caroline Colton & Associates, and Penny Bowring and Ray
Parslow of Emery Vincent Associates.

At Thames & Hudson, this book has been shepherded by a superior
team: Lucas Dietrich, Philip Watson, Tim Evans, Igor Astrologo and
Johanna Neurath in London, and Peter Shaw and Michelle Brasington
in Melbourne.

We are also grateful to our families, especially Abbey, Matilda and
Eliza Johnson, and Hugo, Anita and Jeremy Jackson, for their support.

DEDICATED TO JANE, PETER, LIZ AND THE MEMORY OF GAINOR.

CONTENTS

INTRODUCTION

This book is intended to clarify the key political dynamics, aesthetic approaches and built achievements of Australian architecture during the last six years of the twentieth century. This was the most productive construction boom (of comparable length) in the nation's history.

From 1994 to 1999, Sydney and Melbourne's cores literally turned around to face previously ignored waterfronts with major facilities for commerce and leisure. Smaller cities and towns linked into the continent's expanding tourist circuit by building distinctive visitor centres to display their idiosyncracies and histories. There also has been exceptional activity in building iconic university facilities and 'designer' housing.

Australian Architecture Now is an unusual history book, because it scans across a diverse and momentary scene instead of recording a longer continuum of crucial achievements. Our format provides two essays, twenty-two case studies of outstanding public and domestic projects (Exemplars) and many chapters which compare buildings according to similarities of either genre (Types) or style (Tendencies).

Our Tendencies and Types scans may be controversial. As British writer Charles Jencks discovered after publication of his themes of postmodernism, most architects hate to have their creativity and professional prospects limited by categorisation. Australians often claim that their buildings 'have no style'. But all humans are unique organisms – and their productions inescapably express their minds and circumstances.

Artistic architects increasingly are being marketed as 'brand-name' stylists of prestige monuments and housing. Architecture can't be disengaged from cultural imagery and its practitioners are generally trying to produce precedent-topping visions. This document certainly offers evidence that Australian architecture more often reflects the personal styles and social conditions of its creators than the poetic ideal of *genius loci* – a unique sense of place arising from the weather patterns, geography and history of a site.

By juxtaposing selected pictures on double page spreads, we want to show that similar concepts are successfully being realised in diverse places, by architects who may not know each other's work and despite differences of climate. But because we are documenting only built structures, we can't confirm the opposite reality (which shows up in ideas competitions) that various aesthetics can be applied convincingly to one site.

Australian Architecture Now displays almost all of the built works which interested us during the late 1990s, but several excellent projects could not be included because their architects or owners have declined to allow them to be displayed in either this document particularly or publications generally.

DAVINA JACKSON, CHRIS JOHNSON, SYDNEY 2000

CURRENT SURGES
IN AUSTRALIAN ARCHITECTURE

DAVINA JACKSON

1 MARTON MAROSSZEKY, OF THE UNIVERSITY OF NEW SOUTH WALES BUILDING RESEARCH CENTRE, HAS REVEALED AN IRONIC 1990s DISCREPANCY BETWEEN THE CONSTRUCTION INDUSTRY'S GOVERNMENT-ENFORCED COMMITMENT TO CHECKLISTS OF QUALITY ASSURANCE AND ITS DELIVERY OF BUILDINGS TO STANDARDS DIMINISHED FROM THOSE OF THE 1980s ('QUALITY ASSURANCE: A GOOD IDEA GONE WRONG?', *ARCHITECTURE AUSTRALIA*, SEP/OCT 1996).

2 PHILIP DREW, *THE COAST DWELLERS*, PENGUIN, 1994.

3 HOWEVER, STRATA TITLES SUGGEST A FUTURE PROBLEM: THE FRAGMENTATION OF LARGE SITES INTO MANY SMALL LEGAL ENTITIES WHICH WILL BE DIFFICULT TO COMBINE AGAIN FOR REDEVELOPMENT WHEN CURRENT USES NEED REVISION.

4 JOHN RALSTON SAUL, *THE UNCONSCIOUS CIVILIZATION* (1995 MASSEY LECTURES), PENGUIN, 1997. ON PAGE 34, HE NOTES: 'TO BE PRECISE, WE LIVE IN A CORPORATIST SOCIETY WITH SOFT PRETENSIONS TO DEMOCRACY. MORE POWER EVERY DAY IS SLIPPING OVER TOWARDS THE [INTEREST] GROUPS.' THIS VIEW HAS BEEN SUPPORTED BY MANY COMMENTATORS: MOST RECENTLY BY THOMAS FRIEDMAN IN *THE LEXUS AND THE OLIVE TREE*, HARPER COLLINS, 1999.

5 ROBIN BOYD WROTE, IN *AUSTRALIA'S HOME*, MELBOURNE UNIVERSITY PRESS, 1952: 'ARCHITECTURE WAS THE WHITE MAN'S IDEA; THE BLACKS HAD NO USE FOR IT.' THE NEW GENRE OF ABORIGINAL CULTURAL CENTRES IS MOSTLY DESIGNED BY WHITE ARCHITECTS. THE ONLY ARCHITECTURAL OFFICES DIRECTED BY ABORIGINALS ARE TANGENTYERE DESIGN IN ALICE SPRINGS, OWNED BY AN ABORIGINAL LAND COUNCIL, AND THE MERRIMA DESIGN UNIT – LED BY AUSTRALIA'S FIRST INDIGENOUS ARCHITECT, DILLON KOMBUMERRIE – AT THE NSW DEPARTMENT OF PUBLIC WORKS AND SERVICES.

More than two centuries after the British military first pitched tents at Port Jackson, Sydney, in 1788, Australian architecture is displaying the impulses of late adolescence. During the construction boom of the six years before 2000 – the phase surveyed in this book – there were palpable swellings of independence and creative vigour, and new signs of maturity and confidence in dealing with the world offshore.

These urges clearly have been fostered by rising national prosperity since the stock market crash of October 1987. But economic buoyancy can only support artistic visions; it cannot create them. And the concepts are cooking. There is much more originality and diversity – though not always refinement[1] – in Australia's architecture of 1994–99 than was evident during the construction boom leading up to its 1988 Bicentennial.

Why is this country's architecture suddenly more interesting?

While it was always destined to advance from primitive huts and sheds, town buildings copied from Georgian and Victorian pattern books, and public edifices drafted in London, antipodean architecture was set back by a 1980s surfeit of romantic retrospection. Like Europe and America, Australia was 'infected', as the veteran Sydney modernist Harry Seidler termed it, by postmodern tendencies to emulate Palladian monuments and embellish buildings with decorative features of historic and 'contextural' rather than futuristic inclination. Despite their declared commitment to the aesthetics of technological progress, modernists also were looking backwards: to boxy precedents dating back to the 1920s.

Of course, 1990s architecture is not suddenly cleansed of retrospection – and only the notion of revolution, rather than evolution, demands that it should be. While the Palladian influences have dissipated, retro-modern concepts still inspire many designers – and will continue to do so even after the construction industry is computerised enough to support emerging visions of structures in less orthogonal geometries. Even so, this book's scan across many of the best recent works shows a progressive and dynamic situation.

Australian architecture originates mainly from studios set up around the perimeter of the continent – a fringe described as the nation's verandah by Sydney writer Philip Drew.[2] Clockwise from the north-east, the key sources of 1990s activity were Noosa (the resort centre of Queensland's Sunshine Coast), Brisbane, Sydney and Melbourne. Gems also emerged from drawing boards in Cairns, Byron Bay, Canberra, Merimbula, Hobart, Adelaide, Perth, Darwin and Alice Springs.

If those cities and towns could be said to form a necklace of architectural culture, some of the jewels would be considered large, multi-faceted sparklers; some bright, new nuggets, and others lacking lustre – at the moment – beyond the dim glow of colonial glories.

From those places of origin, Australian architects are building on sites scattered widely around the country – and some of the most memorable works of the last five years are in places remote from large populations. For instance, there's been a recent boom in building charismatic visitor centres at points of interest to travellers, including Uluru (the central desert monolith also known as Ayers Rock), Ballarat (on the site of an 1854 goldfields massacre) and Port Arthur (a colonial convict settlement in Tasmania).

All cultures reveal their economic structures and political priorities by the types of buildings that they design and budget to high standards. And Australian enthusiasm for architect-designed, postcard-conscious visitor centres is one expression of its immersion in the embryonic world of rapid, affordable travel and instant transfers of words, images and money.

Australia's hierarchy of architectural types is headed no longer by classic stone symbols of the authority of government (Town Halls, Post Offices, Public Service Offices, Customs Houses). Bureaucracies rent offices in commercial blocks and debate how to administer crumbling nineteenth-century artefacts in the context of general policies to slash expenses and sell services to corporate providers. Meanwhile, public opinion opposes sales of government assets and demands that heritage buildings be subsidised for cultural uses.

Also obsolete are large twentieth-century industrial complexes near rail stations, and the warehouses and wharf sheds of shipping ports. These are being subdivided into dense residential compounds for growing populations in the 'attractor' cities of Sydney, Melbourne and Brisbane (and, to a limited extent, Perth, Adelaide, Hobart and Darwin). Again, community groups oppose attempts to develop prime tracts for housing and marinas. Yet residences – whether hotel suites, apartments, houses or warehouse studios – are joining, and sometimes replacing, offices as sites of international business. Housing is no more nor less privately owned[3] than offices or factories, and marinas are usually more accessible to the public than docks. But when housing is proposed for high-status sites, concerns about private weath erupt in the letters columns.

In today's digital age, public architecture is being used more and more as a commercial marketing tool. Many architects are in shock or denial about this corruption of the discipline's historic role to create the cornerstones of civic culture which used to be financed by the Crown, the church, the military and (this century) elected forms of government. Nevertheless, contemporary circumstances confirm the view of Canadian writer John Ralston Saul that developed societies are corporate oligarchies rather than democracies.[4] The invincible new rulers are the leaders and courtiers of planet-wrapping communications organisations. Even so, architecture will continue to signify the values of the people who design it, the aspirations of the people who pay for it and the status of the people intended to occupy it – as it has since Vitruvius.

Public Australian buildings now are conceived mainly to help produce and sell packaged experiences of culture – to offshore and out-of-town customers as well as local markets. Since 1994, the scene has been dominated by university buildings (designed to attract Asian students and research funds from corporations, not just to contain acts of teaching and research); sports arenas and halls; trade exhibition and convention centres; Aboriginal cultural centres;[5] and various commercial developments, often including unit housing. Only a few office towers have been built since 1994 – a cyclical trough – but many columns of apartments have thickened the high-rise density (rarely with distinction) of Sydney and Melbourne's cores.

In most new city developments, it has been imperative to include indoor-outdoor facilities for the convivial consumption of cappuccino. It might be worth debating (as a diversion in that kind of context) how much truth inhabits an idea that coffee is the essence which fuels architecture in the telecommunications era as powerfully as oil facilitated the buildings of the industrial age.

Architecture increasingly is serving the nexus of FAME industries – food/fashion, arts, media and entertainment – in spite of fundamental ethical tensions. On one hand, the FAME industries thrive by exploiting the tastes of prosperous and young people, whose consumption patterns are mostly about absorbing pleasures and projecting personal appeal. In contrast, architecture has consistently represented conservative 'civic' values of permanence, power, stature, quality and refinement. Even architects steeped in the once-revolutionary values of twentieth-century modernism rarely aspire to design buildings that look groovy, spunky or ephemeral. They most appreciate 'authentic' aesthetics which invoke the theme of monastic austerity – a kind of sensuality which contradicts the hedonism that will increasingly drive leisure societies.

CURRENT SURGES

6 AUSTRALIAN WRITER ROBERT HUGHES, WHO HAS LIVED IN MANHATTAN FOR SEVERAL DECADES, CONVINCINGLY CRITICISED SYDNEY'S TRAJECTORY OF HERITAGE OBLITERATION AT HIS 1998 HERITAGE WEEK LECTURE FOR THE NATIONAL TRUST. YET HE DESCRIBED NEW YORK'S COMPARABLE RECORD AS THAT OF 'A CITY OF CONSTANT RENEWAL.' IN 1999, SYDNEY WRITER DAVID MARR, IN A CATALOGUE ESSAY FOR THE NSW HISTORIC HOUSES TRUST EXHIBITION 'DEMOLISHED HOUSES OF SYDNEY' SUGGESTED THAT IT IS GENERALLY AN INCLINATION OF PROSPEROUS AND ENERGETIC CULTURES TO DESTROY THEIR HISTORIC BUILDINGS.

As architects negotiate rapidly changing opportunities, they are faced with new challenges to the principal role for which they have been trained: designing buildings and environments. Regardless of the creative and organisational talents of individuals, architects are the only professionals who can boast a five-year base of university training in how to conceive the look and feel of structures and spaces.

Despite their qualifications, architects are not entirely trusted to create socially acceptable buildings and places. Their creative propositions are being supervised far more intensively, by a wider range of empowered but design-illiterate stakeholders, than ever before. This situation suggests widening discrepancies of ethics and expectations between architects, property developers, community lobby groups and governments.

Today, most large Australian buildings are planned by multi-disciplinary teams led by project managers who are skilled in 'on-time, on-budget' production processes more than design creation or appreciation. Government planners, also rarely trained in design, are encroaching on architects' concepts by imposing increasingly detailed aesthetic guidelines which enforce design choices as fundamental as roof shapes, structure outlines and heights, building materials and colours. Architects need exceptional powers of persuasion to navigate these complex political conditions without surrendering the cohesion and detailed quality of their designs.

As a contradictory trend, there has been a significant recent increase of design consciousness among the people who buy, facilitate and occupy architecture. Four causes in Australia are: increased coverage of design in the public media; increased availability of international journals in city bookshops; a boom in conferences and seminars on architectural and planning topics (providing more opportunities for debate among various disciplines); and increased access to international travel (allowing many antipodeans to regularly visit the latest and greatest works of the northern hemisphere).

One outcome of this escalation of awareness is flourishing public debates about architectural issues. Most memorable was the 1998 campaign of outrage about a new Sydney apartment building, nicknamed 'the Toaster', which was internationally vilified, in a campaign driven by *The Sydney Morning Herald*, for defiling views of the Opera House and Royal Botanic Gardens. Although the city had tolerated a line of taller, and no more distinguished, office blocks on the same site since the 1960s, the Toaster controversy registered the often overlooked notion of architectural quality on Sydney's political agenda. It was found that many architects influenced the design (two firms working for the developers and more than six architects representing or advising arms of government), but a series of owner-developers and builders controlled production. Although the controversy calmed down after the opening of a colonnade of waterfront shops and restaurants leading to the Opera House, it highlighted serious quandaries about Sydney's systems of land development.

A second effect is the birth of a market for buildings (particularly apartment buildings) which are signature-branded as designs from an architect of recognised talent. The first recent example of this phenomenon was the marketing of Melbourne Terrace, an externally decorative block of city housing designed and produced by Nonda Katsalidis in 1994. His development met the aspirations of affluent and trend-conscious city professionals with interesting configurations of interior space leading to wide balconies, fashionable fixtures and finishes, with emphasis on glamorous kitchens and bathrooms, and street entrances marked by commissioned sculptures. Despite, or because of, design individuality and quality, Melbourne Terrace and subsequent Katsalidis housing projects have sold before construction – giving the architect enough bankability to rise above his profession's usual client-attraction concerns, to now be assembling his own development consortia.

A third by-product of the public's sharper appetite for design is a new tendency by progressive politicians to press property developers to commission well-designed buildings. For example, Sydney's Lord Mayor, Frank Sartor, recently introduced city bylaws and an annual mayoral prize to reward developers for building a design obtained either from an architectural competition or an architect which his city council recognises as a good designer. This proposition was opposed by several of the city's most successful architects – all winners of design awards – because they claimed that the rules would be manipulated to serve biased agendas. A Melbourne example of similar political pressure is the last Victorian Liberal government's suggestions to some developers that its then Planning Minister, Rob Maclellan, would find it more appropriate to waive local council height limits if he could justify his approvals of towers on the grounds of their attractive architecture.

Within this new climate of public demand for good design, architects continue to argue about what, if any, designs can be deemed good. Significantly, awards juries for the Royal Australian Institute of Architects repeatedly declined during the 1990s to honour Sydney's annual crops of public buildings, housing and other urban sites. The judges blamed government for failing to ensure that the city's most talented architects were delivered key projects (not forced to audition) then supported with satisfactory budgets and shepherded through the political systems to allow them to produce works of detailed quality. It was noted that some of Sydney's most respected senior architects – for example, Glenn Murcutt, Harry Seidler, Richard Leplastrier – did not receive commissions for Olympics 2000 sports facilities. However, some small Games facilities (e.g., the archery pavilion and amenities blocks) were given to talented emerging offices, with excellent results.

Despite criticism of Sydney's recent constructions, only a few cities around the world have built – during this decade and on the ground rather than on computer – more new works of architecture at higher standards. Rotterdam, Berlin, Melbourne, London and perhaps Paris are among those cities, but New York, Copenhagen, Singapore, Tokyo and Barcelona are among the majority which are not currently considered hot-spots for architecture of high distinction. Also, the aesthetic calibre of Sydney's Olympics precinct – criticised locally for mediocrity – is only bettered during the twentieth century by the Games venues of Munich (Frei Otto's tensile structures) and, in certain respects, Barcelona, Tokyo, Montreal and Rome.

However, Sydney's presence – displaying all the economic forces of the late twentieth century – is best interpreted as a skyline viewed from a boat navigating its fabulous harbour. On the ground, the postwar flaws in its complexion are brutally apparent. Like New York and other American capitals, it has ringed its business district with waterside expressways and thrown up hosts of banal office and housing towers to obliterate coherent precincts of nineteenth-century terraces.[6] Even prestige developments are inclined towards bland and Classical aesthetics. Like Los Angeles, Sydney's suburbs of triple-garage brick veneer villas sprawl for more than an hour's drive west of its business centre.

Sydney's architecture has been dominated for two decades by steel-framed pavilions varying what has become known as 'the Murcutt section'. This strategy, led by Glenn Murcutt since the late 1970s, tops a Miesian box (often a long, square-ended box) of minimally divided 'universal' space with a gestural roof of corrugated steel. The outcomes are celebrated as sophisticated yet authentic refinements of early Australian farmhouses and sheds.

Variations of the Murcutt section can be seen in skeletal structures by four generations of Sydney architects: including Philip Cox (especially his Australian Pavilion at the Venice Gardens), Alex Tzannes, Ken Maher, Alex Popov, James Grose, Ed Lippmann, Peter Stutchbury, Drew Heath and the architects of many schools and small

7 THIS MURCUTT IS GLENN'S SON, NICK.

8 IN *LEARNING FROM LAS VEGAS* (1972), VENTURI DESCRIBED AS 'DUCKS' THE MONUMENTS OF A CITY WHICH ARE CONCEIVED AS INDEPENDENT SCULPTURES AND NEED AIRSPACE TO HIGHLIGHT THEIR OUTLINES. HIS 'DECORATED SHEDS' ARE BOXES FITTED INTO STREETS OF EXISTING BUILDINGS, DISPLAYING GRAPHIC FACADES.

9 ANOTHER SUNSHINE COAST ARCHITECT, GERARD MURTAGH, HAS PRODUCED A HOUSE (AT SUNSHINE BEACH, 1996) WHICH USES FINE WOODEN BATTENS AS A MONOLITHIC CLADDING. THIS IDEA HAS BEEN TESTED ALSO BY JOHN WARDLE AND KERSTIN THOMPSON IN MELBOURNE.

10 FROM THE 1960s TO THE 1980s, SYDNEY ARCHITECT JOHN ANDREWS WORKED IN NORTH AMERICA ON INSTITUTIONAL BUILDINGS. HIS KEY PROJECTS WERE SCARBOROUGH COLLEGE IN TORONTO (COMPLETED 1965), THE MIAMI PASSENGER TERMINAL (1970), GUND HALL AT THE HARVARD GRADUATE SCHOOL OF DESIGN IN BOSTON (1972), THE CANADIAN NATIONAL TOWER IN TORONTO (1972), THE KENT STATE UNIVERSITY SCHOOL OF ART, CLEVELAND, OHIO (1972) AND THE INTELSAT HEADQUARTERS IN WASHINGTON (1988).

civic buildings. Their roofs range from shallow barrel vaults to folded or twisted skillions; from hovering aerofoils to sequences of hyperbolic paraboloids. Meanwhile, Murcutt's latest works include interesting shifts of strategy; some contradicting his famous exhortation to 'touch this earth lightly'.

Certain Sydney practices, including Burley Katon Halliday, Engelen Moore, Stanic Harding and Melocco & Moore, are less interested in Murcutt's roof plays, but are influenced, as he has been, by the rectilinear minimalism of Ludwig Mies van der Rohe, Willem Dudok and Tadao Ando. Other offices – including Durbach Block Murcutt,[7] Luigi Rosselli, Virginia Kerridge, Tonkin Zulaikha, Walter Barda, Stephen Varady and Sam Marshall – are more expressively contemporary.

Overshadowing Sydney for design exuberance, urban cohesion and intellectual exploration is Australia's second largest metropolis, Melbourne – which has regularly amazed observers with controversial feats of architectural innovation during the 1990s. The culture is characterised by constant rivalry between modernists refining abstract, ordered compositions in steel, concrete and glass (an approach exemplified by Denton Corker Marshall, Wood Marsh and Metier 3) and expressionists developing organic structures using various geometries and materials (notably Gregory Burgess and Ashton Raggatt McDougall). Between those extremes are the collages of progressive postmodernists (Nonda Katsalidis, Allan Powell, NeoMetro).

Some Melbourne practices – especially ARM, Ivan Rijavec, Carey Lyon and the semi-imported Lab Architecture Studio – have been venturing well ahead of architecture's mainstream to exploit computer design techniques and science's complexity theories. The outcomes are geometrically elaborate, not necessarily expensive, buildings which subvert post-Renaissance reliance on rectilinear grids – and will be recognised mostly as millennial versions of Robert Venturi's ducks.[8]

Melbourne's architectural culture of intensive academic inquiry, uninhibited argument and bold built works has been galvanised since the Second World War by three architects who have led the city's crucial debates and aesthetic advances. The first tastemaker was Robin Boyd, a 1950s and 1960s modernist whose commentaries (including nine books and many newspaper articles and lectures) set key agendas for modern city life and introduced the oft-exploited term, 'the Australian ugliness.' The second motivator is Peter Corrigan, who generated the current wave of anti-modern debate in the 1970s, stimulated a lively design culture at the Royal Melbourne Institute of Technology, and inspired many younger practitioners with his ebullient buildings collaging 'banal' features borrowed from houses in the suburbs and popular media imagery.

In the 1990s, Melbourne's architectural culture has been orchestrated by South African academic Leon van Schaik, Dean of RMIT's Faculty for the Constructed Environment. A former teacher at London's Architectural Association during its 1970s–1980s heyday under Alvin Boyarsky, van Schaik transformed RMIT's staff and structures to produce the country's most dynamically competitive, creatively progressive, theoretically dense and glamorously promoted school of architecture and design. His crucial performance has been to shepherd RMIT's current phase of building new facilities at several campuses – arranging commissions for some of the city's most imaginative architects – to create a collection of arresting icons which declare the university's vigour, deliver new landmarks to the city and offer novel precedents for architecture generally.

In south-east Queensland, key architects are conducting a silent contest – often within their own oeuvres – between light, breezy pavilions of slatted timber and glass louvres, and monolithic buildings of rendered masonry. The former strategy has been celebrated as the one most appropriate to Queensland's patterns of sun and wind, and most authentic to its vernacular lineage of farm sheds and verandahed houses on stumps. Yet masonry has been chosen repeatedly for key civic buildings in Brisbane   for example, Robin Gibson's cultural facilities on the south bank of the river and earlier institutions by James Birrell. Masonry buildings are considered by many energy-efficiency engineers to be more effective at cooling and heating interiors than glassy, permeable structures. Also, romantic adobe dwellings are much sought-after by Queensland's escalating population of migrants from Melbourne and other southern cities.

Most Queensland architects experiment with both light and heavy forms of construction. At Noosa on the Sunshine Coast, veteran Gabriel Poole alternates between tent-inspired houses of steel and canvas, and gleaming, white-washed casas. His protegés, Lindsay and Kerry Clare and John Mainwaring, sometimes anchor their buildings with emphatic walls of masonry but are mainly committed to the skeletal aesthetic possibilities of timber and steel.[9] However, Mainwaring and the Clares recently began working as government architects in Brisbane and Sydney, so their involvement in defining the Coast's architecture has been interrupted. In Brisbane, practitioners like Geoffrey Pie, Andresen and O'Gorman, John Hockings, Bud Brannigan and Rex Addison remain associated with light pavilions, while a young office, Donovan Hill, is combining monumental concrete and fine timber battens in complex and decorative ensembles oriented around indoor-outdoor 'ambiguous rooms.'

Although Queensland, Sydney and Melbourne architects are designing most of Australia's prime buildings and places, international figures, including Renzo Piano and Mario Bellini of Italy, Britain's Norman Foster and American landscape architects George Hargreaves, Peter Walker and Martha Schwartz, have won key recent commissions in some of the main cities. French architect Philippe Robert is working with Australian developers of urban renewal schemes in both Sydney and Paris. At the commercial level, Dutch architect Rem Koolhaas's signature is tagged to new warehouse apartments in Sydney – a project handled through his Hong Kong partner, Aaron Tan.

Meanwhile, Australian architectural practices are building extensively across Asia, the Middle East and Europe. The most active multinationals are Bligh Voller Nield, the Buchan Group, Cox Architects, Daryl Jackson, Denton Corker Marshall (building in Poland), DesignInc (a 1999 fusion of Brisbane, Sydney and Melbourne firms, some with work in China), Hames Sharley, Harry Seidler (building in his birthplace, Vienna), Nation Fender Katsalidis and Peddle Thorp. Three more of the largest international practices – Hassell, Woodhead International and Woods Bagot – expanded from the provincial city of Adelaide.

Finally, it's significant, yet rarely mentioned, that some of Australia's most outstanding architects are headquartered in other countries. Melburnian Peter Wilson is based in Münster, Germany, with his partner, Julia Bolles, and constructs commercial and public buildings 'across the Eurolandschaft.' Perth-educated Kerry Hill directs a practice in Singapore which is building luxurious resorts and residences across Asia and Australia. Melburnians Hendrik Koning and Julie Eizenberg work in Los Angeles on award-winning housing and small public projects. Sydney's Carl Pickering, based in Rome, designs prestigious interiors, furniture and exhibitions around Europe. Ken Sowerby, also living in Italy, travels the world to design state-of-the-art newspaper printing halls. In the rarified air of international scholarship, Professors William J. Mitchell and Peter Rowe, both graduates of the University of Melbourne, now head the architecture faculties of MIT and Harvard in Boston and are authors of numerous books and essays which are repeatedly footnoted by other writers. While they are not the first or only antipodeans to establish remarkable careers offshore,[10] their buildings and texts certainly add muscular definition to Australian architecture's current phase of energetic adolescence.

TENDENCIES

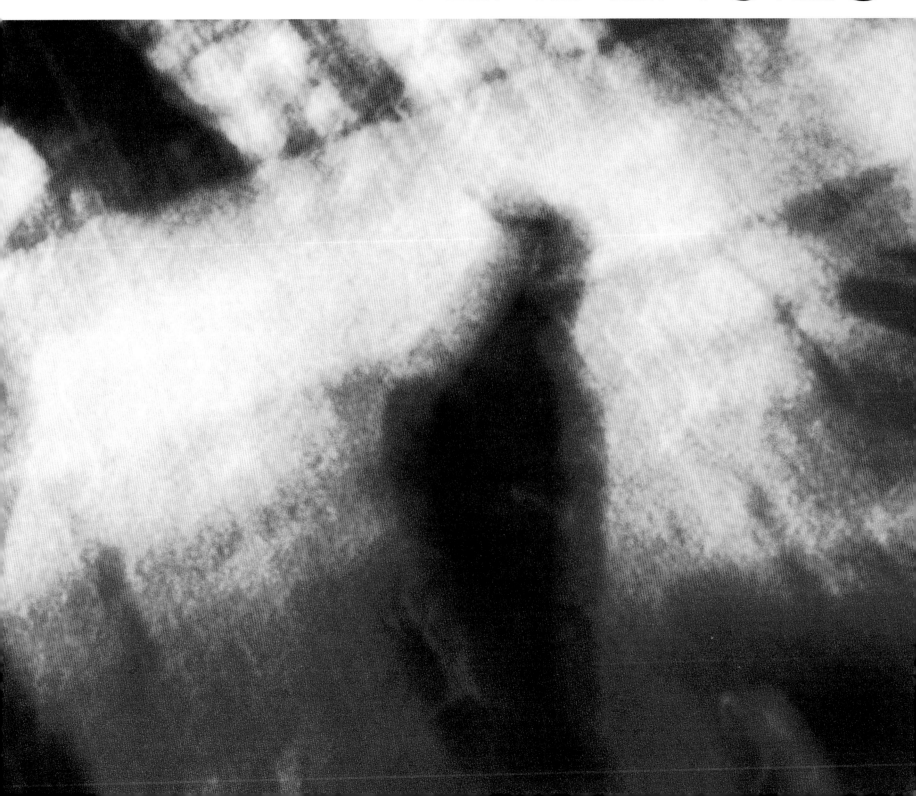

FREE GEOMETRIES

AS COMPUTERS SPEED COMPLEX DESIGN PROCESSES,
AUSTRALIAN ARCHITECTS ARE TESTING AMBITIOUS IDEAS FOR
ANTI-RECTANGULAR STRUCTURES

THIS PAGE WAVES OF CEILING IN THE
UPSTAIRS FOYER OF THE IMAX CINEMA AT
SYDNEY'S DARLING HARBOUR LEISURE
PRECINCT; ARCHITECTS HBO + EMTB
(LIONEL GLENDENNING), 1996.
PHOTO SIMON KENNY.

OPPOSITE TOP IMAX DIGITAL PERSPECTIVE,
TOWARDS THE NORTH ENTRY.

OPPOSITE LEFT SYDNEY'S IMAX CINEMA
OCCUPIES AN AWKWARD HARBOURSIDE
SITE, JOSTLED BY TWO FLYOVERS AND
DIVORCED FROM THE CITY BY AN
EXPRESSWAY. AN EYE-SHAPED FLOOR PLAN
IS EXTRUDED VERTICALLY AND CLAD
EXTERNALLY WITH STRIPES OF SILVER
ALUMINIUM. THE YELLOW-CHEQUERED
BULGE CONTAINS THE GIANT SCREEN AND
SIGNALS ACROSS THE CITY A CONCEPT
OF THE BUILDING 'SPILLING ITS GUTS'.
PHOTO SIMON KENNY.

OPPOSITE RIGHT OPTICAL GYMASTICS:
ELENBERG FRASER'S DAZZLE SHED IN
A MELBOURNE BACK GARDEN, 1996.
PHOTO ISAMU SAWA.

Modernism's reliance on Euclidean geometry and orthogonal grids is being contradicted by several coteries of designers reacting to diverse influences and impulses.

First, architects like Gregory Burgess in Melbourne and Christine Vadasz in Byron Bay are making complex and circuitous buildings in timber, stone, brick and ceramics. These rustic concepts are inspired by the structures of Nature, the Gaia philosophy, cosmic myths and motifs, traditional timber buildings in Hungary and 20th century houses by, in particular, Frank Lloyd Wright and Bruce Goff.

Organic architecture in Australia often incorporates ecological and climate-responsive strategies developed by progressive social movements of the 1960s and 1970s. It also expresses the mentalities of oblique arrival, informality and meandering which are honoured by Australia's native communities and often suggested as female in style.

A second anti-orthogonal direction stems from Robert Venturi's 1960s arguments about complexity and contradiction, in which he urged modernists to learn to like the ugly chaos of structures and signage along metropolitan main roads. Melbourne architect Peter Corrigan was strongly inspired by Venturi during his studies at Harvard – and his firm, Edmond & Corrigan, later influenced other Melbourne architects (initially Norman Day and Peter Crone) to contribute to a genre of low-rise buildings which pastiched features adapted from suburban housing and the images of consumer commerce.

In the 1990s, the baton of Australia's Venturian brand of anti-modernism passed from Edmond & Corrigan to proteges Ashton Raggatt McDougall – a transition marked by their adjacent edifices on the Swanston Street edge of RMIT University, Melbourne.

Building 8 (E&C with Demaine Partnership, 1994) is a post-modern 'decorated shed' which colourfully represents images from contemporary tribal cultures. It also alludes to 19th century debates on the supposed polychromy of ancient Greek monuments. Sydney scholar Peter Kohane has compared its facade to Gottfried Semper's 1854 law of building, which is sometimes claimed to have inspired the curtain walls of modernist high-rises by suggesting that the earliest tropical huts were simply frames to support woven cloths.

Two years after Building 8, ARM's Storey Hall, 1995, shocked the public with another elaborate and colourful facade. But this project (geometrically complicated inside and out) moved on to express the creative potential of computers and scientific and religious theories on the workings of the universe.

ARM and fellow Melburnians Carey Lyon, Hamish Lyon and Nikolas Koulouras are also interpreting current theories about non-linear time and collapsing space with schemes exploiting the mathematics of folds, ribbons, loops, waves and knots. Topology, a branch of geometry, produces convoluted forms like the torus and the Mobius band, which might now be buildable via computerised laser cutting of sheet materials.

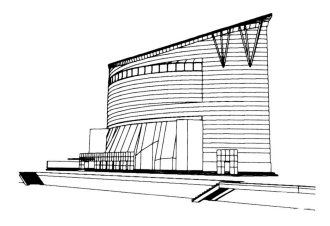

TOP DISTORTED BOXES ON SPLAYED POLES SHELTER THE CENTRAL COURT OF FORWARD VINEY WOOLLAN'S FORWARD-FURMAGE HOUSE, 1995, FROM ANTARCTIC WINDS ACROSS HOBART'S DERWENT RIVER. PHOTO RICHARD EASTWOOD.

ABOVE BLACKET SMITH'S CRUSTACEOUS PICNIC SHELTER, 1997, AT A PARK BESIDE PERTH'S SOUTH COOGEE BEACH. PHOTO MARTIN FARQUHARSON.

TOP RIGHT FOLDED WALLS OF GLASS AND STEEL LATTICE FORM A TRIANGULAR LONG HOUSE FOR CULTIVATING PLANTS. THE ROBERT CLARK HORTICULTURAL CENTRE, BALLARAT, VICTORIA, BY PETER ELLIOTT, 1995. PHOTO JOHN GOLLINGS.

BELOW RIGHT AND OPPOSITE GAMES OF PERSPECTIVE AND COMPLEXITY BY ASHTON RAGGATT MCDOUGALL AT THE PROMEDICUS MEDICAL CENTRE, ST KILDA, MELBOURNE, 1995. PHOTOS TREVOR MEIN.

Some architects are testing the limits of conventional circular and triangular geometries. For instance, Peter Elliott's Ballarat glasshouse, 1995, uses a frame of steel lattice to tension a triangular pavilion into concertina folds like an origami napkin. Equally rhythmic are the hyperbolic paraboloid roofs of two long and large sheds: the Brisbane Convention Centre by Cox Rayner, 1995, and Hassell's Olympic Park Railway Station, Sydney, 1998.

Australia's king and crown prince of curves are Melburnians Ivan Rijavec and Tom Kovac. Rijavec uses complex radial geometry (more feasible since the arrival of computer-aided design and construction systems) to assemble ambitiously gymnastic white-lined houses that are intended to tease the eye with methods he researches from science and psychology. Kovac's comparable sculptures (he trained with Rijavec) are conceived more intuitively – beginning with intensively scribbled sketches, although the Kovac Malone office is computerised.

Both Rijavec and Kovac tend to obscure their frames and shaping fins with skins of painted board. In this respect, they relate to the Los Angeles construction protocol of plywood and stucco (without the same danger of earthquakes).

Around Australia, many architects are distorting ideal forms – skewing boxes into trapezoids; folding and twisting roofs; splaying poles at awkward angles, and pushing arcs into irregular bulges.

Of course these adventures are conceived to amaze observers and compel them to wonder: How does that structure stand up?

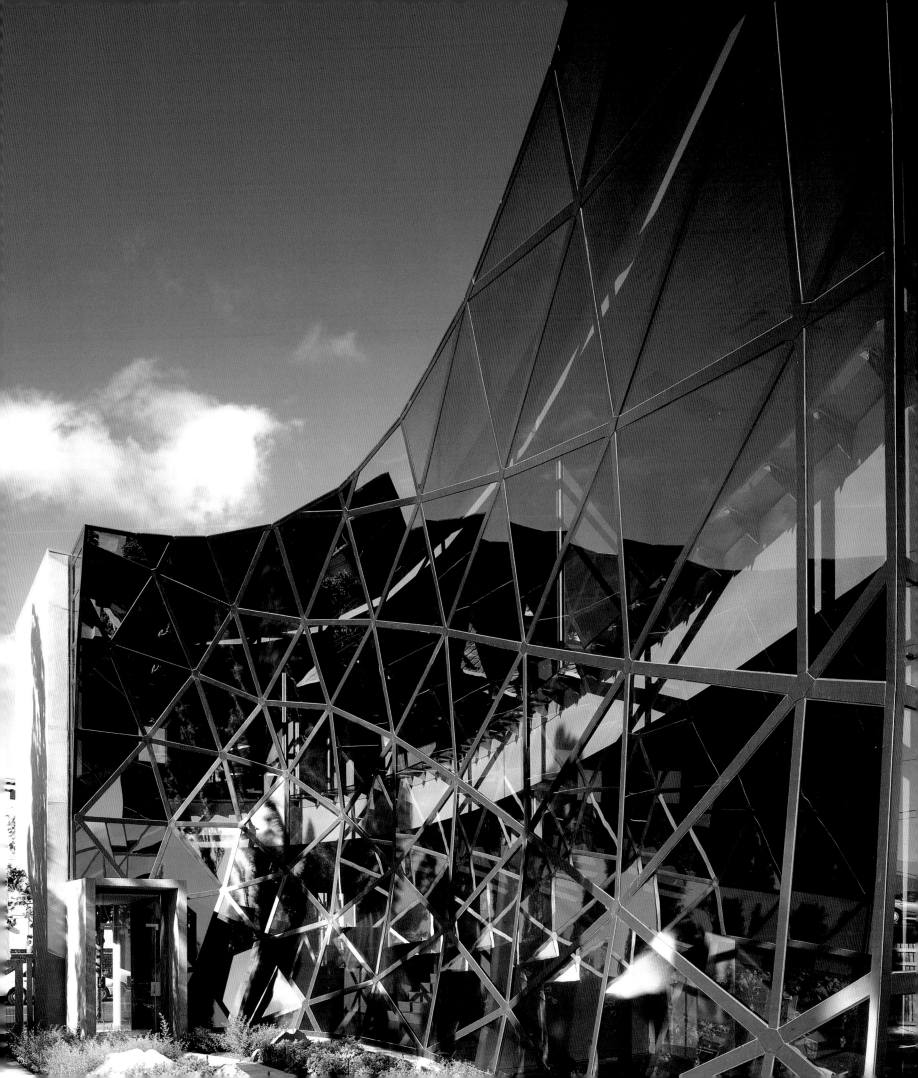

TOP LEFT FOLDED METAL FORMS AND HOT MATT COLOURS DISTINGUISH THE FIBRE RESEARCH CENTRE AT GEELONG'S DEAKIN UNIVERSITY, BY BSA-SINCLAIR KNIGHT MERZ (HAMISH LYON). PHOTO JOHN GOLLINGS.

LEFT A STEALTH BOMBER'S NOSE MARKS THE ENTRANCE TO ART AND TECHNICAL STUDIOS AT MOWBRAY COLLEGE, MELBOURNE, BY NORMAN DAY, 1996. PHOTO ADRIENNE WENTWORTH.

ABOVE A SWOOPING STAIRCASE AND SINUOUS CHIMNEY IN IVAN RIJAVEC'S RESIDENTIAL CONVERSION OF BRICK STABLES, FITZROY, MELBOURNE, 1994. PHOTO JOHN GOLLINGS.

OPPOSITE AND FLOOR PLAN THE ALESSIO HOUSE, MELBOURNE, 1997, IS ONE OF A SEQUENCE OF RADIALLY COMPLEX RESIDENCES DESIGNED BY IVAN RIJAVEC. PHOTO JOHN GOLLINGS.

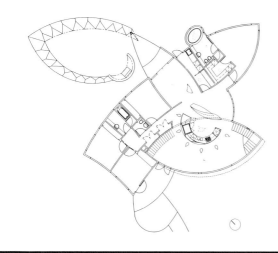

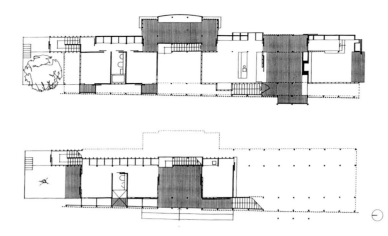

MATCHSTICK MANNERISM

FINE TIMBER BATTENS AND STEEL POLES ARE DEFINING NEW
AESTHETICS OF FRAGILITY AND INSTABILITY, COMPOSING
STRUCTURES OF PLAYFUL ASSYMETRY OR INTENSE RHYTHM

Queensland is the spiritual home of an architectural style which brings new poetic qualities to the subtropical tradition of building breezy enclosures with screens of timber battens.

Meanwhile, some Melbourne and Sydney architects are arranging coloured sticks and poles in slanted arrays of either orderly or disorderly appearance.

Both of these 'matchstick' scenarios owe debts of inspiration to Japan, and certain projects allude to a natural Australian prototype: the eucalypt forest.

Queensland's 'batten school' is one of the most regionally authentic of Australia's 1990s aesthetics – despite its obvious associations with the screening systems of Japanese rural houses and temples. It advances the State's climate-sensitive tradition of using lattice screens to dress the verandahs, line the breezeways (airy corridors) and wrap the undercrofts of weatherboard 'Queenslander' villas. These sun and air-conditioning treatments were popularised by Brisbane architect Robin Dods and his contemporaries during the early 20th century, and have since been reprised for speculative housing in other States.

In the 1970s, Queensland's slatting style took a southerly and diagonal turn, with many Sydney and Melbourne architects (including Daryl Jackson, Max May, Ian McKay and Andrew Metcalf) using battens nailed at 45 degrees to create screens to filter sun, breezes, outlooks and privacy.

However, the current emphasis on meticulous and lavish battening

as a lyrical strategy stems primarily from the works and teachings of two influential lecturers at the University of Queensland, Brit Andresen (a Norwegian who arrived from Britain in 1977) and Peter O'Gorman (a local architect who recently left UQ for full-time design and building).

Since completing two key houses at Mt Nebo and on Stradbroke Island in 1986, Andresen and O'Gorman have become increasingly sophisticated and intense in their use of humble slats, crafting them on site and arranging them like notes in symphonic scores.

Like Renaissance humanists such as Alberti, they appreciate harmonics – rhythms in music, mathematics, art and architecture. And like the makers of Gothic cathedrals, they want to create sublime performances of light and shadow with structural techniques that (pragmatically for the tropics) 'fracture the sunlight.'

Andresen's concurrent interest in 20th-century Italian architect Carlo Scarpa (she visited his Castelvecchio renovations in 1972 after winning a competition for the Burrell Museum in Glasgow) also has germinated in works by her former students Brian Donovan, Timothy Hill and Alice Hampson. They have built several Scarpa-esque houses in which boxes and planes of fine hardwood slatting delicately embellish brutal masonry monoliths.

In a different use of battens, John Hockings, another UQ teacher/practitioner, recently reclothed a Brisbane bungalow with screens of wide, black-stained boards laid horizontally. This project

OPPOSITE LEFT AND RIGHT AT THE
HIGHGATE HILL HOUSE, BRISBANE, 1998,
BRIT ANDRESEN AND PETER O'GORMAN
HAVE STRUNG TWO TIERS OF INDOOR AND
OUTDOOR LIVING AND SLEEPING SPACES
ALONG A GULLY. PHOTOS JON LINKINS.

ABOVE CLARE DESIGN'S SALES PAVILION
FOR THE TWIN WATERS CANAL ESTATE AT
NOOSA, QUEENSLAND, 1998. ROMANTIC
IMAGERY HELPS TO SELL A SUBDIVISON OF
CONVENTIONAL BRICK AND TILE VILLAS –
AND SIGNALS A TEST OF THE MARKET BY
DEVELOPER LEND LEASE. THE LOOKOUT
TOWER UPDATES THREE 1986 PRECEDENTS
BY RUSSELL HALL, PETER O'GORMAN AND
BRIT ANDRESEN WITH TIMOTHY HILL.
PHOTO BART MAIORANA.

MATCHSTICK MANNERISM

TOP DONOVAN HILL'S 'T' HOUSE, SUNSHINE COAST, 1996. PHOTO JON LINKINS.

ABOVE HOUSE ADDITION, SYDNEY, BY DREW HEATH, 1999. PHOTO BRETT BOARDMAN.

TOP RIGHT AND SECTION DRAWING ALICE HAMPSON'S BRISBANE COURTYARD, 1997. PHOTO PATRICK BINGHAM-HALL.

RIGHT HAYMARKET CAFÉ SHELTER, SYDNEY, 1998, BY MCCONNEL SMITH & JOHNSON. PHOTO BART MAIORANA.

OPPOSITE LEFT AND RIGHT FACULTY OF ART AND DESIGN, MONASH UNIVERSITY, CAULFIELD, MELBOURNE, 1999, BY DENTON CORKER MARSHALL. PHOTOS TIM GRIFFITH.

showed the potential of battens to define outdoor rooms and transition zones to create a sense of privacy without loss of prospect.

In Sydney, McConnel Smith & Johnson (Mark Willett) began to test a deconstructivist strategy of steel poles akimbo: sometimes splayed in irregular support of substantial masses (Westmead Hospital, 1995) and elsewhere seeming to fall in disarray (Haymarket Café Shelter, 1998).

Scrupulously disorderly poles also appear in 1990s works by Garry Forward in Hobart, Odden Rodrigues in Perth and Bligh Voller Nield (Shane Thompson), Brisbane.

In Melbourne, Denton Corker Marshall has been playing various games of matchstick mannerism. First, the firm arranged coloured battens in barcode and Fibonacci formats on exterior walls at the Adelphi Hotel (1992). Then it marshalled ranks of either strictly vertical or dangerously angled columns to define passages and mark the edges of structures (Monash Caulfield Campus, 1993, 1999; Melbourne Exhibition Centre (MEC), 1996). Later, the practice began to dramatise the entrances of civic buildings with imposingly upthrusting blades pierced by fine, slanted sticks (MEC; Melbourne Museum, 1999).

Recently, DCM employed coloured sticks to compose a gigantic motorway entry portal to Melbourne city from its Tullamarine Airport (City Link Gateway, 1999). This ensemble, heralded by undulating road walls of yellow concrete, ironically symbolised the city's millennial cultural thrusts while threatening imminent collapse.

CUBIC ABSTRACTION

SYDNEY AND MELBOURNE ARE REVIVING
THE HEROIC SIMPLIFICATIONS OF HIGH MODERNISM;
UPDATED WITH UNPRECEDENTED PRECISION

ABOVE LEFT ENGELEN MOORE'S NEUTRAL
BAY HOUSE, SYDNEY, 1997, WITH A
SAWTOOTH ROOF STRUCTURE ORIENTED
TO SCOOP NORTH LIGHT. PHOTO ROSS
HONEYSETT.

ABOVE RIGHT CONCRETE HOUSE IN SOUTH
MELBOURNE BY KERSTIN THOMPSON, 1998.
PHOTO BEN WRIGLEY.

OPPOSITE ALLAN POWELL'S PERFORMING
ARTS CENTRE AT MONASH UNIVERSITY'S
CLAYTON CAMPUS, MELBOURNE, 1995.
PHOTO TREVOR MEIN.

Some of architecture's aesthetic dilemmas of the 1980s and 1990s stem from a state of flux between the last gasps of the industrial society and the yet-to-be-finalised cultural structures of the digital age. How to react to this condition of instability? Some architects aim to express the chaos of the time; others interpret Nature. Another group is continuing to be guided by the machine-age concepts of pioneer modernists in both architecture and art.

Australian architects long ago abandoned the ocean liner curves of the streamlining style which launched modernist architecture in the southern hemisphere during the 1930s. (A prominent example was Burnham Beeches, a Melbourne mansion by Harry Norris, 1930, and the mode soon spread to hospitals and factories.) However, the cubic models set up by Holland's De Stijl coterie (Gerrit Rietveld, Willem Dudok, Theo van Doesburg) have been continuously influential since Seabrook & Fildes completed the MacRobertson Girls High School in Melbourne in 1934.

Dudok particularly influenced Sydney government architects and his latest Australian legacy can be seen at the Olympic Village: Bruce Eeles' white apartment complexes with HPA, Vote, Hassell and Peddle Thorp & Walker, 1999.

Dutch ideas of interlocking boxes of form and space – combined with Corb's spatial strategies of the 1920s – also appear in recent works by Sydney offices Geoform, Virginia Kerridge, Stephen Varady, Melocco & Moore and Marsh Cashman with Curve 9, as well as Melbourne projects by Shelley Penn, Chris Connell, McGaurin Soon, Geoff Crosby, Nic Gioia and John Wardle. These modernists often overlay the De Stijl principles with moves to deconstruct the box along the lines of mid-century Venetian architect Carlo Scarpa.

Many Australians admire the bare contemporary minimalism of John Pawson in London, Peter Zumthor in Switzerland and Tadao Ando in Japan. Their works have been linked with the Japanese concept of *wabi*, explained by Bruce Chatwin (in his introduction to Pawson's 1996 book, *Minimalism*) as a sense of serenity stemming from solitude and poverty.

Many of these Australians, along with Sydney's Burley Katon Halliday and Melbourne's NeoMetro and Kerstin Thompson, also have interpreted the monumental planes of Luis Barragán's Mexican casas. In a compatible way, Allan Powell of Melbourne paid homage to the strangely disturbing architecture of Giorgio de Chirico's metaphysical paintings (the *piazze d'Italia* series) with his design for Monash University's Centre of Performing Arts, Melbourne, 1995. Intending to propose a new idea of Australian architecture, Powell painted this stark monument red: a reminder to metropolitan scholars of the continent's vast desert.

In Sydney and Melbourne, the once-daring concepts of absolute abstraction have reached the level of mainstream fashion and are regularly exploited by property developers to sell designer apartments. This may signal a cyclical peak of interest in minimalism. A leading exponent of the style, Iain Halliday, declared in

CUBIC ABSTRACTION

1999 that 'it's gone as far as it can,' mentioning that his firm is now testing eclectic schemes.

Of course, for many modernists around Australia, the vital sources are Mies and Le Corbusier's early cubic works. Their models have been influential since the 1950s (Sydney, Melbourne and Perth remain strongly associated with minimalism) and are often reinterpreted with references to recent skeletal and thin-skin structures by Norman Foster, Renzo Piano, Richard Rogers and Jean Nouvel.

Australian Miesians of the 1990s include Alexander Tzannes, James Grose (now with Bligh Voller Nield), Ed Lippmann and Engelen Moore in Sydney; Sean Godsell, Peter Elliott and Geoff Crosby in Melbourne; and David Langston-Jones, a London-trained architect who built several corrugated tin houses in tropical Cairns.

Modernist curtain walls were also an inspiration for Denton Corker Marshall's Governors Towers in Sydney, 1994, and Hassell's Commonwealth Law Courts in Melbourne, 1999. The former employs vertical and square grids on two towers; the latter is a back-to-back L configuration cloaked with a tapestry of tinted glass and fine mullions arranged in dissonant rhythms. With this treatment, the law courts promotes a late-modern fusion of sleek and universal corporate styling with elaborate, pseudo-structural surface patterns.

While elaborate pattern obviously is the antithesis of minimalism, the challenge of creating a successful synthesis is, like many feats of balance, dangerously thrilling.

ABOVE NEOMETRO'S PROVAN HOUSE, TOORAK, MELBOURNE, 1996. PHOTO TREVOR MEIN.

RIGHT MCGAURIN SOON'S ORCHARD STREET HOUSE, BRIGHTON, VICTORIA, 1998. PHOTO JOHN GOLLINGS.

FAR RIGHT DINOSAUR DESIGNS, A MELBOURNE SHOP SELLING VIVID RESIN JEWELLERY AND HOMEWARES, BY CHRISTOPHER CONNELL, 1996. PHOTO TREVOR MEIN.

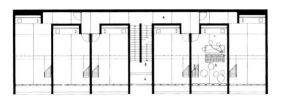

TOP, PLANS AND RIGHT RUTLAND STREET STUDIO APARTMENTS IN SURRY HILLS, SYDNEY, BY BURLEY KATON HALLIDAY, 1997. FLOOR PLANS TOP. PHOTOS SHARRIN REES.

ABOVE IN AN OTHERWISE BAROQUE REFURBISHMENT OF MELBOURNE'S PRINCE OF WALES HOTEL, 1998, ALLAN POWELL CONTAINED PART OF THE ENTRY FOYER AND A STAIRCASE IN A BLACK GLASS BOX, PROJECTING INTO A COURTYARD. PHOTO TIM GRIFFITH.

FRAGMENTS, LAYERS, COLLAGE

AUSTRALIA'S CULTURAL DIVERSITY IS BEING REPRESENTED BY NEW BUILDINGS OF AESTHETIC AND METAPHORIC COMPLEXITY

OPPOSITE BREAMLEA HOUSE, VICTORIA, BY MCGAURIN SOON, 1998. PHOTO JOHN GOLLINGS.

TOP RIGHT JOHN WARDLE'S KITAMURA HOUSE IN THE MELBOURNE SUBURB OF KEW, 1995. PHOTO TREVOR MEIN.

BOTTOM RIGHT A POLYCARBONATE-SHEATHED TOWER HINGES THE WEATHER-BOARDED ARMS OF A NOOSA HOUSE RENOVATED BY WEIR & PHILLIPS, 1998. PHOTO PAUL GOSNEY.

Although the tag 'pomo' is now an insult to architects, the profession recognises postmodern concepts of racial diversity and environmental complexity as key mentalities of global culture.

Even so, it's a challenge to translate emerging recognitions of cultural differences into visually coherent, habitable structures.

Certainly architects trained in modernist ethics of abstraction, truthful expression and universal culture are uneasy about designing the theatrical buildings and theme interiors which are now being demanded by the leisure industry.

There have been numerous clashes of integrities between Australian architects (steeped in rationality) and American imagineers (enthusiastic about fantasy) working on the Darling Park, Sega World and Fox Film Studios developments in Sydney, and the Melbourne and Sydney casinos.

In recent Australian architecture, theories about diversity mostly have been interpreted as collages of fragments, arranged either in dynamic collisions or as hierarchies of ordered layers.

The dynamic collision approach was being tested by Edmond & Corrigan and other Melbourne offices in the 1970s and 1980s; before Jacques Derrida's tactics of literary deconstruction were discussed by Australian architects.

Inspired by Robert Venturi's complexity arguments from 1966, these Melburnians boisterously juxtaposed exactly the kinds of popular suburban features which local critic Robin Boyd had roundly disparaged in *The Australian Ugliness* (1960). In retrospect,

their works can be understood as premonitions of a late-century breakdown of modernist agendas for international uniformity.

In the 1990s, the Melbourne impulse towards irregular collages has been continued by Nonda Katsalidis, Allan Powell, Ashton Raggatt McDougall and NeoMetro.

Sydney architects who have built dynamic and elaborative ensembles include Cox Richardson, Gordon & Valich, certain architects at Allen Jack & Cottier, Jahn Associates, Campbell Luscombe and two Italians who trained with leading postmodernists, Luigi Rosselli and Renato D'Ettorre.

In northern Australia, collages often arise from rural tendencies towards 'do-it-yourself' bricolage with whatever bits of timber and tin can readily be found. Gabriel Poole, Phillip Follent, John Mainwaring, Arkhe Field and Russell Hall are Queensland exponents of this approach, which often results from budget constraints. In the Northern Territory, works of bricolage have been assembled by Hully Liveris, Tangentyere Design and (less often) Troppo. In South Australia, Nick Tridente is one of the most adventurous practitioners of collage – and other Adelaide firms have worked with community artists to elaborate their schemes.

The alternative strategy of layered collage updates the rectilinear formats of modernism's De Stijl movement with more varied forms, finishes and spatial volumes.

Australian interest in layering has been fostered by discussions about palimpsest (the notion of exposing and erasing historical layers of cultural expression). In recent years,

FRAGMENTS, LAYERS, COLLAGE

ABOVE GERARD HOUSE AT NORTH HAVEN MARINA, ADELAIDE, BY NICK TRIDENTE, 1996. PHOTO TREVOR FOX.

LEFT TREATMENT & DIAGNOSTIC BUILDING AT WODEN VALLEY HOSPITAL, CANBERRA, BY LAWRENCE NIELD & ASSOCIATES, 1994. PHOTO JOHN GOLLINGS.

RIGHT IN AN ALLUSION TO DUCHAMP, DESCENDING PANELS SIGNIFY THE STAIRS AT STEPHEN VARADY'S GREEN ADDITIONS, SYDNEY, 1998. PHOTO MICK BELL.

OPPOSITE FIRST FLOOR PLAN AND NORTH-EAST VIEW OF RENATO D'ETTORRE'S SOUTH COOGEE HOUSE, SYDNEY, 1994. PHOTO BART MAIORANA.

this theory has been demonstrated most convincingly by Tonkin Zulaikha on several Sydney recycling projects: the Casula Powerhouse Arts Centre and Verona Cinema Complex, both 1996, and Customs House, 1998.

Initially a word that describes overlaying texts, palimpsest was promoted in Australia's architectural debate by Lawrence Nield as Professor of Architecture at the University of Sydney, 1992–96.

In his civic buildings of that period – two hospital blocks, a community centre and several university buildings – he has drawn metaphors liberally from all of civilisation rather than attempting to represent the histories of specific sites. Only at the Sunshine Coast University Library in Queensland, with John Mainwaring, 1997, do the fragments – sunscreens and skylights – seem certainly linked to the local climate.

A significant Melbourne example of layered collage is the Crown Casino – a giant complex of five building types – by Bates Smart, Perrott Lyon Mathieson and Daryl Jackson, 1997.

Of the Australian firms designing layered ensembles, three are prolific and remarkably meticulous in both composition and detail: Clare Design (now in Sydney after building an international reputation for houses and civic buildings on the Sunshine Coast); Donovan Hill, a newly prominent firm in Brisbane, and John Wardle, a Melbourne specialist in houses and commercial interiors. In different ways, these architects aim to express not just many ideas but immaculate fusions of them.

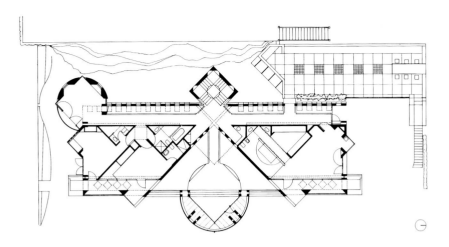

ROMANTIC AUSTERITY

**MODERN URBAN AUSTRALIANS CONTINUE TO CELEBRATE
THE RIGOURS OF ISOLATED LIVING ON THE LAND**

ABOVE LEIGH WOOLLEY'S 'THE FISHERIES'
RETREAT, 1995, NESTLES INTO A ROCKY
SLOPE IN A NATIONAL PARK ON TASMANIA'S
FREYCINET PENINSULA. THE TIMBER
FRAMED AND STEEL-CLAD HOUSE IS RAISED
ON A STEEL SUB-STRUCTURE DESIGNED TO
BE BUILT BY TWO PEOPLE AND TO MINIMISE
DISTURBANCE OF THE ECOLOGICALLY
FRAGILE SITE. TIMBER DECKS ARE SHAPED
TO AVOID A STAND OF OYSTER BAY PINE
TREES. PHOTO LEIGH WOOLLEY.

OPPOSITE AND CROSS-SECTION A BUSH
HUT IN SYDNEY'S BLUE MOUNTAINS, 1998,
DESIGNED AND BUILT BY DREW HEATH, AN
ARCHITECT EDUCATED IN TASMANIA. IT
CONTAINS A PRIVATE LIBRARY. PHOTO
BRETT BOARDMAN.

Most of Australia's 19 million people live comfortably in suburbs and towns close to the shores of the continent. Yet the nation's culture sentimentally reveres its colonial memories of living rough in the outback. In architecture, these bush mentalities often blend with modernist ideals of authenticity and meticulous simplicity.

When juries for architecture awards explain their choices of design excellence, words like 'tension', 'rigour', 'raw' and 'tough' are often employed as terms of appreciation. On the other hand, adjectives like 'comfortable' and 'decorative' are commonly understood to imply failings of intellectual and creative discipline.

Among architects specialising in domestic design, the mythology of the primitive hut – the fire, the simple shelter from rain, the place to recline safely – remains a compelling inspiration.

Of course, there are many kinds of primitive hut – from prehistoric shelters framed with mammoth bones to igloos in the Arctic. French writer Antoine Chrysostome Quatremère de Quincy (1755–1849) distilled all the world's species into three types: rock dwellings for nomadic hunters, tents for shepherds and wood cabins for farmers. The last category prevails throughout Australia: indeed, all the islands and continents of the eastern Pacific.

Contemporary Australian cabins, especially those constructed on rural or bush sites in the warmer latitudes, are often inspired by the village structures of Australia's equatorial neighbours: the islands of Indonesia and Melanesia, and particularly Papua New Guinea.

Some key Australian architects, including Rex Addison in Brisbane and Glenn Murcutt, Richard Leplastrier and Peter Stutchbury in Sydney, have lived in PNG and/or are strongly inspired by its huts of poles and matting with floors raised above the ground.

Many PNG pavilions are visually charged by thatched roofs in towering forms, usually steeply pitched to sluice tropical rains and symbolise the paternal control of most Melanesian societies.

In current Australian architecture, the shape of a domestic roof is a phrase of code which can convey to sophisticated aesthetes both the inventiveness of the architect (executing a visually exceptional and technically difficult gesture) and the architect's level of concern (low to high) to offer occupants a sense of protected shelter.

As historian Joseph Rykwert has clarified, the peaked roof has always symbolised shelter in art (an evocative example being Filarete's 15th century sketches of Adam holding his hands above his head in the first rainstorm).

Even today, psychological studies suggest that most Westerners respond positively to prototypal images of hip and gable roofs – and this primal affection is reflected in the designs of mass-built suburban houses.

Among elite architects, however, there's a strong tendency to design roofs in non-homely forms. These usually are modified from the tin skillions of farm sheds – but in a provocative house and studio by Addison, 1998–99, gables have been installed upside down.

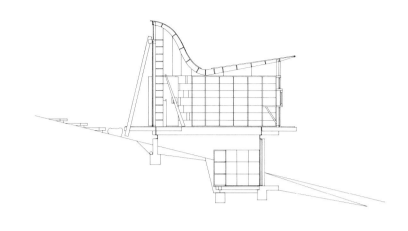

ROMANTIC AUSTERITY

TOP STAIRCASE OF RECYCLED HARDWOOD AND BRASS BUILT BY PHILIP STICKLEN AT A SYDNEY WAREHOUSE CONVERTED BY KERRIDGE WALLACE, 1995.
PHOTO SIMON KENNY.

ABOVE CONCRETE STAIRCASE WITH PLYWOOD SCREEN BY SAM MARSHALL, 1999, IN HIS UPDATE OF A WAREHOUSE BESIDE KERRIDGE WALLACE'S IN SYDNEY.
PHOTO PATRICK BINGHAM-HALL.

RIGHT HUNT-REEVES HOUSE, CLAREVILLE, SYDNEY, 1999; A CLIFFSIDE BUSH DWELLING OVERLOOKING PITTWATER HARBOUR.
PHOTO PATRICK BINGHAM-HALL.

Although counter-domestic rooflines are resisted by many local councils, steel skillions have been cautiously (and profitably) tested by developers Mirvac and Lend Lease in some architect-designed houses at the Olympic Village, Newington, Sydney, 1999.

In other impulses to express austerity, many designers have been exposing the robust structures and battered surfaces of old warehouses – and there's much enthusiasm to build with common and recycled materials.

New floors and cabinets of reused, refinished Australian hardwoods are prized as being more environmentally sensitive than using the same species straight from the forest.

Meanwhile, leading Australian style magazines are encouraging readers to furnish their homes with utilitarian tables, benches and shelving rescued from obsolete warehouses. This strand of bric-a-brac decor is known as industrial salvage – and it's more fashionable among some aspiring urban professionals than furnishing with European antiques.

Alongside those directions, there's continuing appreciation of Japan's Zen tradition of austerity: architecturally expressed with elegant timber craftsmanship and serene, minimally furnished spaces, with sliding walls opening to the landscape.

A spectacular landscape context is an essential element in producing an astonishing work of architectural austerity. Relating a cool, monastic chamber to a prospect of lush Nature creates a juxtaposition of almost magical enchantment.

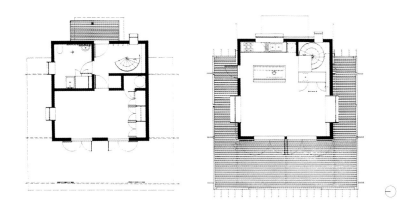

ABOVE A HOUSE OF CORRUGATED
GALVANISED STEEL AT DEWHURST,
VICTORIA, BY LINDSAY HOLLAND, 1996.
PHOTO PETER HYATT.

RIGHT AND FLOOR PLANS WOODWARD
BEACH HOUSE BY PETER MADDISON, 1996:
A MECCANO ASSEMBLY OF RAW MATERIALS
ON MELBOURNE'S PHILLIP ISLAND.
PHOTO TREVOR MEIN.

TYPES

PUBLIC WORKS
ICONS OF EDUCATION

**RMIT BUILDING 220, WOOD MARSH
WITH PELS INNES NIELSON KOSLOFF,
BUNDOORA, VICTORIA, 1998**
DESCRIBED BY AN AWARDS JURY AS
'SCULPTURE IN THE LANDSCAPE', RMIT
BUILDING 220 SWEEPS IN A BOLD ARC
TOWARDS A STAND OF RED GUMS ON A
SEMI-RURAL CAMPUS. THE MASONRY
STRUCTURE IS PINNED BY ONE SERVICE
CORE AND CLAD WITH ROCK-TEXTURED
CONCRETE AND RED METAL PANELS THAT
ARE APPLIED TO LOOK LIKE IMPROBABLY
VERTICAL BRICKWORK. THE INTERIOR PLAN
HAS MANY TEACHING ROOMS AND
OFFICES ALIGNED ALONG ONE CORRIDOR
PER FLOOR. PHOTOS TIM GRIFFITH.

Construction industry cycles can be differentiated by the types of public buildings that are deemed important enough to need fine architects. In Australia, the 1980s cycle was led by prestige office towers. In the 1990s, the flat market for corporate skyscrapers is being contrasted with a national boom in university buildings.

Ironically though, this academic upswing has been driven by brutal trimming of government subsidies. Universities now are expected to sell rather than offer education – and the largest markets for potential fee-paying students are in Asia.

To attract enrolments, some institutions have been developing new facilities with compelling visual qualities. Photos of these icons are often included in faculty brochures, and they may win attention in the general media. In symbolic terms, bold architecture conveys the spirit of competitive commerce which is, by force, slowly seeping through academic culture.

Certain universities have reacted to academia's new economic conditions more promptly than others. Novel buildings are mostly being commissioned by RMIT, Deakin and Monash (in Victoria), New South Wales, Newcastle and the Sunshine Coast.

The most active patron of new academic architecture is RMIT, which is building extraordinary landmarks on its city and suburban campuses. These represent all three of Melbourne architecture's current themes: anti-modern complexity, postmodern collage and progressive modernism.

RMIT's principal works, fronting Melbourne's Swanston Street, are Building 8 by Edmond & Corrigan with Demaine, 1994, and Storey Hall by Ashton Raggatt McDougall, 1995. With lurid colours, intense patterns and unorthodox forms, these buildings shriek of an anti-rationalist revolt, one aided by digital technologies.

Around the corner, Building 94, by Allan Powell with Pels Innes Nielson Kosloff, 1995, is a collage of brutalist sculptural forms in sensual materials, set up in a tense composition with a cleavage.

On RMIT's pastoral campuses at Bundoora, in Melbourne's northern suburbs, Building 220 by Wood Marsh with Pels Innes Nielson Kosloff, 1998, is a modernist gesture – a sweeping arc modified by graphic contrasts of materials in orange and grey.

More neo-modernist buildings are planned for the other Bundoora site: student housing by Durbach Block, a long multi-purpose building by Kerstin Thompson, research pavilions by Sean Godsell and a biomedical sciences block by John Wardle with Eggleston Macdonald.

Further along Swanston Street from RMIT's city icons, the University of Melbourne unveiled in 1998 a fresh face to its campus: the Ian Potter Museum of Art by Nation Fender Katsalidis. This ensemble of layered planes and cubic frames (relieved by an ornate white frieze) is a hip yet orderly contrast to the frantic facades of the former technical college uphill.

Both RMIT and Melbourne have been using Peter Elliott to tidy up neglected parts of their campuses and judiciously introduce small new structures to link with and add amenities to existing buildings.

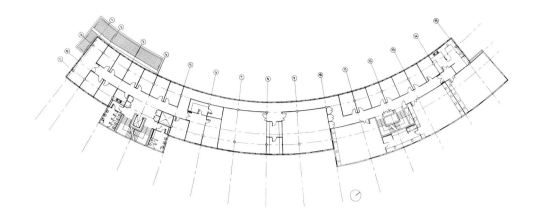

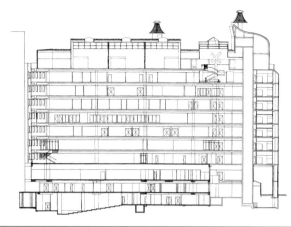

At Monash University's Caulfield campus in Melbourne, Denton Corker Marshall recently completed a neo-modernist, silver-sheathed Faculty of Art and Design, 1999, to supplement its Computer Sciences Building, 1993, and several engineering, medical and computer buildings by Bates Smart McCutcheon, 1993–94.

On another Monash campus at Clayton, Allan Powell produced a monolithic Performing Arts Centre, 1994, which was coloured in deep red oxide as a reminder of the Australian desert.

In Geelong, Victoria's second largest city, Deakin University has completed three interesting projects. The first was a recycling of old waterfront woolstores for its architecture school, by McGlashan & Everist, 1996. The latest, by BSA-Sinclair Knight Merz at Waurn Ponds, 1999, is a wool research shed distinguished by its folded, metal-sheathed form and jolts of saturated pink and yellow.

On a satellite campus at Burwood, north of Melbourne, Deakin also has built some graphic icons by Wood Marsh with Pels Innes Nielson Kosloff. Buildings C–G,.1996, and Building J, 1998, are primal forms – radiating from a central stair and elaborated with facade materials of contrasting textures in white, grey and black.

Modernist aesthetics also define the Callaghan bush campus of the University of Newcastle and the Kensington (Sydney) campus of the University of NSW. Both were mainly developed during the 1960s and 1970s heyday of the Sydney School – whose members often mixed British brutalism with the

OPPOSITE
RMIT BUILDING 8, EDMOND & CORRIGAN WITH DEMAINE PARTNERSHIP, MELBOURNE, 1994
SURMOUNTING A TWO-STOREY BRUTALIST BUILDING BY JOHN ANDREWS, THIS 11-STOREY DECORATED SHED HERALDED THE UNIVERSITY'S 1990s PROGRAM OF PROGRESSIVE BUILDING. THE SWANSTON STREET ELEVATION (ABOVE LEFT) IS A HIGHLY FIGURED TAPESTRY OF MOTIFS WHICH ALLUDE TO AUSTRALIA'S MULTI-CULTURAL CIRCUMSTANCES – 'WARTS AND ALL.' OTHER FACADES ARE ELABORATED IN POLYCHROMATIC BRICK AND STRIPED STEEL PANELLING. CROSS SECTION TOP. PHOTO JOHN GOLLINGS.

ABOVE
IAN POTTER MUSEUM OF ART (UNIVERSITY OF MELBOURNE), NATION FENDER KATSALIDIS, MELBOURNE, 1999
SET BESIDE AN EXISTING GALLERY, THIS MUSEUM PRESENTS A NEW FACE FOR THE UNIVERSITY TO ONE OF MELBOURNE'S BUSIEST STREETS. THE EXTERIOR IS AN ABSTRACTED, CUBIC COLLAGE OF MASONRY AND METALS, ELABORATED BY A WHITE WALL FRIEZE CALLED 'CULTURAL RUBBLE', BY CHRISTINE O'LAUGHLIN. THE INTERIOR HAS OFFICES AND GALLERIES AROUND AN ATRIUM.
PHOTO JOHN GOLLINGS.

ABOVE AND RIGHT
BOX HILL INSTITUTE OF TAFE, STAGE 2
NELSON CAMPUS, LYONS, BOX HILL,
VICTORIA, 1999
A NEW FOYER LINKING TWO COLLEGE
BUILDINGS WAS DESIGNED AS A 'SPHERE
WITHIN A SPHERE.' THE CENTRAL DOME
CONTAINS A LECTURE THEATRE
OVERLOOKED BY AN UPSTAIRS GALLERY.
WALLS OF THE OUTER SPHERE HAVE BEEN
CLAD WITH FIBREBOARD TILES IN
TOPOGRAPHIC COLOURS INSPIRED BY
SATELLITE PHOTOS OF THE EARTH. AS AN
OPTICAL TRICK, THESE COLOURFUL
CURVED WALLS APPEAR 'COMPRESSED'
BETWEEN AN OPAL SKYLIGHT AND PALE
VINYL FLOOR. PHOTOS TREVOR MEIN.

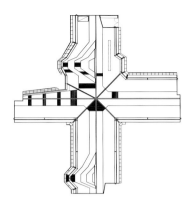

humane, organic models of Alvar Aalto and Frank Lloyd Wright.

Among the gum trees at Newcastle, this tradition has been compatibly updated in concrete, steel and glass by Stutchbury & Pape with EJE Architecture (Faculty of Design, 1995; Faculty of Nursing, 1999); Grose Bradley (Architecture Studios, 1997) and Jackson Teece Chesterman Willis (Pacific Power Laboratories, 1994). Further projects are being developed by Stutchbury & Pape with Suters (a medical link building) and S&P with Richard Leplastrier and Sue Harper (an education and cultural centre for Aborigines and Torres Strait Islanders).

At the University of NSW, there is a powerful contrast between the brick classicism of Peddle Thorp's Quadrangle Building, 1994, and Cox Richardson's Barker Street Housing, 1998, and interpretations of modernist Italian rationalism from Guiseppe Terragni to Renzo Piano.

The latter works are in masonry, steel and glass, with climate-sensitive facades of fritted glazing, louvres and sunscreens. Examples are Lawrence Nield's Graduate School of Management, 1996; Bligh Voller Nield's Webster Building refurbishment, 1999, and Mitchell/ Giurgola & Thorp's Faculty of Architecture, 1998, and Scientia Building, 1999.

In Perth, polychrome brick has been used creatively at Curtin University of Technology – where Philip Cox Etherington Coulter & Jones formed the bold Kahnian triangles of the New Technologies Building, 1994, with brickwork in variegated streaks – like the exposed strata of ocean cliffs.

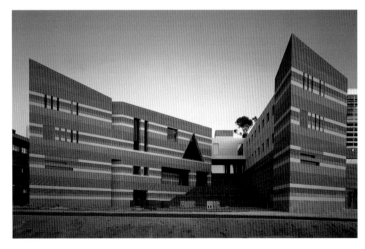

TOP (PLAN) AND MIDDLE
GOULBURN OVENS INSTITUTE OF TAFE, PERROTT LYON MATHIESON WITH CAREY LYON, BENALLA, VICTORIA, 1998
DESIGNED AS THE FIRST BUILDING OF A NEW RURAL CAMPUS, THIS STEEL SHED BEGINS WITH A CRUCIFORM PLAN RECALLING THE PEGS USED BY SURVEYORS TO MAP GROUND FOR DEVELOPMENT. THE BUILDING SHELL IS CONTOURED AND COLOURED TO REPRESENT UNDULATING LAND. THE ENTRANCE IS AT THE CENTRE OF THE CROSS: TRAINING ROOMS ARE IN THE WINGS. PHOTO TIM GRIFFITH.

ABOVE LEFT
NEW TECHNOLOGIES BUILDING, CURTIN UNIVERSITY, PHILIP COX, ETHERINGTON COULTER & JONES, PERTH, 1994
BUILT ON A CAMPUS OF BLAND BRICK AND CONCRETE BLOCKS, THIS FOUR-STOREY BUILDING UPDATES THE PRISMATIC FORMS OF LOUIS KAHN WITH ONE OF AUSTRALIA'S MOST FLORID RECENT EXAMPLES OF POLYCHROME BRICKWORK. ON PLAN, ONE OF TWO LINKED RECTANGULAR BLOCKS IS DIAGONALLY SLICED TO OPEN UP AN ARRIVAL COURT AND A BROAD STAIRCASE TO THE THIRD FLOOR ENTRANCE. PHOTOS PATRICK BINGHAM-HALL.

ABOVE RIGHT
BUILDING B, SWINBURNE UNIVERSITY (TAFE), PERROTT LYON MATHIESON WITH CAREY LYON, LILYDALE LAKE, VICTORIA, 1997
SITE SURVEY PLANS INITIATED THE DESIGN FOR THIS THREE-STOREY BUILDING, HOUSING A LIBRARY AND COMPUTER RESOURCES CENTRE, SURROUNDED BY TRAINING ROOMS. THE ARCHITECTURE CAN BE INTERPRETED METAPHORICALLY AS A SLICE OF SUBTERRANEAN LANDSCAPE RAISED TO GROUND LEVEL. IN RESPONSE TO THE STEEP SITE, THE ENTRY IS AT MID-LEVEL. PHOTO JOHN GOLLINGS.

Geological allusions also appeal to Melbourne's Carey Lyons, who has interpreted landforms and rock schisms in masonry, at Swinburne University's Building B, Lilydale, 1997, and in steel, at Goulburn Ovens College, Benalla, 1998. These artfully contoured buildings, both credited to Lyon Architecture with Perrott Lyon Mathieson, are centrepieces of new campuses on rural sites which are mainly flat.

At Sippy Downs, Queensland, the University of the Sunshine Coast is also growing from scratch on flat pastures. Its first buildings switch between light expressions of the 'Sunshine Coast Style' (Clare Design's Recreation Club, 1997), and substantial blocks in masonry (six initial buildings by Mitchell/Giurgola & Thorp with Geoffrey Pie, 1995; the Faculty of Science by Daryl Jackson with Down & Neylan, 1997, and Bligh Voller Nield's Faculty of Art, 1999). Both genres have steel roofs, skylights, slatted sunscreens and systems for natural ventilation.

Sunshine Coast's focal building is a three-storey library by Lawrence Nield of Sydney with Noosa architect John Mainwaring, 1997. With its casual demeanour (beach shack materials, barbeques on the Great Verandah) and sun-responsive screens and sawtooth roof-lights (reminding some observers of flipping pages), it's a vital step in the development of original Australian architecture.

In a different way to RMIT's city spectacles, it usurps European conventions of classical academic civitas with exuberant and witty interpretations of local traditions and idiosyncracies.

ABOVE AND TOP RIGHT
FACULTY OF DESIGN, UNIVERSITY OF NEWCASTLE, STUTCHBURY & PAPE WITH EJE ARCHITECTURE, NEW SOUTH WALES, 1995
CONTINUING THE ROBUST ARCHITECTURE OF A BUSH CAMPUS, THIS NATURALLY VENTILATED, ECOLOGY-CONSCIOUS BUILDING HAS A SAWTOOTH ROOF FACING EAST AND A DECK AND COURT TO THE NORTH. THREE LEVELS OF WORKSHOPS, STUDIOS AND OFFICES ARE PUNCTURED BY A CENTRAL LIGHT VOID/STAIRWELL. PHOTOS PATRICK BINGHAM-HALL, DAVE CUBBY.

BOTTOM RIGHT
FACULTY OF NURSING, UNIVERSITY OF NEWCASTLE, STUTCHBURY & PAPE WITH EJE ARCHITECTURE, NEW SOUTH WALES, 1995
A 450-SEAT LECTURE THEATRE SITS BETWEEN TWO BLOCKS OF OFFICES TOPPED WITH STEEL SKILLIONS. THESE FLYING ROOFS DEFLECT BREEZES DOWN TO TWO COURTYARDS. GLAZING ON THE NORTH-EAST FACADE ALLOWS OUTLOOKS TO GUM TREES. LIKE THE UNIVERSITY'S OTHER RECENT BUILDINGS, THE NURSING FACULTY IS PLAINLY BUILT TO A TIGHT BUDGET, USING NATURAL VENTILATION AND ENERGY-EFFICIENCY STRATEGIES. PHOTO TIM LINKINS.

OPPOSITE
ARCHITECTURE STUDIOS, GROSE BRADLEY, UNIVERSITY OF NEWCASTLE, NEW SOUTH WALES, 1997
IN RESPONSE TO A MINIMAL BUDGET, THE STUDIOS PAVILION IS A BASIC BOX FORMED FROM STEEL WAREHOUSE FRAMES, SANDWICH PANELS, CONCRETE BLOCKS AND CORRUGATED ZINCALUME. THE SQUARE PLAN IS CENTRALLY SLICED BY A NORTH-SOUTH ENTRY RAMP WHICH BECOMES A BRIDGE OVERLOOKING THE GROUND FLOOR OF STUDENT WORKSTATIONS. THE SKILLION ROOF IS SKYLIT. PHOTO TOM BALFOUR.

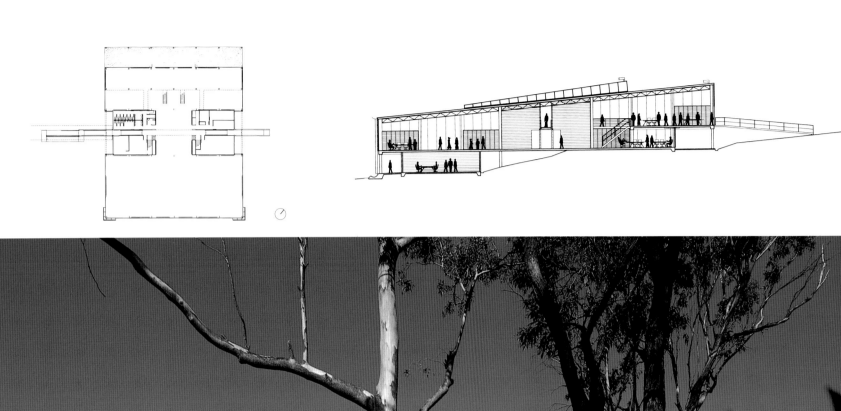

PUBLIC BUILDINGS

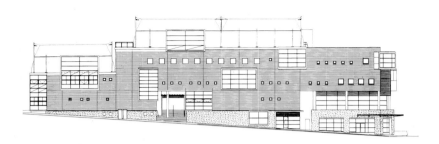

While the world reconfigures its cultural structures and commercial systems, civic buildings are beginning to regain some of the ceremonial and metaphorical qualities which were mostly avoided during modernism's war against adornment. But there is much debate between modernists and expressionists about the morality of architectural imagery.

The last great discussion on architectural aesthetics occurred in the 19th century, when industrial societies began to ignore hand-made decorative art to focus on mass-produced goods. In high Victorian England, from the 1840s to the 1880s, leading architecture theorists like James Ferguson and John Ruskin resisted the diminution of arts and crafts by glorifying the idea of buildings gaining elegance through superfluous elaboration. Theirs was a reactionary position, invoking a high ethical ideal about the supremacy of human creativity over the mindless efficiency of steam machines. In *The Seven Lamps of Architecture* (1849), Ruskin defined buildings as merely functional structures and claimed for architecture a greater, decorative, role to create 'those characters of an edifice which are above and beyond its common use.' Of course in architecture's 20th-century intellectual framework, the reverse has prevailed as truth.

Today, because of the ubiquity of visual communication and the need for cities to compete within a planet-wide marketplace, there's revived demand for 'postcard' architecture: a commercial need for singular expression rather than uniformity in building aesthetics.

ABOVE LEFT
MANDURAH PERFORMING ARTS CENTRE, HAMES SHARLEY, MANDURAH, WESTERN AUSTRALIA, 1998
ON THE WATERFRONT OF A GROWING CITY SOUTH OF PERTH, A 2-STOREY CULTURAL CENTRE PROVIDES THEATRES, AN ART GALLERY, PERFORMANCE STUDIOS AND A RESTAURANT. GLASSY FACADES ALLOW WIDE VIEWS FROM AND INTO THE FOYERS. THE FLAT ROOF PROJECTS TO STEEL PYLONS WHICH DEFINE THE ENTRY PATH AND ADJACENT REFLECTION POND AS A COLONNADE. BOARDWALKS ENCOURAGE PROMENADES ALONG THE RIVER AFTER PERFORMANCES. PHOTO MARTIN FARQUHARSON.

ABOVE RIGHT
ULTIMO COMMUNITY CENTRE, LAWRENCE NIELD & PARTNERS, SYDNEY, 1997
BUILT ON A PRIME CORNER OF A HISTORIC NEIGHBOURHOOD, THIS COMMUNITY COMPLEX WRAPS AROUND A COURTYARD AND UPDATES THE ANCIENT TRADITION OF WALLED VILLAGES. HERE, HOWEVER, THE MASONRY ENCLOSURE IS PUNCTURED WITH SUDDEN CHANGES TO MODERN MATERIALS (RIPPLE STEEL, GLASS), AND AN IRREGULAR ARRAY OF BALCONY WINDOWS, ONE ELLIPTICAL OPENING (AN EYE TO THE SKY) AND A ROOFTOP VEIL OF BLACK TENNIS NETS. SOUTH ELEVATION TOP. PHOTO FARSHID ASSASSI.

OPPOSITE
COMMONWEALTH LAW COURTS, HASSELL, MELBOURNE, 1999
CORPORATE MODERNISM'S CURTAIN WALL IS RE-DRAPED ON THIS 17-STOREY TOWER AS AN INTRICATE AND GLOSSY TAPESTRY. THE DISSONANT PATTERNING OF WINDOW MULLIONS IS INTENDED TO PROVOKE A SENSE OF TENSION BETWEEN POISED STABILITY AND SUDDEN MOVEMENT. THE BUILDING IS PLANNED AS TWO BLOCKS – ONE CONTAINING FEDERAL COURTS AND THE OTHER HOLDING PUBLIC AREAS AND OFFICES. THESE REALMS ARE LINKED BY BRIDGES ACROSS A SKYLIT CENTRAL 'STREET'. PHOTO JOHN GOLLINGS.

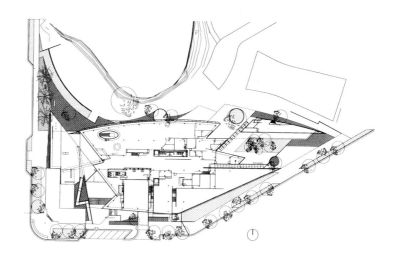

This shift is provoking argument between architects who celebrate 'authentic' tectonics and primal forms and others who hope to revive applied decoration and metaphoric imagery.

In Australia, the authenticity position is supported by Sydney architect Richard Francis-Jones, who writes that 'architecture should not be reduced to a market-dependent consumerable, as at this point it becomes merely decorated building, within the flux of fashion' ('The [Im]possibility of Slowness' in *UME* 10, 1999). The elaboration position is put by Melbourne architect Carey Lyon, who recognises that 'decorating the outside of the box is superficial not deep' and claims that 'an archeology for the contemporary city won't be discovered by digging deep but by scratching at the surface' ('Another City for a Thin World' in *Transition* No. 40, 1993).

These questions of surface versus substance, along with impulses to 'transform the box', show up strongly in several government administration and public cultural buildings developed during the 1990s.

One strategy has been to 'slice open' a building by splitting it with an internal chasm. This becomes a skylit central street overlooked by balconies and sometimes linked by bridges. Examples are the Wagga Wagga Civic Centre by Garner Davis (Wagga Wagga, NSW, 1999) and Hassell's Commonwealth Law Courts (Melbourne, 1999).

Another approach has been to animate a building's street facades with shapely cutouts and dynamic arrangements of projecting

WAGGA WAGGA CIVIC CENTRE, GARNER DAVIS, WAGGA WAGGA, NEW SOUTH WALES, 1999
A RURAL CITY HAS BUILT A THREE-STOREY ARTS/ADMINISTRATION CENTRE BESIDE ITS LAGOON. ITS DESIGN STEMS FROM A 'CONCEPTUAL MAP' OF AXES DRAWN ACROSS THE SITE, TO LINK TO KEY PLACES AROUND THE CITY. THESE 'LEY LINES' GUIDED THE COMPLEX'S PLAN IN RELATION TO AN EXISTING COUNCIL CHAMBER AND THEATRE. THE MAIN NEW BUILDING IS TRANSPARENT AND HAS SEVERAL ENTRANCES. VARIOUS FACADES (OF EQUAL STATUS) ARE ERODED BY PLAZAS TO THE WEST AND EAST. GROUND FLOOR PLAN TOP. PHOTOS PATRICK BINGHAM-HALL.

NEXT PAGES THE WAGGA WAGGA CIVIC CENTRE'S NORTH FACADE OF PERFORATED METAL OVER GLAZING, SEEN AT NIGHT, LOOKING SOUTH ACROSS THE WOLLUNDRY LAGOON. PHOTO PATRICK BINGHAM-HALL.

**NEVILLE BONNER BUILDING,
DAVENPORT CAMPBELL WITH
DONOVAN HILL AND POWELL DODS
THORPE, BRISBANE, 1999**
A SIX-STOREY GOVERNMENT OFFICE
COMPLEX OCCUPIES AN AWKWARD CITY
BLOCK BORDERED BY A FREEWAY
OVERPASS AND HISTORIC MONUMENTS.
IT IS BUILT OF CONCRETE, WITH GLAZED
CURTAIN WALLS SHIELDED BY MASSIVE
PRECAST SUNSCREENS AND ALUMINIUM
LOUVRES. TERRACED COURTS AT TWO
CORNERS ARE LANDSCAPED WITH PONDS.
A BRIDGE AND WHEELCHAIR RAMP ALLOW
ACCESS FROM THE HIGHER STREET.
PHOTOS ANTHONY BROWELL.

balconies and windows. This tactic is demonstrated at the Ultimo Community Centre by Lawrence Nield & Partners, Sydney, 1996 (where the bay windows have been likened by writer Philip Drew to the tribunas projecting from Moroccan harems) and at Hassell's courts.

At the Neville Bonner Building in Brisbane, by Davenport Campbell with Donovan Hill and Powell Dods Thorpe, 1999, the block walls around the entrance are energised by a dissipated arrangement of projecting ledges and window frames, ornamented by four art installations. The other facades are cloaked with either computer-controlled metal sun louvres or fixed masonry sunscreens in highly figured geometric patterns. This strategy of decorative masonic plays with sunlight and shadows is also seen in several 1990s houses by Donovan Hill and is reminiscent of the 1930s incinerators of Walter and Marion Griffin (pupils of Wright) and (in monumentality) some of Harry Seidler's sunscreens.

While some architects are puncturing solids, others are using glass and overlays of perforated metal to show that civic buildings can be transparent, sunny and permeable. At Mandurah, Western Australia, the waterfront cultural centre by Hames Sharley, 1998, is fully glazed on both of its key facades, so its foyers glow at night as lanterns of human activity.

One intriguing aspect of recent civic architecture is that most new works are landscaped with black reflection ponds. This suggests that architects now want citizens to appreciate stillness – and the illusion of endless depth.

LIBRARIES

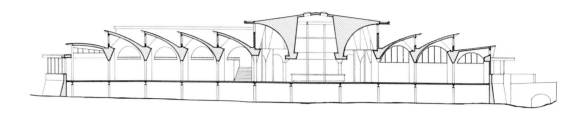

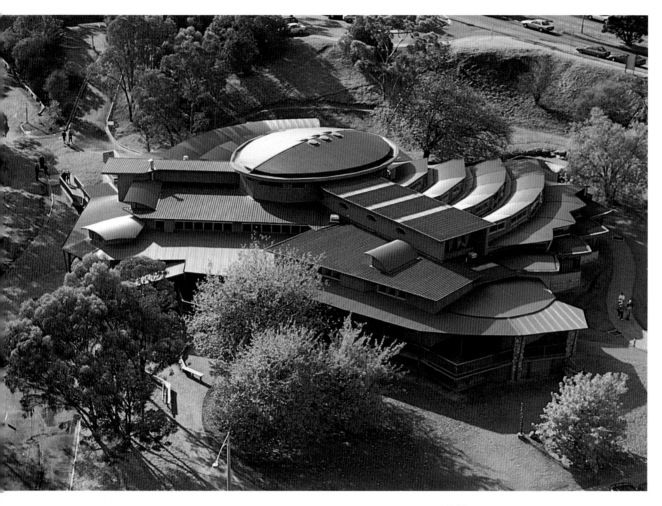

'This will kill that: the book will kill the edifice,' wrote Victor Hugo in *The Hunchback of Notre Dame*. Two centuries later, the architecture of libraries is a demanding matter of how to display the contemporary significance of repositories dating back to monks in the Middle Ages. And the future of the printed book is clouded by the advent of on-screen communications.

In the early 1990s, when Ashton Raggatt McDougall conceived additions to Enrico Taglietti's 1969 St Kilda Library in Melbourne (along with a major refurbishment of the fire-gutted Town Hall across the road), there was a belief among futurists that books would not be published on paper in the digital age. (This now seems less certain.)

As a solemn farewell to literature of the Gutenberg age, ARM fronted the new library with a bluestone grave like monumental tomes found in local cemeteries. The open pages are devoid of text but supply one 'active illustration': a window (screen) which reveals activities in the reading room to pedestrians outside. Inside the library, this facade wall is curved to read as the book's back view.

No other Australian library offers such literal symbolism, although Nield-Mainwaring's Sunshine Coast library includes metaphoric gestures. Another recent example is Greg Burgess' Eltham Library, 1995, which provides an artistic community with an organic place to dwell within, yet apart from, the bush. At Gordon, on Sydney's north shore, Schwager Brooks built a polychrome brick library and police station around a community plaza in 1994.

ELTHAM LIBRARY, GREGORY BURGESS, MELBOURNE, 1995
ELTHAM IS A BUSH COMMUNITY SENSITIVE TO THE ARTS AND NATURE. ITS NEW LIBRARY IS AN ORGANIC PAVILION MADE OF CLAY AND MUD BRICKS AND TIMBER, WITH A MULTI-LAYERED, RED STEEL ROOF SEEN FROM HIGHER GROUND. THE ARCHITECTURE IS INTENDED TO BALANCE NOTIONS OF PRIVACY AND SHARING, IMAGINATION AND WISDOM, THOUGHT AND CALM. THERE IS A HIERARCHY OF BRIGHT CENTRAL SPACES, GLOOMIER CORNERS AND PERIPHERAL BALCONIES SERVED BY A CAFÉ. PHOTO TREVOR MEIN.

ST KILDA LIBRARY AND TOWN HALL,
ASHTON RAGGATT MCDOUGALL,
MELBOURNE, 1994
A NEW SUBURBAN LIBRARY IS SIGNALLED
BY A GIANT BLUESTONE TOME WITH A
'PICTURE' WINDOW (ABOVE). ACROSS THE
ROAD, A VICTORIAN TOWN HALL HAS BEEN
RENOVATED WITH FEATURES LIFTED FROM
FOREIGN PRECEDENTS. NEW REAR
OFFICES MIMIC ALVAR AALTO'S FINLANDIA
HALL (RIGHT) AND A WHEELCHAIR RAMP
REVISES AMERICAN SCULPTOR RICHARD
SERRA'S 1960s 'TILTED ARC' (FAR RIGHT).
PHOTOS JOHN GOLLINGS, TREVOR MEIN.

HOSPITALS

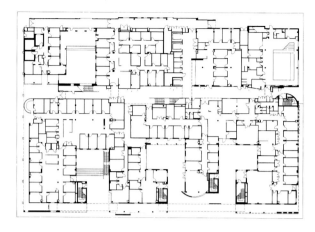

After British surgeon Joseph Lister produced the first antiseptics in the 1870s, fresh air began to be considered less essential to treat the sick. As a result, and to save costs and staff walking time, 20th-century hospitals mostly have been designed as towers of stacked dormitories and services.

In Australia now, however, the hospital high-rise is shrinking and fragmenting to become a 'hospital-as-village'. Although this idea is more expensive to build, it is more appropriate to the industry's new commercial conditions, which emphasise patient satisfaction as well as efficiencies of treatment. Computers and fibre-optic surgery are also likely to change hospital floor plans because they are transforming many procedures.

Appropriately, the village concept was recently tested for a children's facility, where low buildings were desired to avoid an institutional sense of intimidation.

In 1993, the Royal Alexandra Hospital for Children commissioned four three-storey complexes to establish a new site at Westmead. These buildings were designed by four offices of architects, with deliberately diverse aesthetics. Government architects at NSW State Projects supervised the development and delivered tropical-style wards in pale brick laced with white awnings. Woods Bagot expressed the clinical services block with masonry grids of white and yellow. With the administration building, Lawrence Nield combined grids and sinuous rooflines. And McConnel Smith & Johnson planned the outpatients' facility as cubes in scorching colours.

ABOVE
ROYAL ALEXANDRA HOSPITAL FOR CHILDREN ADMINISTRATION BUILDING, LAWRENCE NIELD & PARTNERS, WESTMEAD, NEW SOUTH WALES, 1995
THIS CHILDREN'S HOSPITAL ARRIVAL COMPLEX IS FIRST SEEN ACROSS A FORECOURT LANDSCAPED WITH SCULPTURES. TO REDUCE ITS LARGE SCALE, THE ARCHITECTURE IS FRAGMENTARY: COMBINING UNDULATING ROOFLINES AND LAYERED STRUCTURES WITH PERFORATED METAL SUNSCREENS ON THE NORTH AND WEST SIDES. INSIDE, THE GALLERIA (LEFT) IS BRIGHTLY DAYLIT, WITH AN AERIAL SCULPTURE BY MIKE KITCHING. PHOTOS JOHN GOLLINGS.

OPPOSITE
ROYAL ALEXANDRA HOSPITAL FOR CHILDREN OUTPATIENTS BUILDING, MCCONNEL SMITH & JOHNSON, WESTMEAD, NEW SOUTH WALES, 1995
CONTRADICTORY GAMES OF AESTHETICS ARE COMBINED IN THIS DESIGN FOR CHILDREN. FIRST, THE FACADE OF A LARGE BLOCK IS INTERRUPTED BY COURTYARDS SUITABLE FOR PLAY. BUT THE REMAINING BOXY FORMS, INSPIRED BY DI CHIRICO'S DISTURBING PAINTINGS, RETAIN A POTENTIALLY INTIMIDATING SENSE OF MONUMENTALITY – WHICH IS SUBVERTED BY HAPPY COLOURS. THE PLAN (TOP) IS ORDERED BY A SKYLIT CENTRAL HALL. PHOTO FARSHID ASSASSI.

INDIGENOUS PAVILIONS

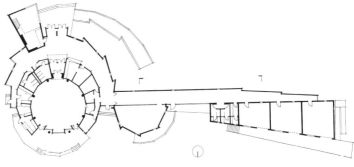

In 1952, Robin Boyd claimed that Australia's blacks had no use for architecture. With this comment in *Australia's Home*, he overlooked three kinds of climate-responsive 19th century indigenous structures: the light elevated huts of the north, stick and bark wind-breaks in the desert and stone 'igloos' in Victoria.

Although there's less evidence of those dwellings today, new types of indigenous community buildings are being developed to express tribal identity and educate visitors.

There's no known record of an indigenous architecture graduate until the 1990s. So the key Aboriginal visitor and cultural centres have been conceived by whites: Glenn Murcutt with Troppo, (Kakadu National Park, NT, 1994), Anthony Styant-Browne (at Healesville, Victoria, 1996) and Gregory Burgess (Uluru, NT, 1996).

National facilities for Aboriginal and Torres Strait Islander culture are being built beside Lake Burley Griffin in Canberra, as an informal precinct of buildings in assorted forms and colours. The design is by two Melbourne firms, Ashton Raggatt McDougall with Robert Peck von Hartel Trethowan.

In these early days of conceiving pavilions of Aboriginality, it is often expected that they should represent values other than those of the male-oriented European culture which has dominated the mobs since the mid 19th century. Most schemes incorporate the ideas of oblique arrival rather than formal axial entrances, meandering rather than lineal paths, outdoor meeting places and cave-gloomy rooms, and curvy, assymetrical structures and spaces rather than rectangular forms. The visitor centres by Burgess and Styant-Browne also allude to bush creatures in their plans or forms.

The ARM-RPVHT Canberra scheme has no obvious animalistic connotations – and nor does a significant new education complex in Sydney: the teaching facilities added to Tranby Aboriginal College by Cracknell Lonergan with Merrima, 1998. This project is a series of copper-roofed cylinders built in red and yellow cement blocks, set around a sinuous gathering place.

At Alice Springs, in the central desert, the Tangentyere Council, administering local Aboriginal affairs, owns an office employing white architects, led by Sue Dugdale. This group plans housing, renovations and small structures.

Australia's only 'authentic' Aboriginal design office is the Merrima unit set up in the NSW Department of Public Works and Services in 1995. It is managed by three of Australia's first indigenous architecture and interior design graduates: Dillon Kombumerrie, Kevin O'Brien and Alison Page.

In 1998, Kombumerrie made history as the first Australian Aborigine to be credited for a work of architecture in contemporary mode: the Girrawaa Creative Work Centre beside Bathurst Gaol, NSW.

This timber and steel pavilion signals Merrima's agenda to build zoomorphic representations of tribal totems and supernatural Dreamtime figures – abstracted as skeletal structures with thin skins. At Girrawaa, the totem is a locally hallowed goanna lizard, with its tail transformed into an entry ramp.

ABOVE
TRANBY COLLEGE ADDITIONS,
CRACKNELL LONERGAN WITH
MERRIMA/NSW DPWS, SYDNEY, 1998
NEW TEACHING FACILITIES HAVE BEEN
BUILT BEHIND THE GEORGIAN VILLA
HEADQUARTERS OF THE TRANBY
ABORIGINAL CO-OPERATIVE IN GLEBE.
A SERIES OF TWO-STOREY CIRCULAR
PAVILIONS ARE CLUSTERED TOGETHER
AROUND A SINUOUS GATHERING PLACE
(SEE PLAN, TOP). BUILT IN SPLIT FACE
CONCRETE BLOCK, THEY ARE WRAPPED
WITH BRASS-BALUSTRADED BALCONIES
OVERLOOKING THE COURTYARD AND
TOPPED WITH COPPER DOMES.
PHOTO SIMON KENNY.

LEFT AND ABOVE
GIRRAWAA CREATIVE WORK CENTRE,
MERRIMA DESIGN/NSW DEPARTMENT
OF PUBLIC WORKS & SERVICES,
BATHURST, NEW SOUTH WALES, 1998
THE GIRRAWAA (FORMERLY GOOGAR)
WORK CENTRE IS A STEEL AND PLYWOOD
PAVILION BUILT OUTSIDE THE WALLS OF
A COUNTRY GAOL AS A FACILITY FOR
INDIGENOUS PRISONERS TO LEARN CRAFT
TECHNIQUES. AFTER CONSULTATION WITH
USERS, THE ARCHITECTS PLANNED THE
BUILDING TO REPRESENT A LACE MONITOR
GOANNA LIZARD: TOTEM OF THE LOCAL
WIRADJURI PEOPLE. INSIDE, THE ROOMS
ARE IRREGULARLY SHAPED. PHOTOS
PATRICK BINGHAM-HALL.

HALLS OF WORSHIP

**CENTRAL SYNAGOGUE, JACKSON
TEECE CHESTERMAN WILLIS, BONDI,
NEW SOUTH WALES, 1998**
AT THE SYNAGOGUE ENTRY (ABOVE),
A STAINLESS STEEL ARCH PROJECTS
FROM A SANDSTONE FACADE. INSIDE, AN
OCULUS ILLUMINATES THE OCTAGONAL
SHULE (OPPOSITE TOP), WHICH ALSO HAS
FOUR CEREMONIAL WINDOWS OF STAINED
GLASS LAYERS (ABOVE AND TOP LEFT)
CREATED BY ARTISTS JANET LAURENCE
AND JISUK HAN. IN THE FOYER (OPPOSITE
BOTTOM), HAN'S MEMORIAL WALL HAS
PERSPEX NAME PLATES ILLUMINATED BY
HALOGEN CANDLES FOR ANNIVERSARIES.
PHOTOS JOHN GOLLINGS.

Houses of religion have been a declining type in Australia since the neo-Gothic churches of the late 19th century. But the diminishing congregations of European parishes are being offset by waves of customers for American and Asian courses in spiritual fulfilment and health. This shift of community mentality, from serving a supreme being to satisfying the self, has affected the architecture of places of worship. No longer planned as intimidating symbols of godly authority, they now tend to project an egalitarian demeanour.

Contradicting the Gothic tradition of interior gloom pierced by sublime shafts of heavenly light, Australian churches often are designed in the Scandinavian style of gentle illumination, white walls and pale timber pews. There is still a crucial need to orchestrate daylight to introduce a sense of enlightenment above serene spaces.

A significant new religious building is the Central Synagogue at Bondi, NSW, 1998. Designed by Jackson Teece Chesterman Willis (Damian Barker), with symbolic installations by artists Janet Laurence and Jisuk Han, it replaces an earlier synagogue destroyed by fire.

Although the shule and minor sanctuary can contain more than 2000 worshippers, this two-storey complex modestly relates to nearby houses with a horizontal sandstone and glass front, relieved simply by a sweeping entry arch of steel tube.

That unpretentious facade is a contrast to the ornate pagoda architecture of several massive Buddhist temples recently built in different parts of the country.

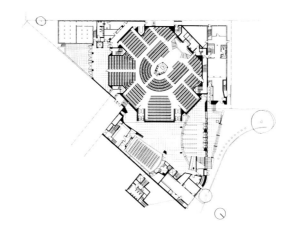

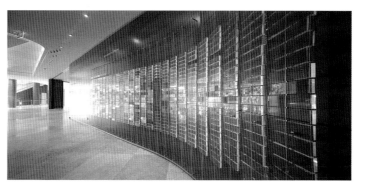

ENVIRONMENTAL ART

Australia's main change in public art during the 1990s was a rise in the patronage of artworks conceived to fuse with and metaphysically enrich specific sites. This can be partly explained by reaction against the earlier habit of placing discrete sculptures in parks and plazas.

There are three common approaches to commissioning site-specific art. One is to appoint a community artist to work with local adults or children in a creative therapy program which produces authentic expressions of the community. Another method is to marry artists who think in three dimensions with architects and other designers of environments. The third system is for developers of major projects to commission one artist to produce a work for a chosen part of the property.

The most notable, permanent public artworks of the 1990s were created by Sydney teams involving Janet Laurence (concerned with alchemy), Richard Goodwin (who assembles steel exo-skeletons and protheses), and Jennifer Turpin with Michaelie Crawford (who creatively manipulate water).

In Victoria, Herring Island in the Yarra River opened as a park of seven environmental installations. Melbourne architects Nation Fender Katsalidis formed the Visible Art Foundation to commission artists to produce provocative works for display on their building sites.

The Sydney and Melbourne city councils regularly add new works to their already extensive sculpture walks. And the Queensland state government now requires building developers to apply two percent of their budgets to artworks.

TOP LEFT RICHARD GOODWIN'S CORVETTE MEMORIAL AT GARDEN ISLAND, SYDNEY, 1995. PHOTO ANTHONY BROWELL.

TOP RIGHT 'VEIL OF TREES', BY JANET LAURENCE AND JISUK HAN, AT MRS MACQUARIE'S CHAIR, 1999. AN EARLY INSTALLATION FOR THE SYDNEY SCULPTURE WALK. PHOTO BRETT BOARDMAN.

LEFT ROBYN BACKEN'S 'CHRIST KNOWS' WINDOW INSTALLATION AT THE CASULA POWERHOUSE ARTS CENTRE IN WESTERN SYDNEY. PHOTO CHRIS FORTESCUE.

OPPOSITE PAGE BOTTOM RIGHT
'THE MEMORY LINE' IS A RIBBON OF
RYE GRASS MARKING A SUBURBAN
SYDNEY CREEK BED; BY JENNIFER
TURPIN AND MICHAELIE CRAWFORD
WITH SCHAEFFER BARNSLEY AND THE
FAIRFIELD COMMUNITY, 1996. PHOTO
IAN HOBBS.

LEFT STATUE OF FORMER AUSTRALIAN
PRIME MINISTER BEN CHIFLEY BY SIMEON
NELSON, AT CHIFLEY SQUARE, SYDNEY,
1998. PHOTO SIMEON NELSON.

TOP LIGHT WALLS IN THE DEVONSHIRE
STREET TUNNEL, SYDNEY, BY MERILYN
FAIRSKYE, 1999. PHOTO PATRICK
BINGHAM-HALL.

ABOVE LEFT PATRICIA PICCININI'S 'PROTEIN
LATTICE'; A STREET DISPLAY FOR THE
VISIBLE ARTS FOUNDATION AT THE REPUBLIC
APARTMENT TOWER, MELBOURNE, 1999.
PHOTO JOHN GOLLINGS.

ABOVE RIGHT 'TANK', AT SYDNEY'S
DOWNING CENTRE TUNNEL, BY JENNIFER
TURPIN AND MICHAELIE CRAWFORD WITH
PEDDLE THORP, 1997. PHOTO IAN HOBBS.

TRAFFIC STRUCTURES

Transport infrastructure has only lately become a realm of possible (indeed interesting) activity for architects and artists. This is an outcome of the rising influence of urban designers; a new discipline which adds aesthetic concerns to the town planning and engineering agendas of government authorities. Until the 1990s, road and rail planning agencies consistently ignored the design professions in their schemes for highways, bridges, rail systems and interchanges. But during the past decade, a handful of architects and artists have been commissioned to design bridges, freeway noise barriers and sculptural installations at intersections. The results, mostly in Sydney and Melbourne so far, are inspiring a generally more creative attitude to infrastructure.

Melbourne's key roadwork projects – by Wood Marsh with Pels Innes Nielson Kosloff and by Denton Corker Marshall – are graphic gestures in coloured and textured concrete (with subsidiary materials), apparently influenced by 1960s art concepts. The road walls of both projects undulate and swerve in direct response to the speed of observers and the behaviour of tyres on the tarmac.

Sydney's key traffic schemes – by Richard Goodwin, Margaret Petrykowski of DPWS with Merilyn Fairskye, and Buzacott Caro – are metal and/or concrete structures elaborated with wall designs, sculptural assemblages and/or towers adorned with metal ribbons or baubles.

Australian governments are continuing to expand road and rail networks across the continent.

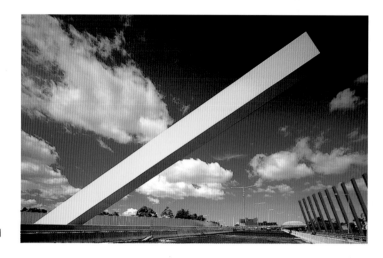

LEFT
EASTERN FREEWAY EXTENSION SOUND BARRIERS, WOOD MARSH WITH PELS INNES NIELSON KOSLOFF, WEST MELBOURNE, VICTORIA, 1998
TEN KILOMETRES OF FREEWAY THROUGH A DEGRADED CREEK VALLEY HAVE BEEN LINED WITH SOUND-REDUCING WALLS IN DIVERSE MATERIALS. THESE ARE BUILT AS ROBUST, SEPARATE ARCS TO CREATE AN OSCILLATING EFFECT WHEN SEEN FROM VEHICLES AT HIGH SPEED. SOME WALLS ARE IN ROCK-TEXTURED CONCRETE; OTHERS ARE TRANSPARENT: ALL ARE INTENDED TO BE SEEN FROM BOTH SIDES. PHOTO TIM GRIFFITH.

ABOVE AND OPPOSITE
CITY LINK GATEWAY, DENTON CORKER MARSHALL, MELBOURNE, 1999
MELBOURNE'S NEW NORTH ENTRANCE FROM ITS TULLAMARINE AIRPORT IS A BRAVURA ENSEMBLE OF UNDULATING NOISE BARRIERS, STEEL PORTALS REPETITIVELY FRAMING A FLYOVER AND GIANT STICKS PROJECTED AT ANGLES NEAR COLLAPSE. THESE ELEMENTS ARE OPTICALLY STIMULATING WHEN SEEN AT MOTORWAY SPEED. THIS ENSEMBLE ALSO RECREATES THE MEDIEVAL SYMBOLISM OF THE GATE AS A THRESHOLD TO A WALLED CITY. AND THERE ARE LINKS TO THE HYPER-REAL MOTORWAY PAINTINGS OF JEFFREY SMART. PHOTOS TIM GRIFFITH.

OPPOSITE
GLEBE ISLAND ARTERIAL SOUND
WALLS (BURLEY GRIFFIN DESIGN),
RICHARD GOODWIN, SYDNEY, 1997
CONCRETE NOISE WALLS ARE CLIPPED TO
A CITY FLYOVER WITH A SEQUENCE OF
TUBULAR STEEL BRACES FIXED UNDER
THE ROAD TO RESIST HIGH WINDS. THE
WALLS ARE STAMPED WITH MOTIFS
DRAWN FROM THE ART DECO PYRMONT
INCINERATOR (WALTER BURLEY GRIFFIN
AND MARION MAHONEY GRIFFIN, 1935)
WHICH WAS DEMOLISHED ON A NEARBY
SITE IN 1992. BENEATH THE FLYOVER, ITS
COLUMNS HAVE BEEN SHEATHED WITH
SCULPTURAL 'PROSTHESES'. PHOTO
ANTHONY BROWELL.

TOP LEFT
RAILWAY SQUARE BUS STATION, NSW
DEPARTMENT OF PUBLIC WORKS AND
SERVICES (MARGARET PETRYKOWSKI)
WITH CITY OF SYDNEY AND MERILYN
FAIRSKYE, SYDNEY, 1999
MARKING A FIVE-WAY INTERSECTION AT
THE SOUTH AND WEST ENTRANCES TO
CENTRAL SYDNEY, THIS BUS STATION HAS
EXUBERANT SHELTERS OF DARK STEEL
AND GLASS (LIKE FLYING SHARDS)
BENEATH FOUR LIGHTING, SIGNAGE AND
STORAGE PYLONS HIGHLIGHTED BY
RIBBONS OF MULTI-COLOURED METAL.
PHOTO PATRICK BINGHAM-HALL

LEFT AND ABOVE
KING STREET FOOTBRIDGE, BUZACOTT
CARO, SYDNEY, 1998
SPANNING ACROSS A MOTORWAY TO
LINK SYDNEY CITY WITH ITS DARLING
HARBOUR LEISURE PRECINCT, THIS
FOOTBRIDGE IS PLANNED AS A BALCONY
LEADING TO A MONUMENTAL STONE-CLAD
STAIRCASE WHICH DESCENDS TO THE
WATER. THE NORTH WALL (EDGE BEAM)
OF THE BRIDGE IS WRAPPED WITH ZINC;
THE SOUTH SIDE IS OPEN ABOVE GLAZED
SCREENS. THE TIMBER DECK RESTS ON
OUTRIGGER BEAMS CANTILEVERED OFF
THE PRIMARY BOX GIRDER. PHOTOS
PATRICK BINGHAM-HALL.

69

COMMERCE & LEISURE
METROPOLITIAN MAGNETS

As cities compete for tourism, they are building more megastructures to attract and cater to masses of people. Three types of these halls have been built in Australia recently. All have been designed as commercial facilities rather than public institutions; with photogenic roofs or iconic features and perhaps a hotel tower.

Large halls for trade exhibitions have been built on the Yarra River in Melbourne (Denton Corker Marshall, 1996), at Southbank, Brisbane (Cox Rayner, 1995) and on the Sydney Olympic site at Homebush (Ancher Mortlock & Woolley, 1998). The latter two have segmented rooflines of paraboloids and domes, while the Melbourne centre has a planar roof highlighted by a soaring blade at the entry.

New air terminals have been built in Brisbane (Bligh Voller Nield's international terminal, 1996) and Sydney (Hassell's Qantas domestic, 1999). Renovations are also under way at the Melbourne and Adelaide airports. After Norman Foster's seminal Stansted Airport near London, these are all designed for maximum transparency, with serene, skylit interiors and ceilings often held by quadrapod pillars.

A third type of megastructure is the waterfront entertainment-retail-restaurant complex – sometimes linked to a major casino and hotel. Recent projects are Melbourne's Crown casino (Bates Smart, Perrott Lyon Mathieson, Daryl Jackson, 1997); Star City casino, Sydney (Cox Hillier, 1998); and Cockle Bay Wharf, Sydney (Eric Kuhne for Lend Lease, 1999). All of these have been designed as ensembles of forms, to diminish their total scale.

ABOVE
CROWN ENTERTAINMENT CENTRE, BATES SMART WITH PERROTT LYON MATHIESON AND DARYL JACKSON, MELBOURNE, 1997
ON THE SOUTH BANK OF THE YARRA RIVER, THIS COMPLEX COMBINES FIVE FUNCTIONS WHICH USUALLY REQUIRE SEPARATE BUILDINGS: HOTEL, SHOPPING MALL, HEALTH AND SPORTS COMPLEX, RIVERFRONT DINING PROMENADE BENEATH NIGHTCLUBS AND FUNCTION ROOMS, AND A STACK OF CASINO HALLS. THE ARCHITECTURE CONTAINS MOST OF THE PUBLIC FUNCTIONS WITHIN A THREE-STOREY PODIUM TO THE HOTEL TOWER. PHOTO JOHN GOLLINGS.

TOP
BRISBANE CONVENTION AND EXHIBITION CENTRE, COX RAYNER, BRISBANE, 1995
THIS RIVERSIDE TRADE CENTRE IN QUEENSLAND'S CAPITAL CITY HAS FIVE COLUMN-FREE EXHIBITION HALLS (EACH 72 METRES SQUARE), WHICH ARE SIGNALLED BY ROOF SHELLS FORMED IN STEEL LATTICE USING HYPERBOLIC PARABOLOID GEOMETRY. THE UNDULATING ROOF DESCENDS ON ALL SIDES TO APPEAR TO LOWER THE HEIGHT OF THE COMPLEX. IN A SEQUENCE ALONG THE STREETFRONT, CONCRETE CLAD TOWERS CONTAIN AIRCONDITIONING AND OTHER SERVICES. PHOTO PATRICK BINGHAM-HALL.

ABOVE
COCKLE BAY WHARF, ERIC KUHNE WITH LEND LEASE, SYDNEY, 1999
ALONG THE EAST SIDE OF SYDNEY'S DARLING HARBOUR LEISURE PRECINCT, THIS THREE-STOREY RESTAURANT AND RECREATION COMPLEX COMBINES POST-MODERN COLLAGE, DECONSTRUCTIVIST AND MARINE MATERIALS AND IMAGERY. THE DEVELOPMENT HAS THREE DINING PAVILIONS ON THE ROOF GARDEN, CONFERENCE, CASUAL DINING AND SHOPPING FACILITIES BELOW, A LARGE COURTYARD BAR, A NIGHTCLUB AND A MARINA. PHOTO BRETT BOARDMAN.

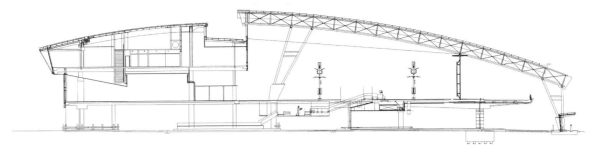

ABOVE AND RIGHT
QANTAS DOMESTIC AIR TERMINAL,
HASSELL, SYDNEY, 1999
SYDNEY AIRPORT IS UPGRADING FOR NEW
WAVES OF TRAVELLERS. THE QANTAS
TERMINAL NOW PROVIDES SPACIOUS,
HALLS WHICH ARE EVENLY SKYLIT VIA
DIFFUSERS IN THE CURVED ROOF. THE
TARMAC AND ARRIVAL FACADES ARE
GENEROUSLY GLAZED TO FOSTER AN
ATMOSPHERE OF OPEN TRANSPARENCY.
CROSS SECTION TOP. PHOTOS PATRICK
BINGHAM-HALL.

DISTRICT HUBS

Cities are constitutions of villages which foster community values that are contested on the football field and honoured in public artworks. Yet the key buildings of Australia's suburbs mostly have expressed either European classical or American corporate aesthetics rather than antipodean conditions. Now there are signs of change.

As the old icons of government become obsolete, the architectural foci of some urban districts are turning out to be small centres of commerce and leisure. These groovy complexes of mixed uses almost always provide at least one dispensary of coffee to indoor and outdoor tables. Some contain cinemas supplemented by a late night bookshop, music store and/or gift boutique, with offices or apartments on the highest floors. Other imaginative permutations of use – luxury car showrooms, boutique grocery stores, potted plant shops – are also profitable.

An interesting aspect of many recent urban leisure complexes is a tendency to eschew the imagery of glamour that usually is associated with retail centres and cinemas. Instead, they project a distinct sense of grungy discord by exposing the old brickwork of existing warehouse shells and combining raw, rugged, cold and noise-activating materials in treatments reminiscent of old factories and workshops, dockyards and cattle sheds. While these gutsy schemes are often vaguely interpreted as Australian in intent, they do not literally reflect local characteristics.

A notable recent example of industrial expression is Tonkin

ABOVE AND TOP
THE POINT AT ALBERT PARK, PETER MADDISON, MELBOURNE, 1997
A MODERN EXCLAMATION AT THE END OF A LAKESIDE ROW OF OLD BOATSHEDS, THIS PAVILION PROVIDES BOAT HIRE AND COFFEE ON THE GROUND FLOOR AND A FORMAL RESTAURANT, FUNCTION ROOM AND OFFICES ABOVE. THE NAUTICAL-MODERNIST ARCHITECTURE INCLUDES A CONSTRUCTIVIST OBSERVATION TOWER. MATERIALS INCLUDE BLUE-BLACK STEEL FRAMING, PRECAST CONCRETE PANELS, IRONBARK DECKING AND SUNSHADES AND A LAKESIDE SKIN OF TINTED GLASS. PHOTOS TREVOR MEIN.

ABOVE
LUXE, NEOMETRO, ST KILDA, VICTORIA, 1999
A RECYCLED WAREHOUSE AND A NEW 'MINI-TOWER' (ABOVE) PROVIDE STUDIOS, OFFICES, A GALLERY, A RESTAURANT/WINE BAR AND A CAFÉ. THE MATERIALS AND FORMS OF THE ARCHITECTURE RESPOND TO THE ROUGH AND DIVERSE NATURE OF THE LOCALITY – AND TO THE AESTHETICS OF A NEW COMMUNITY OF PROFESSIONAL PEOPLE. STREET ELEVATION TOP. PHOTO PETER CLARKE.

OPPOSITE
NORTON STREET CINEMAS, TONKIN ZULAIKHA, LEICHHARDT, NEW SOUTH WALES, 1998
A 1970s WAREHOUSE HAS BEEN CONVERTED INTO CINEMAS, A RESTAURANT AND BOOK AND MUSIC SHOPS, WITH BASEMENT PARKING. THE AUDITORIA ARE ARRANGED AT THE REAR OF THE BUILDING TO ALLOW ACTIVE RETAIL AND DINING TO FACE THE STREET. THE NEW ACTIVITIES ARE SIGNALLED BY AN ILLUMINATED ENSEMBLE ABOVE THE ENTRANCE STAIRS. PHOTO PATRICK BINGHAM-HALL.

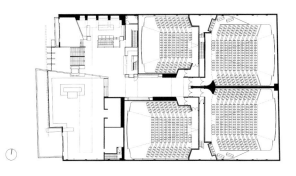

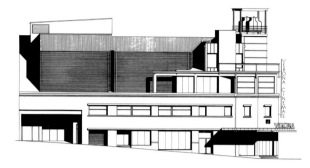

Zulaikha's 1995 conversion of an old Sydney paper factory into the Verona cinema/retail/restaurant/yoga centre. Although the realm of the cinema is carpeted according to acoustics-conscious convention, the building's foyer and circulation core have an anti-hospitable atmosphere generated by black floor tiles and an aggressive steel staircase. Patrons appear to appreciate these treatments.

Boutique commercial centres often signal their presence with a thrusting sculptural gesture. At the Verona, a rooftop stack of frames and boxes has been piled on the prime corner to allude to the vigour and disharmonies of modern urban life. A comparable roof ensemble – boxes and sticks in galvanised steel – crowns NeoMetro's Luxe complex (studios, wine bar and art gallery) built on a key corner at St Kilda, Melbourne, in 1999.

One noted development which doesn't have a roof gesture is 490 Crown Street – a three-storey building in Surry Hills, Sydney, which fills a block between an old hotel and a former warehouse: both retained as part of the complex. Designed principally by Alexander Tzannes, this 1997 infill is good-mannered and unusually climate-responsive for a commercial block. Its main facade is distinguished by sliding timber sunscreens and its rear elevation includes a wide sundeck off a first floor showroom and party venue.

Behind the glazed shopfronts of that domestically scaled container is the remarkable spectacle of MG cars and Land Rovers prominently displayed within restaurants. They can be ordered from the menu.

ABOVE AND RIGHT
VERONA CINEMA COMPLEX, TONKIN ZULAIKHA, PADDINGTON, NEW SOUTH WALES, 1995
AN OLD BRICK PAPER FACTORY HAS BEEN CONVERTED INTO THREE STREET-LEVEL SHOPS, A FOOTPATH TICKET KIOSK FOR FOUR UPSTAIRS CINEMAS, A RESTAURANT, A YOGA STUDIO AND TOP FLOOR OFFICES OPENING TO A DECK. THESE MIXED USES ARE SIGNALLED BY A PILE OF SCULPTURAL FORMS ON THE BUILDING'S MAIN CORNER. INSIDE, THE FOYER AND STAIRS ARE TREATED WITH RUGGED INDUSTRIAL MATERIALS, WITH RICH COLOURS AND CARPETING IN THE CINEMA ZONES. SIDE ELEVATION TOP. PHOTOS BART MAIORANA.

BELOW LEFT
490 CROWN STREET, ALEXANDER
TZANNES, SURRY HILLS, NEW SOUTH
WALES, 1997
THIS TWO-STOREY DEVELOPMENT
UPGRADES A SUBURBAN BLOCK BETWEEN
A HISTORIC HOTEL AND AN OLD
WAREHOUSE. THE INFILL BUILDING
ACCOMMODATES RESTAURANTS, CAR
SHOWROOMS, A BOUTIQUE GROCERY
AND AN ENTRY FOYER ON THE GROUND
FLOOR, WITH A FURNISHING PRODUCT
SHOWROOM AND OFFICES ABOVE. THE
NEW FACADE IS DISTINGUISHED BY
SLIDING PANELS OF TIMBER LOUVRES.
PHOTO BART MAIORANA.

ABOVE AND TOP LEFT
FUEL AND MG GARAGE (AT 490 CROWN
STREET), SYNMAN JUSTIN BIALEK,
SURRY HILLS, NEW SOUTH WALES, 1997
KEY ATTRACTIONS OF THE 490 CROWN
STREET DEVELOPMENT ARE TWO
RESTAURANTS WHICH ALSO SELL LUXURY
CARS. FUEL IS AN INFORMAL BRASSERIE
AND GROCERY STORE WHICH HAS A
RECTANGULAR CENTRAL BAR AND SIDE
WALLS OF STACKED STONE. MG GARAGE
IS A MORE SOPHISTICATED RESTAURANT
DRESSED WITH LUXURY FINISHES. PHOTOS
SIMON KENNY, SHARRIN REES.

TOURIST CHECKPOINTS

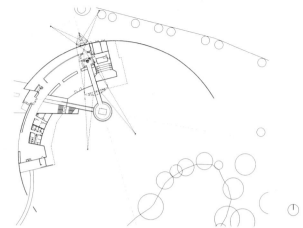

Charisma is the crucial element in designing contemporary visitor centres. Unlike the quotidian district information booths which used to dispense maps to Australian families in caravans, they are built to attract international tourists, and the architecture is supposed to be memorable enough to sell as calendars and postcards.

Many regional cities and towns have been constructing visitor centres in order to join the network of destinations recommended in round-Australia backpacker guidebooks. Perhaps for this reason, the imaginative centres are often found in places remote from large cities. Key 1990s examples are located near the crocodile swamps and monolithic landforms of the Northern Territory, in several Queensland coastal towns, at certain Victorian, South Australian and NSW rural centres of late 19th-century goldmining activity, and at special points of heritage or landscape significance on the southern island of Tasmania.

Most Australian visitor centres are externally distinguished by a spectacular roof or pinnacle, and many are internally planned to encourage a circuitous route through rooms displaying local memorabilia. There is always a large parking area on site and usually a refreshment kiosk.

The architectural languages of visitor centres are more varied than those of almost any other type of Australian building. And because they are small buildings of cultural significance, budgets often stretch to include extravagances which would be unfeasible in larger commercial or civic projects.

EUREKA STOCKADE INTERPRETIVE CENTRE, COX SANDERSON NESS, BALLARAT, VICTORIA, 1998
THE 1854 MASSACRE OF GOLDMINERS PROTESTING ABOUT BRITISH TAXES IS A RESONANT POINT OF AUSTRALIAN HISTORY. INSIDE A HILLTOP STOCKADE, 400 MINERS SWORE ALLEGIANCE TO THE 'EUREKA' FLAG OF THE SOUTHERN CROSS BEFORE COLONIAL TROOPS MURDERED 35 OF THEM. THE NEW VISITOR CENTRE WHICH COMMEMORATES THIS EVENT HAS BEEN DESIGNED AS A CIRCULAR PAVILION WITH MODIFIED ELEMENTS THAT ALLUDE 'IN A NON-LITERAL WAY' TO KEY ASPECTS OF THE STORY. THE STOCKADE PICKETS ARE REPRESENTED AS A CURVED SCREEN OF HORIZONTAL OREGON SLATS; THE EUREKA FLAG IS FLOWN VERTICALLY IN A DRAMATIC GESTURE REMINISCENT OF THE TUNNEL VENTILATION SOCKS WHICH WERE FLOWN THROUGHOUT THE GOLDFIELDS. THE PAVILION APPEARS TO BE SPIKED BY THE 50-METRE-HIGH FLAG MAST, WHICH IS HELD AT AN ANGLE BY CABLES AND TRUSS BEAMS. INSIDE, VISITORS TAKE A CIRCULAR ROUTE THROUGH THE BUILDING, PARTLY UNDERGROUND, TO CULMINATE IN A CONTEMPLATION SPACE AND A COMMEMORATIVE LAWN ON THE ROOF. SITE PLAN TOP. PHOTOS PATRICK BINGHAM-HALL.

TOP, ABOVE AND LEFT
'WORLD OF THE PLATYPUS', GREGORY BURGESS, HEALESVILLE, VICTORIA, 1995
THIS PAVILION IN A WILDLIFE SANCTUARY EXHIBITS THE NOCTURNAL FOREST LIFE OF THE PLATYPUS. SITED IN A FERN GULLY NEAR A CREEK AND LAKE, THE BUILDING IS MADE IN EARTHY MATERIALS – MUD BRICK AND TIMBERS WITH A COPPER ROOF – TO SEEM TO EMERGE FROM THE LANDSCAPE. ITS STRUCTURE IS IRREGULAR AND ITS PATHWAYS MEANDER. INTERNAL SPACES ARE MAINLY GLOOMY TO EMPHASISE THE EXPERIENCE OF WATCHING THE ANIMAL IN ITS HABITAT. PHOTOS JOHN GOLLINGS.

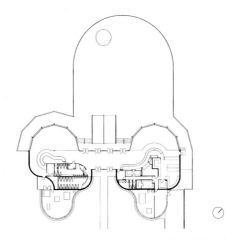

ABOVE
MOUNT LOFTY SUMMIT, RAFFEN MARON, SOUTH AUSTRALIA, 1998
ON THE HIGHEST PEAK OF THE ADELAIDE HILLS, A NEW VISITOR CENTRE PROVIDES A RESTAURANT, CAFÉ, INFORMATION BOOTH AND SOUVENIR SHOP. THE DESIGN HAS A GLAZED PASSAGE LINKING TWO CIRCULAR PAVILIONS WITH OUTDOOR DINING AREAS SHADED BY THE WIDE BRIMS OF INVERTED PARASOL ROOFS (PLAN TOP). INSIDE, FACETED GLASS PANELS ALLOW 180 DEGREE VIEWS AROUND THE HILLS. THE ENTRANCE IS ALIGNED ON AXIS WITH THE RESTORED FLINDERS COLUMN, BUILT IN 1885 AS A TRIG STATION AND LANDMARK. PHOTO TREVOR FOX.

RIGHT
PORT ARTHUR VISITOR CENTRE, PHILIP LIGHTON WITH DARYL JACKSON, TASMANIA, 1999
PORT ARTHUR WAS ONE OF AUSTRALIA'S BLOODIEST COLONIAL CONVICT SETTLEMENTS. ITS NEW VISITOR CENTRE BRINGS TOGETHER FORMERLY SCATTERED FACILITIES UNDER A ROOF INTENDED TO ECHO THE SHAPE OF THE HILL BEHIND. THE SCALE OF THIS LARGE STRUCTURE IS VISUALLY REDUCED BY CHIMNEYS, BAY WINDOWS AND OTHER ELEMENTS, AS WELL AS CHANGES OF MATERIALS (TIMBERS, ZINC, CONCRETE). PHOTO PETER WHYTE.

81

TOP LEFT
OLYMPIC FERRY WHARF, ALEXANDER TZANNES, HOMEBUSH, NEW SOUTH WALES, 1997
ONE ROUTE TO HOMEBUSH IS TAKEN BY FERRY BOATS ALONG THE PARRAMATTA RIVER FROM SYDNEY CITY. AT THE TERMINAL, A SHALLOW-VAULTED ROOF OF CORRUGATED STEEL MARKS AN L-SHAPED PATH FROM THE DOCK TO A PLAZA, ROAD AND CAR PARK. TEMPORARY SHADE CANOPIES ARE SOMETIMES SET UP FOR OFFICIAL CEREMONIES.

BOTTOM LEFT
NEWINGTON VILLAGE APARTMENTS, HPA WITH BRUCE EELES, VOTE AND HASSELL, NEWINGTON, NEW SOUTH WALES, 1999
ACROSS HASLAM'S CREEK NORTH OF THE OLYMPIC SPORTS PARK, A 90-HECTARE TOWN IS BEING BUILT ON NEW URBANISM PRINCIPLES FOR GAMES ATHLETES (IN BASIC FORMAT) THEN SYDNEY RESIDENTS. THE PRIME EDGE OF THIS NEW SUBURB IS A SEQUENCE OF CUBIST WHITE APARTMENT BUILDINGS, STEPPING BACK TO CREATE LARGE TERRACES ON EVERY LEVEL. LIKE THE WALLS OF A MEDIEVAL FORTRESS, THESE ALSO GIVE A VISUAL IMPRESSION OF SECURITY.

TOP RIGHT
SYDNEY INTERNATIONAL AQUATIC CENTRE, COX RICHARDSON WITH PEDDLE THORP, HOMEBUSH, NEW SOUTH WALES, 1994
BUILT BEFORE SYDNEY'S OLYMPICS BID, THE AQUATIC CENTRE HAS BECOME A POPULAR VENUE FOR FAMILIES IN SUBURBS WITHOUT BEACHES. ITS WHITE ROOF TRUSS ALLUDES TO THE DISTANT HARBOUR BRIDGE AND AN EARTH BERM SUPPORTS RACKS OF TEMPORARY SEATING DURING OLYMPICS MODE. A TUNNEL THROUGH THE BERM ALLOWS ENTRY TO AN OBSERVATION BRIDGE ACROSS A GIANT HALL CONTAINING COMPETITION AND LEISURE POOLS.

BOTTOM RIGHT
SHOWRING (BASEBALL STADIUM), COX RICHARDSON WITH PEDDLE THORP AND CONYBEARE MORRISON, HOMEBUSH, NEW SOUTH WALES, 1998
FIVE ROOF CANOPIES, REMINISCENT OF BASEBALL CAPS, ARE SUSPENDED FROM RED LIGHTING TOWERS IN THE GRANDSTAND AROUND THE ARENA TO BE USED FOR OLYMPICS BASEBALL GAMES. LOCATED IN THE CENTRE OF THE RAS SHOWGROUNDS AT HOMEBUSH, THE VENUE IS OTHERWISE USED FOR EQUESTRIAN, AGRICULTURAL AND OTHER OUTDOOR DISPLAYS.

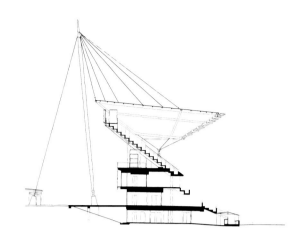

ABOVE
ANCHER MORTLOCK & WOOLLEY,
STATE HOCKEY CENTRE, HOMEBUSH
BAY, NSW, 1998
SIGHTLINE STUDIES GENERATED THE
CROSS-SECTION (TOP) OF THIS 1500-SEAT
GRANDSTAND WITH PLAYER AND
ADMINISTRATION FACILITIES TUCKED
BELOW THE SEATING TIERS. ITS DYNAMIC
ROOF IS SEPARATELY HUNG FROM A
CENTRE-REAR MAST AND TIED DOWN BY
STEEL CABLES AT THE SIDES AND REAR.
RAIN IS CONDUCTED FROM THE FRONT
EDGE TO WATER RECYCLING TANKS. FOUR
PITCH-LIGHTING PYLONS ARE DESIGNED
TO LOOK LIKE HOCKEY STICKS AND TO BE
ADJUSTED LIKE DESK LAMPS.

**ABOVE AND RIGHT
COUNTRY ROAD HEADQUARTERS,
METIER 3, MELBOURNE, 1997**
A HISTORIC BRICK POWER STATION BESIDE
MELBOURNE'S YARRA RIVER HAS BEEN
CONVERTED AND EXPANDED FOR THE
MAIN PREMISES OF A FASHION AND
HOMEWARES CORPORATION. THE
ARCHITECTURE IS INTENDED TO EXPRESS
THE COMPANY'S CONTINUUM FROM THE
PAST (BRICK) TO THE FUTURE (METAL AND
GLASS). PHOTOS TIM GRIFFITH.

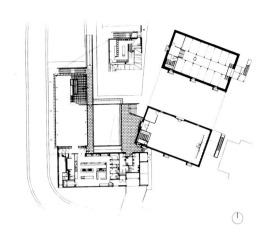

ABOVE AND RIGHT
**MAGILL ESTATE WINERY, ALLEN JACK +
COTTIER, ADELAIDE, 1996**
A MODERNIST GLASS BOX ON A STONE
BASE FORMS A NEW DINING PAVILION AT
A REFURBISHED SOUTH AUSTRALIAN
WINERY. FROM THIS RAISED PLATFORM,
PATRONS LOOK WEST ACROSS THE
VINEYARDS OF MAGILL ESTATE, KNOWN AS
THE BIRTHPLACE OF PENFOLD'S GRANGE
HERMITAGE. TO THE EAST IS A WATER
COURT. INTERIOR FINISHES ARE
TRAVERTINE, TIMBER VENEER AND
STAINLESS STEEL. HISTORIC BRICK CELLAR
BUILDINGS HAVE BEEN UPGRADED FOR
VISITORS. PHOTOS FARSHID ASSASSI.

RECYCLED WHARVES

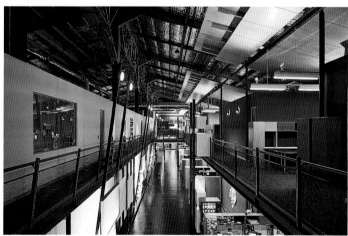

Three port cities – Sydney, Hobart and Darwin – have been recycling obsolete finger wharves which were once frequented by freighters before the advent of much larger container ships and super-tankers.

In Hobart's Sullivans Cove, Darwin Harbour, and Sydney's Walsh Bay, decaying timber storage sheds have been successfully updated for restaurants, offices of cultural groups, public performance spaces and hotels.

The results most appreciated have been those which preserve and restore the main structures and as much of the cladding and hardwood flooring as possible, while judiciously opening up some walls with new windows designed to continue the proportional rhythms and scales of the original layers of external timberwork.

Exterior colours are preferred to relate to the faded institutional greys and grey-blues which often characterise these sheds. Interior fitouts tend to be deliberately modern, but in rugged maritime-industrial styles using raw or black steel, recycled hardwoods and marine plywood, accented with strong but often dull-toned colours.

In Sydney, however, there has been a great deal of controversy about a series of government-brokered commercial developments which are converting more than a dozen city wharves into high-priced apartments and hotel suites. Architects worry that these projects are being clumsily procured, managed and designed. And socialists suggest that prime waterfront sites are being alienated from the public for consumption by wealthy citizens and foreigners.

ABOVE AND RIGHT
FOXTEL HQ AND PLAYOUT CENTRE, BATES SMART, SYDNEY, 1996
A TELEVISION STATION HAS BEEN INSTALLED INSIDE AN OLD FINGER WHARF. TWO FLOORS OF OFFICES ARE ARRANGED ON BOTH SIDES OF A CENTRAL STREET AND A SYSTEM OF 'WORKING WALLS' ALLOWS SPACES TO BE REARRANGED TO SUIT CHANGES OF STAFF AND PROJECTS. THE NEW ARCHITECTURE CONTINUES THE MARINE-INDUSTRIAL CHARACTER OF THE BUILDING. PHOTOS JOHN GOLLINGS.

OPPOSITE
BANGARRA DANCE THEATRE (WALSH BAY WHARVES 4–5), COX RICHARDSON, SYDNEY, 1997
DANCE AND SOUND REHEARSAL SPACES, OFFICES AND A RESTAURANT HAVE BEEN INSERTED INTO A HISTORIC TIMBER FINGER WHARF ON SYDNEY HARBOUR. INSIDE THE LONG SHED, THESE FACILITIES ARE ORGANISED TO THE WEST OF A HALL DEFINED BY A SERPENTINE, SLOPING WALL OF PLYWOOD AND GLASS. PHOTO PATRICK BINGHAM-HALL.

NEXT PAGES
ELIZABETH STREET PIER, HEFFERNAN BUTTON VOSS, HOBART, 1998
AT SULLIVAN'S COVE, THE MAIN BAY OF TASMANIA'S PRINCIPAL CITY, A 1930s FINGER WHARF HAS BEEN CONVERTED INTO A SERVICED APARTMENT AND FUNCTION COMPLEX ABOVE GROUND FLOOR CAFÉS OPENING TO PUBLIC PROMENADES. THE ROOF OF THE SHED HAS BEEN RAISED AND THE FACADES HAVE BEEN ENLIVENED BY BALCONIES WITH COLOURED GLASS PRIVACY PANELS. PHOTO RICHARD EASTWOOD.

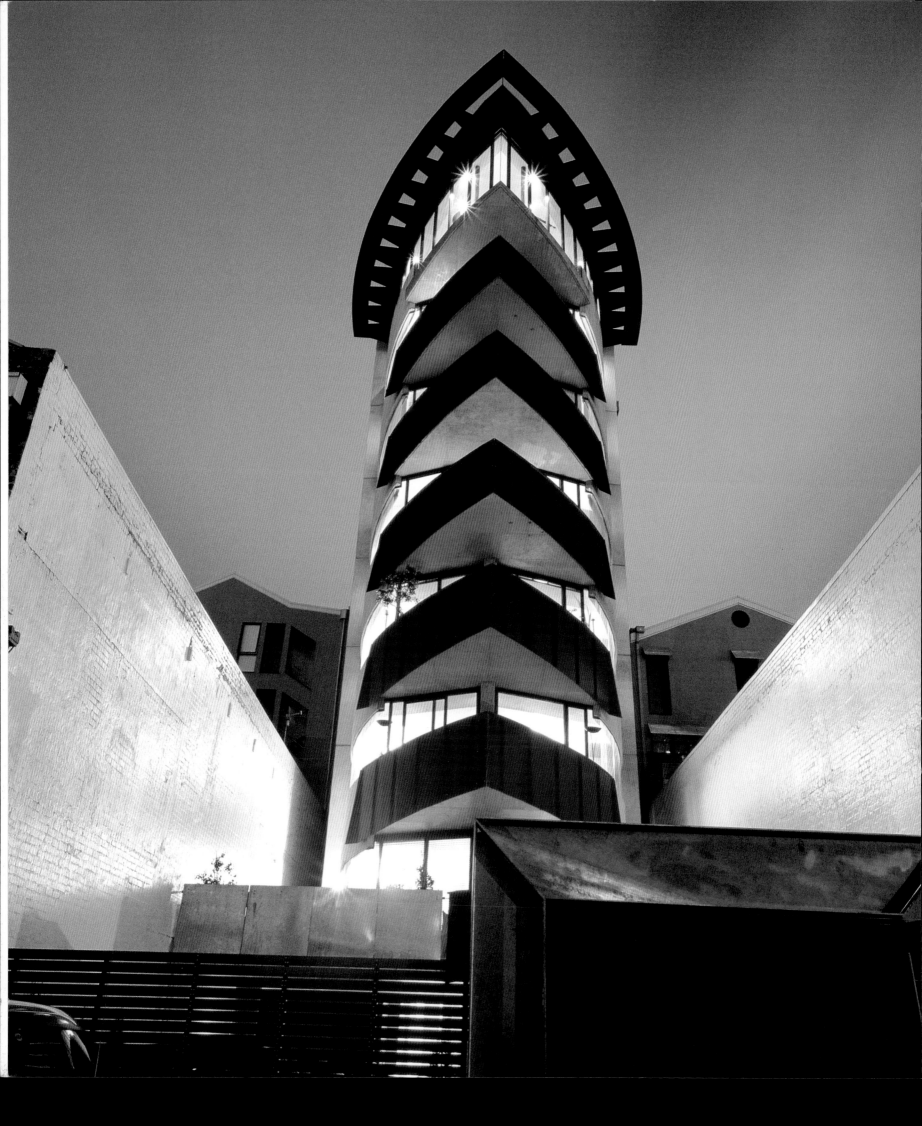

HOUSING
VERTICAL LIVING

In the 1990s, many apartment and hotel towers arose near columns of offices in the cores of Sydney and Melbourne. They were encouraged by the 'Postcode' and 'Living City' incentive programs offered to property developers by the city councils in 1993 and 1994.

Most of these new buildings are spatially stingy and aesthetically clumsy, but they serve increasing numbers of young and single people, foreign university students and foreign workers on location.

A more prestigious high-rise housing market is also proving profitable: 'signature' developments by admired architects and sold off-the-plan as desirable investments.

The stellar creator of designer apartment towers is Melbourne's Nonda Katsalidis, who travels with a coterie of disciples from one building to the next. His portfolio includes the 13-storey Melbourne Terrace (1994), the nine-level Richmond Silos refurbishment (1997), and the 36-level Republic (1999). The first is an externally decorative, internally austere complex occupying a city block; the others are expressively sculpted, upthrusting structures. All are distinguished by sensuous finishes, including patinated metals.

In Sydney, the most prestigious residential tower is the Macquarie Apartments by Italian architect Renzo Piano (2000): it has a rectangular core and balconies protected by two curved veils of glass panels and louvres.

Other remarkable Sydney towers are Harry Seidler's Horizon (1998) and the Moore Park Gardens series by Allen Jack + Cottier (1997–1999). More are on the way.

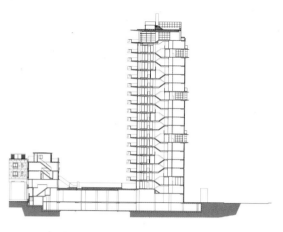

THIS PAGE
MOORE PARK GARDENS,
ALLEN JACK + COTTIER, REDFERN,
NEW SOUTH WALES, 1997–2000
MOORE PARK GARDENS PROVIDES 560
HOUSING UNITS AND COMMUNITY
FACILITIES ON A 2.6 HECTARE SITE WHICH
USED TO BE A BREWERY. NINE NEW
BUILDINGS FACE INWARDS TO GARDENS
AND A CENTRAL, EAST-WEST STREET. FOR
BEST SOLAR ACCESS, ROW HOUSING IS
BUILT TO THE NORTH AND TOWERS TO
THE SOUTH OF THIS AVENUE. THE HIGH-
RISE APARTMENTS ARE ARRANGED IN A
'CROSS-OVER' SECTIONAL FORMAT WHICH
IMPROVES VENTILATION, VIEWS AND
SUNLIGHT. PHOTOS BART MAIORANA.

OPPOSITE
THE HORIZON, HARRY SEIDLER &
ASSOCIATES, SYDNEY, 1998
ONE OF SYDNEY'S MOST PROMINENT
APARTMENT TOWERS IS BUILT ON A
FORMER GOVERNMENT SITE NEAR THE
KINGS CROSS RIDGE. IT IS A 43-STOREY
COLUMN RUFFLED WITH CONCRETE
BALCONIES PAINTED OFF-WHITE AND
INCORPORATING OVERHEAD SUNSHADES.
AT ITS BASE ARE GARDENS, TENNIS
COURTS, A SWIMMING POOL AND
LOW-RISE PERIMETER HOUSING WHICH
RELATES TO THE SCALE OF VICTORIAN
TERRACE HOUSES IN THE VICINITY.
PHOTO TIM GRIFFITH.

RESIDENTIAL BLOCKS

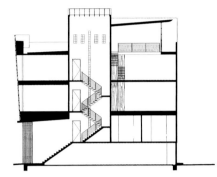

Architectural credentials are driving a hectic market for city apartments. Sumptuous brochures often name designers as a point of prestige, marking a distinct shift of public opinion since the early 1990s. Previously, developers were often squeamish about promoting modern architecture to buyers then steeped in traditional decorating. But a 15-year blizzard of publicity in design journals, combined with increasing overseas travel, has changed the market and made some architects celebrities.

Apartment buildings first came to Sydney and Melbourne in the 1920s and 1930s; many emulating Manhattan's Art Deco skyscrapers. The earliest 'signature' buildings were Harry Seidler's 1960s and 1970s towers on waterside sites around Sydney.

Now there is a strong trend to 'exclusive' low-rise blocks of 2 to 14 storeys, which squat on the street edges of their sites rather than soar in imperial isolation. They may include ground-floor shops or cafés, two-storey or mezzanine penthouses and, if the property is deep enough, a courtyard/lightwell.

There are two main styling themes. One is postmodern collage, first seen in late 1980s townhouses by Melbourne's NeoMetro and Robinson Chen, then in 1990s projects by Nonda Katsalidis and (with polychrome brick) Sydney's Allen Jack + Cottier. The other strategy, dominant in Sydney, is minimalism, led by Burley Katon Halliday, Harry Seidler, Engelen Moore, Alex Tzannes, Stanic Harding, Dale Jones-Evans, Rob Pufflet and Jon Johanssen.

TOP
ANGELO CANDALEPAS WITH WILKINSON CANDALEPAS AND JANET GREY, PYRMONT POINT HOUSING, SYDNEY, 1996
UPDATING THE IDEA OF A WALLED CITADEL ON A HILL, THIS APARTMENT COMPLEX IS INTENDED TO PROVIDE RESIDENTS WITH A SENSE OF REFUGE FROM THE CITY. THE ENTRY ZONE IS DEFINED BY A SOLID STREET WALL OF SANDSTONE QUARRIED FROM THE THE HISTORIC SITE. VARIOUS KINDS OF APARTMENTS ARE ARRANGED IN ZONES TO THE NORTH, SOUTH AND WEST OF A CENTRAL COURTYARD. PHOTO JOHN GOLLINGS.

BOTTOM LEFT
ELWOOD TOWNHOUSES, GEOFF CROSBY, MELBOURNE, 1997
IN A BUDGET DEVELOPMENT OF SEVEN HOUSING UNITS, PANELS OF PRE-CAST, TEXTURE-PAINTED CONCRETE HAVE BEEN TILTED VERTICALLY AND HORIZONTALLY. THIS TECHNIQUE HAS ESTABLISHED TWO DYNAMIC STREET FACADES WHICH GIVE VIEWS TO OCCUPANTS WITHOUT SACRIFICING THEIR PRIVACY, AND ADMIT SLICES OF SUN TO THE UNITS. PHOTO JOHN GOLLINGS.

ABOVE
NIDO APARTMENTS, NEOMETRO, MELBOURNE, 1994
THIS COMPLEX OF 12 APARTMENTS AND CAR PARKING RESPONDS TO THE MELBOURNE CITY COUNCIL'S POSTCODE 3000 PROGRAM TO ENCOURAGE INNER-CITY LIVING. THE BUILDING HAS TWO COLOURFUL STREET FRONTAGES RELATING TO THE SCALE AND DISORDERLY CHARACTER OF THE NEIGHBOURHOOD. THE HIGH-CEILINGED APARTMENTS FACE NORTH AND SOUTH FROM A CENTRAL STAIR AND LIGHTWELL (SEE CROSS-SECTION, TOP). PHOTO PETER CLARKE.

ABOVE
ST LEONARDS APARTMENTS, NONDA KATSALIDIS, ST KILDA, VICTORIA, 1996
IN A RAPIDLY GENTRIFYING SEASIDE SUBURB OF MELBOURNE, THIS LONG BLOCK OF WALK-UP APARTMENTS PROVIDES UNUSUALLY DECORATIVE FRONT AND REAR FACADES, MODULATED BY PROJECTING PRIVACY SCREENS AND BALUSTRADES FORMING EDGES TO DEEP BALCONIES. FOR SECURITY, NOISE CONTROL AND CONVENIENCE, THE BLOCK IS DIVIDED INTO FOUR ZONES OF SIX UNITS SEPARATED BY CENTRAL ENTRANCES. THE PENTHOUSES ARE DOUBLE-STOREYED, WITH WIDE TERRACES LEADING FROM THE LIVING ROOMS. PHOTO JOHN GOLLINGS.

VILLAGES

European architects Leon and Rob Krier enchanted anti-modernists of the 1980s with nostalgic sketches for civilised towns that could salve public fury about the inhumanity of high-rise housing slabs and 1960s concrete megastructures.

Their 'new urbanism' – later interpreted by Americans Andres Duany and Elizabeth Plater-Zyberk with the town of Seaside in Florida – has triggered two significant Australian responses. One is a trend to fragment large institutions like schools and hospitals into compounds of smaller buildings. The other is a revival of interest in villages – the original format for community habitation – among the government planners who regulate voracious property entrepreneurs.

Many Australian developers, along with their architects, are now conscious of pressures favouring multiple housing and tourist resort developments that are human in scale and pedestrian-friendly rather than massive and car-convenient. Seaside's planning has directly influenced various Australian projects since the late 1980s – and a blatant copy of it is being built at Coolum, Queensland, involving local architects Down & Neylan, and other firms.

However, many progressive architects do not admire the new urbanist penchant for 'ye olde cottages' – and they are instead designing villages of sun-reactive modern houses. Queensland versions – like Clare Design's Cotton Tree at Maroochydore (1996) and Daryl Jackson's Couran Cove eco-resort (1999) – have a casual, rugged, nautical character which is naturally Australian.

ABOVE
CORUMBENE, ROBERT MORRIS-NUNN, DERWENT VALLEY, TASMANIA, 1997
THIS 46-BED NURSING HOME IS IN A RURAL AREA WHICH HAS A HISTORY OF GROWING HOPS. THE ARCHITECTURE REINTERPRETS LOCAL FARM BARNS AND HUTS – ESPECIALLY THE OAST HOUSES USED FOR DRYING THE HOPS – TO CREATE A COMFORTABLE AND VISUALLY DYNAMIC REALM SUPPORTING THE EARLY MEMORIES OF ELDERLY RESIDENTS. INSIDE THE BUILDING, RESIDENTIAL SUITES LINE A CENTRAL STREET WHICH INCORPORATES COURTYARDS AND FAMILIAR BUILDING FACADES SCALED DOWN. PHOTO RICHARD EASTWOOD.

ABOVE AND OPPOSITE
COTTON TREE, CLARE DESIGN, MAROOCHYDORE, QUEENSLAND, 1996
ADJACENT BLOCKS OF LAND, ONE OWNED PRIVATELY AND THE OTHER BY THE QUEENSLAND GOVERNMENT, HAVE BEEN RECONFIGURED FOR A DEVELOPMENT OF PUBLIC AND SPECULATIVE HOUSING. THE SCHEME PROVIDES A CLUSTER OF THREE-STOREY, CLIMATE-RESPONSIVE HOUSE AND APARTMENT PAVILIONS BETWEEN EXISTING MELALEUCA TREES. THESE ARE REFINED VERSIONS OF THE OLD BEACH SHACKS OF THE SUNSHINE COAST. SITE CROSS-SECTION TOP. PHOTOS RICHARD STRINGER.

THE ROCKPOOL, ALEX POPOV, MONA VALE, NEW SOUTH WALES, 1999
A 2-STOREY BEACHFRONT APARTMENT COMPLEX DISTINGUISHED BY SHALLOW-VAULTED ROOFS. THESE ARE EXPRESSED ON THE UPPER FACADES BY FRAMES SHAPED FROM STEEL BEAMS AND ARE INTENDED, INTERNALLY, TO LEAD THE EYE THROUGH UPPER LEVEL LIVING ZONES TO THE OCEAN VIEW BEYOND. THE HOUSING IS ARRANGED IN TWO ROWS SEPARATED BY A LANDSCAPED PATH ACROSS THE SITE, WITH BELOW-GROUND PARKING. GROUND PLAN OPPOSITE LEFT; FIRST FLOOR PLAN OPPOSITE RIGHT. PHOTOS KRAIG CARLSTROM.

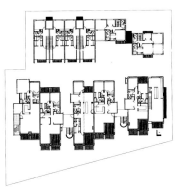

QUEENSLAND FARMHOUSES

In the hinterland between the hills and the beaches of semi-tropical Queensland, the classic dwellings are long sheds and square home-steads. Sheds were often built as shearers' quarters with communal kitchen/dining rooms and are often roofed with corrugated steel skillions falling along their length. Homesteads began as family cabins sheltered by gable or hipped roofs (eternal symbols of domesticity). They are likely to have a front or wrap-around verandah.

Both of these vernacular models were traditionally built of timber, which grows throughout the State and can be practically handled by a man and one or two mates.

The earliest slab huts were built of logs split with adzes and other hand tools, then roofed with sheets of bark. By the 1800s, however, most Queensland farmhouses were made from milled timber stud frames which were internally lined but externally exposed. This construction system is still used by Gabriel Poole, Rex Addison, Clare Design, John Mainwaring, Bark Design, Donovan Hill, Phillip Follent, Bud Brannigan and Arkhe Field. Hot climates do not require double-clad walls with insulating cavities.

Modern Queensland houses are sometimes framed in steel, then walled in with weatherboards, fibre cement sheets or plywood. Sometimes the panel junctions are expressed with gaps or (more nostalgically) cover battens. For roofs, sheets of steel have replaced sheets of bark.

Throughout the 20th century, panels of glass or cedar louvres have been liberally installed in Queensland houses to channel and

'OCEAN VIEW', BRIT ANDRESEN AND PETER O'GORMAN, MOUNT MEE, QUEENSLAND, 1996
THIS SINGLE-STOREY RESIDENCE STREAKS ACROSS A HILLSIDE AND AND BENDS TO MATCH ITS CONTOURS. TO SHELTER FROM STRONG WINDS, IT IS PLACED BELOW THE RIDGE. THE GABLED ROOF, SEEN WHEN ARRIVING FROM HIGHER GROUND, IS CENTERED ALONG A DOWNHILL SPUR AND MARKS THE ENTRANCE AS A SYMBOL OF 'HOME'. TO THE NORTH-EAST, THE FAMILY LIVING ZONE AND MAIN BEDROOM SUITE ARE PLACED TOGETHER, SEPARATED FROM A SOUTH-WESTERN 'TAIL' OF GUEST ROOMS AND UTILITY AREAS BY A CENTRAL SUNDECK. PHOTOS ADRIAN BODDY.

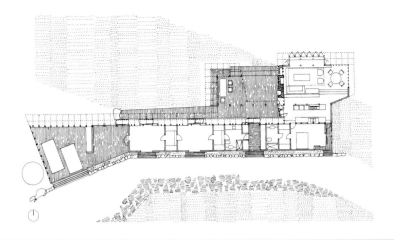

QUEENSLAND FARMHOUSES

**HAMMOND HOUSE, CLARE DESIGN,
COORAN, QUEENSLAND, 1994**
A RETIRED COUPLE OCCUPIES THIS
ECOLOGY-SENSITIVE COTTAGE ON A
HILLSIDE EXPOSED TO EXTREME WINDS.
THE TIMBER-FRAMED STRUCTURE IS
RAISED ON IRONBARK POSTS AND
BRACED WITH WALL FINS AND RODS TYING
THE ROOF TO THE FLOOR. CLADDINGS
ARE PLYWOOD, STEEL AND GLASS PANES
AND LOUVRES. THE FLOOR PLAN IS A
SIMPLE GRID OF SIX MODULES, INCLUDING
A SUNDECK AT THE NORTH ENTRANCE.
THE HOUSE IS EQUIPPED FOR SOLAR
POWER AND WATER AND WASTE
RECYLING. PHOTOS ADRIAN BODDY.

manipulate cross-breezes. Louvres spread quickly to the Northern Territory in the early 20th century and are now also popular among architects in New South Wales and (despite its cold climate) Tasmania.

Noosa architect Gabriel Poole (founder of the 'Sunshine Coast style') also exploited canvas and clear plastic sheeting as roll-up walls for his Tent Houses of the early 1990s and Poole House 3 at Lake Weyba (1996). Canvas was a common Queensland building material in the 19th century.

Around Australia's northern perimeter, houses generally are lifted above the ground – on fat stumps, stilts, cross-braced steel poles or elaborate space-frames like Poole's quadropod systems of 1983–86. Elevation discourages insects and removes floorboards from damp earth (the slab huts had mud or mat-covered floors). It also circulates air under the house, which may cool interior spaces and stabilise the floorboards.

Another historical and ongoing feature of Queensland houses is the popular use of wood battens to construct screens and trellises which filter sunlight, provide privacy, semi-enclose verandahs and breezeways, hide piles of clutter under the house, support climbing vines and decoratively trim important facades.

Queensland's rural sheds and houses are primary inspirations for all architects who pursue the 'vernacular Australian style' that is internationally celebrated through the works of Sydney's Glenn Murcutt. These are antipodean expressions of architecture's eternal Ideal: the primitive hut.

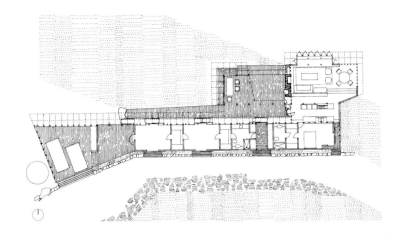

QUEENSLAND FARMHOUSES

ABOVE LEFT
GUEST HOUSE, JOHN MAINWARING, KENILWORTH, QUEENSLAND, 1996
A LONG BUTTERFLY ROOF KINKS FROM NORTH-WEST TO SOUTH DOWN THE SLOPE OF A SUNSHINE COAST FARM. BENEATH THIS CANOPY, THE PRIVATE AND PUBLIC ZONES OF A GUEST HOUSE ARE LINKED BY A WIDE BREEZEWAY WHICH BECOMES A SOLARIUM DURING WINTER. CLERESTORY WINDOWS OF GLASS LOUVRES FACING NORTH-EAST ALLOW GOOD NATURAL LIGHT AND PROTECTION FROM SUMMER SUN. CORRUGATED STEEL AND FIBRE CEMENT SHEET. PHOTO PETER HYATT.

ABOVE
TANK HOUSE, PHILLIP FOLLENT, GOLD COAST, QUEENSLAND, 1995
A MUD-FLOORED LOG CABIN HAS BEEN EXTENDED DOWNHILL WITH A BOISTEROUS TIMBER STRUCTURE SUPPLEMENTED BY A NEW SPILL-EDGE SWIMMING POOL. THE ADDITION PROVIDES TWO BEDROOMS AND SHOWER AND TOILET PODS OFF A CENTRAL HALLWAY/BRIDGE. THIS SPINE LEADS FROM THE EXISTING HOUSE TO A MUSIC ROOM AND DECK OVERLOOKING THE BUSH. IT IS LINED WITH BOOKCASES AND TIMBER LOUVRES (FOR CROSS BREEZES), WITH CLERESTORY WINDOWS ON BOTH SIDES. PHOTO ADRIAN BODDY.

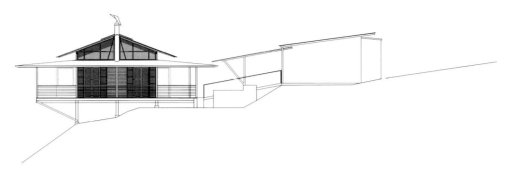

ABOVE AND LEFT
VAUX-OELRICHS HOUSE, GROSE
BRADLEY, COOPERS SHOOT VIA
BANGALOW, NEW SOUTH WALES, 1994
A CLASSIC QUEENSLAND-STYLE
FARMHOUSE IS PERCHED ON A SLOPE
WITH A BROAD PROSPECT TOWARDS THE
PACIFIC OCEAN. WIDE VERANDAHS AND
EAVES SURROUND AND SHADE THE
SINGLE-LEVEL CORE OF LIVING SPACES,
WHICH ARE ENTERED FROM A BRIDGE
ACROSS A LAP POOL. THE ARCHITECTURE
PRODUCES A SENSE OF LIVING ON A
PLATFORM APART FROM THE LANDSCAPE.
THE INTERIOR IS VENTILATED WITH
LOUVRES AND AIR IS EXTRACTED BY ROOF
FANS. PHOTOS ANTHONY BROWELL.

QUEENSLAND FARMHOUSES

**HAMMOND HOUSE, CLARE DESIGN,
COORAN, QUEENSLAND, 1994**
A RETIRED COUPLE OCCUPIES THIS
ECOLOGY-SENSITIVE COTTAGE ON A
HILLSIDE EXPOSED TO EXTREME WINDS.
THE TIMBER-FRAMED STRUCTURE IS
RAISED ON IRONBARK POSTS AND
BRACED WITH WALL FINS AND RODS TYING
THE ROOF TO THE FLOOR. CLADDINGS
ARE PLYWOOD, STEEL AND GLASS PANES
AND LOUVRES. THE FLOOR PLAN IS A
SIMPLE GRID OF SIX MODULES, INCLUDING
A SUNDECK AT THE NORTH ENTRANCE.
THE HOUSE IS EQUIPPED FOR SOLAR
POWER AND WATER AND WASTE
RECYLING. PHOTOS ADRIAN BODDY.

manipulate cross-breezes. Louvres
spread quickly to the Northern
Territory in the early 20th century
and are now also popular among
architects in New South Wales and
(despite its cold climate) Tasmania.

Noosa architect Gabriel Poole
(founder of the 'Sunshine Coast
style') also exploited canvas and
clear plastic sheeting as roll-up
walls for his Tent Houses of the
early 1990s and Poole House 3 at
Lake Weyba (1996). Canvas was a
common Queensland building
material in the 19th century.

Around Australia's northern
perimeter, houses generally are
lifted above the ground – on fat
stumps, stilts, cross-braced steel
poles or elaborate space-frames
like Poole's quadropod systems of
1983–86. Elevation discourages
insects and removes floorboards
from damp earth (the slab huts had
mud or mat-covered floors). It also
circulates air under the house,
which may cool interior spaces
and stabilise the floorboards.

Another historical and ongoing
feature of Queensland houses is
the popular use of wood battens
to construct screens and trellises
which filter sunlight, provide privacy,
semi-enclose verandahs and
breezeways, hide piles of clutter
under the house, support climbing
vines and decoratively trim
important facades.

Queensland's rural sheds and
houses are primary inspirations
for all architects who pursue the
'vernacular Australian style' that is
internationally celebrated through
the works of Sydney's Glenn
Murcutt. These are antipodean
expressions of architecture's eternal
Ideal: the primitive hut.

TROPICAL TIN HUTS

When architects build in the far north of the continent, they need an arsenal of strategies to tame the piercing sun, exhausting humidity and torrential downpours. There's also a constant danger of cyclones. The legendary Cyclone Tracey flattened much of Darwin on Christmas Day in 1974; her terrors still pervade the psyche of the city.

An understandable reaction to Cyclone Tracey has been a plethora of ultra-engineered brick villas on concrete slabs. But some Darwin architects, led by Troppo's Adelaide-trained directors Phil Harris and Adrian Welke, instead responded with light, airy houses to 'work with' local winds rather than block them. (Semi-contrarily, they built a courtyard compound of masonry pavilions in 1999.)

In the Northern Territory and far north Queensland, several other architects (not necessarily local) recently built steel houses which advance the cause of ecology-sensitive tropical design.

These cabins have high-pitched and wide-eaved roofs which quickly propel rain to the ground, allow hot air to rise above the living spaces, hover protectively over sundecks, and allow doors to remain open in torrid afternoon thunderstorms. The roofs often have skylights and revolving ventilators.

Continuing a tropical tradition, floors are usually elevated up to two metres above the ground, creating shady undercrofts for cars, barbeques and workshops.

External stairs lead to front decks which open off the living zone. In tune with the easy sociability of the tropics, there may not be a front door to knock.

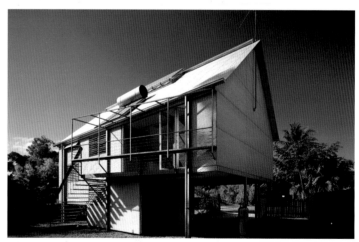

ABOVE LEFT
LIVERIS HOUSE, HULLY LIVERIS, PARAP, NORTHERN TERRITORY, 1995
A 1950s GOVERNMENT HOUSE OF THE COLLOQUIALLY DESCRIBED 'BOOMERANG' TYPE WAS UPGRADED TWO DECADES AFTER NARROWLY ESCAPING DARWIN'S DEVASTATING CYCLONE TRACEY IN 1974. ORIGINALLY ONE ROOM WIDE, WITH A KINKED FLOOR PLAN, THE FIBRE CEMENT STRUCTURE HAS BEEN MODESTLY BUT EXTENSIVELY REVISED WITH PROJECTING DECKS, OVERHANGING ROOFS, LOUVRES, WINDOWS AND AWNINGS.
PHOTO WAYNE MILES.

ABOVE AND TOP
PROWSE HOUSE, DAVID LANGSTON-JONES, CAIRNS, QUEENSLAND, 1995
IN AUSTRALIA'S TROPICS, HOUSES ARE OFTEN RAISED ON STILTS TO ENCOURAGE BREEZES AND PROVIDE A SHADY GROUND AREA FOR SITTING AND CAR PARKING. THIS TIN HUT UPDATES THAT MODEL WITH ADDITIONAL SYSTEMS OF 'BREATHING'. A CENTRAL STAIRCASE CONDUCTS RISING AIR TO ALL ROOMS. AIR ALSO RISES INSIDE THE DOUBLE-SKIN WALLS TO ESCAPE FROM A ROOF VENTILATOR. THE GABLE ROOF IS STEEP (TO SLUICE HEAVY RAIN) AND WIDE (TO SHADE ROOMS AND ALLOW BIFOLD DOORS TO REMAIN OPEN DURING HUMID STORMS). PHOTOS TREVOR MEIN.

OPPOSITE
DE BONO SEMINAR CENTRE, TONE WHEELER, GREAT BARRIER REEF, QUEENSLAND, 1997
AN ISLAND BEACH HUT OPENS TO DECKS ON ALL SIDES. IT IS BUILT OF STEEL WITH THE LIVING PLATFORM ELEVATED TO EXPLOIT OCEAN VIEWS AND BREEZES. ON THE WEST SIDE, TWO LAYERS OF SHUTTERS CONTROL TRANSPARENCY AND WEATHER CONDITIONS BETWEEN THE LIVING ROOM AND DECK. ECOLOGICAL STRATEGIES INCLUDE SOLAR POWER, LPG, COMPOST LAVATORIES AND WATER RECYCLING. INTERIOR FINISHES ARE PLYWOOD, TIMBER AND FIBREBOARD.
PHOTO TIM WHEELER.

SYDNEY'S WHITE HOUSES

Sydney is Australia's centrepoint for pure white temples – from Jørn Utzon's Opera House (completed 1973) and Philip Cox's referential steel pavilions of 1988 at Darling Harbour, back to Sydney Ancher's horizontal residences of the 1940s and 1950s, seminal houses by Ken Woolley and Neville Gruzman in the 1960s and 1970s and Harry Seidler's city towers and suburban houses spanning the last 50 years.

The harbour city's devotion to white forms under blue skies appears to have intensified recently, with new housing by Alex Popov, Burley Katon Halliday, Engelen Moore, Durbach Block, Stephen Lesuik with Nanna Binning and Eeles Trelease.

All these architects have investigated Seidler's oeuvre and are, like him, deeply influenced by early European cubism and its consequent International Style of the three decades after 1950.

Of the contemporary firms noted above, two are modifying classic cubism. Popov, who has travelled widely and lived in China, Majorca and Denmark, brings many subtle allusions to his houses, including Mediterranean qualities faintly reminiscent of the 1920s and '30s residences of Leslie Wilkinson, Sydney University's first professor of architecture. (Wilkinson is said to have been Australia's first importer of Mediterranean architectural themes.) Meanwhile, Neil Durbach and Camilla Block, both from South Africa, have been designing houses where the primary facade reads as a sweeping, irregular curve. Both firms appreciate – and successfully exploit – the defensive power of the massive wall.

**ABOVE AND TOP LEFT
REDFERN HOUSE ALTERATIONS,
ENGELEN MOORE, SYDNEY, 1995**
A 19TH CENTURY TERRACE HOUSE HAS BEEN MODERNISED AND WHITEWASHED THROUGHOUT. THE DOUBLE-HEIGHT LIVING AREA, USED AS A PHOTOGRAPHY STUDIO, IS MINIMALLY FURNISHED AND ITS SOUTH WALL REMAINS SHADOW-FREE ALL DAY. A DESIGN HIGHLIGHT IS A REAR WALL OF GLASS WHICH SLIDES TO A NARROW STACK OF FOLDS (A SYSTEM REMINISCENT OF MIES VAN DER ROHE'S TUGENDHAT HOUSE). PHOTOS ROSS HONEYSETT.

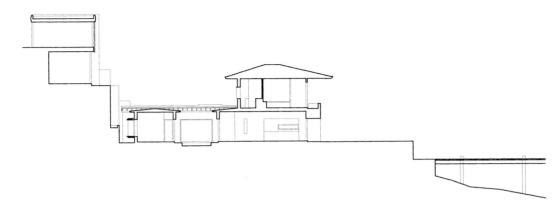

TOP LEFT, ABOVE AND RIGHT
NEUTRAL BAY HOUSE, ALEX POPOV,
SYDNEY, 1999
A NARROW SITE DESCENDS SHARPLY TO
A PLATEAU BESIDE A HARBOUR INLET. TO
MAXIMISE THAT TERRAIN, THREE PAVILIONS
ARE BUILT AT DIFFERENT HEIGHTS. FROM A
GARAGE AT STREET LEVEL, AN INCLINATOR
DESCENDS TO A ONE-BEDROOM GUEST
PAVILION TUCKED ON A LEDGE HALFWAY
DOWN THE CLIFF. THEN IT CONTINUES TO
THE MAIN HOUSE; AN ELEGANT WHITE
TEMPLE WITH A HOVERING ROOF OF
COPPER. THIS TWO-STOREY RESIDENCE
WRAPS AROUND A CENTRAL POOL COURT
AND OPENS TO A HARBOURSIDE TERRACE.
PHOTOS KRAIG CARLSTROM.

ABOVE AND RIGHT
PITT HOUSE, BURLEY KATON HALLIDAY,
SYDNEY, 1996
A 40-YEAR-OLD MODERNIST HOUSE WITH
BROAD HARBOUR VIEWS IS UPDATED IN A
COMPATIBLY CUBIST MANNER. STAIRS RISE
FROM THE STREET TO ARRIVE AT THE
ENTRANCE BEHIND A WALL OF THE POOL
COURT. UPSTAIRS, THE LIVING/DINING
ROOM PROJECTS FROM THE HOUSE
WITHIN A WEST-FACING GLASS BOX.
BEHIND THIS ARE A KITCHEN AND FAMILY
ROOM, WITH BEDROOMS AND A GARDEN
AT THE REAR. A PARENT'S SUITE IS
CENTRALLY PLACED ON THE HIGHEST
FLOOR. PHOTOS SHARRIN REES.

ABOVE AND OPPOSITE RIGHT
HUNTERS HILL HOUSE, DURBACH
BLOCK, SYDNEY, 1998
A 4-BEDROOM, 2-STOREY HOUSE IS
CONTAINED WITHIN A CURVED WHITE
WALL PUNCTURED WITH BLACK AND
WHITE-FRAMED WINDOWS AND OPENINGS
RELATED TO UPSTAIRS TERRACES.
AMENITIES AND SECONDARY BEDROOMS
ARE ON THE GROUND FLOOR; LIVING
SPACES ARE ABOVE. ABUNDANT NATURAL
LIGHT IS PROVIDED FROM A LONG
SKYLIGHT OVER THE STAIRWELL ON
THE NORTH SIDE OF THE HOUSE.
FIRST FLOOR PLAN TOP.
PHOTOS PATRICK BINGHAM-HALL.

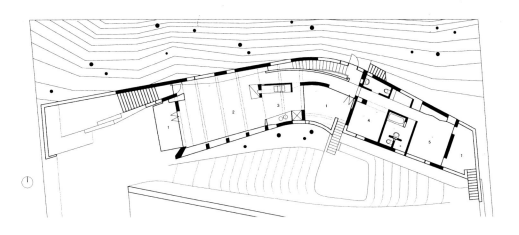

SKELETONS AND SKINS

When 19th-century foundries began to produce iron and sheet glass as building materials, architecture's romantic mythology needed a radical update.

In particular, its lineage of theories comparing buildings to human bodies – ideas dating back to primitive societies – had to be extrapolated to acknowledge the thinness of these novel materials.

The sublime Crystal Palace, built for London's Great Exhibition of 1851, amazed observers with its fine, skeletal strength and taut, stretched translucency. It promptly generated analogies to skin, bones, ribs, sinews and muscles, which have regularly been invoked in architecture ever since.

Scholars apply the metaphor of the naked corpse to some modern buildings which strongly express their structures. Human connotations are also given to the curtain walls of office towers, which are said to drape the body with a fall of woven or diaphanous fabric.

In Australia, architects in diverse climates build similar steel and glass houses to update classic prototypes by Ludwig Mies van der Rohe and Philip Johnson. They are intended to be pure and technically contemporary expressions of primal, universal ideals.

One concept is the platform (or verandah) hovering above an isolated landscape, providing both shelter and a distant prospect. Another, dating back to Classical theories, is the use of plain columns and beams to frame containers for life. And when skeletal houses are warmly treated with honey-toned plywood panels, allusions to ships are inevitable.

ABOVE
TALMAN HOUSE, DALE JONES-EVANS, AIREY'S INLET, VICTORIA, 1997
THIS HOUSE, ON A CLIFF OVERLOOKING VICTORIA'S GREAT SOUTHERN OCEAN, HAS BEEN PLANNED AS A WEATHERPROOF BUNKER – AND ITS LONG AXIS IS IMAGINED AS A LINE OF SEPARATION BETWEEN THE SEA AND THE SHORE. IT SITS ON A GLASS BOX WHICH ALLOWS GROUND-LEVEL VIEWS ACROSS AND BEYOND THE SITE. EXTERNAL MATERIALS – CONCRETE, STEEL, FIBRE CEMENT AND GLASS – RESIST HARSH WEATHER. THE INTERIOR IS FINISHED IN OFF-WHITE PAINT AND TIMBER. PHOTO ASHLEY JONES-EVANS.

ABOVE
CLIFTON BEACH HOUSE, CRAIG ROSEVEAR, TASMANIA, 1997
HOVERING ABOVE SAND DUNES AT THE EDGE OF THE SOUTHERN OCEAN, THIS STEEL-FRAMED HOUSE WAS IMAGINED AS A BRIDGE BETWEEN THE WINDY BEACH AND SHELTERED LAND BEHIND THE DUNES. END WALLS ARE GLAZED TO EXPLOIT DISTANT VIEWS OF A BAY AND LAGOON. THE FRAME WAS ASSEMBLED ON SITE AND IS FILLED WITH PANELS OF GLASS AND CELERY-TOP PINE. PHOTO PETER HYATT.

OPPOSITE
STEEL HOUSE, GROSE BRADLEY, NORTHERN NEW SOUTH WALES, 1997
FACING EAST FROM AN ISOLATED RIDGE TO THE PACIFIC OCEAN, THIS STEEL AND GLASS BOX IS DRAPED WITH MOTORISED BLINDS TO MANIPULATE THE MORNING SUN. INTERIOR FINISHES INCLUDE BRUSHBOX FLOORING AND WALLS OF WHITE PLASTERBOARD AND ZINCALUME. PHOTO ANTHONY BROWELL.

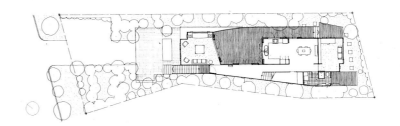

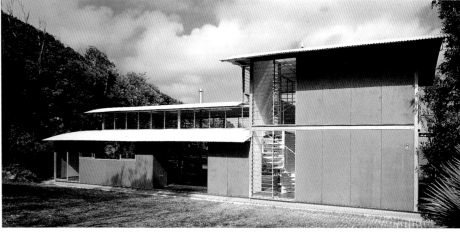

OPPOSITE
BRANNIGAN HOUSE, BUD BRANNIGAN,
ST LUCIA, BRISBANE, 1994
DESIGNED FOR A NARROW BUSH SITE,
THIS HOUSE IS ORIENTED TO THE SIDE
OF THE PROPERTY, WITH LIVING ZONES
ARRANGED AROUND A DECK FACING
NORTH EAST. THE MAIN STEEL FRAME IS
ELEVATED BY A 3600 MM GRID OF POSTS.
WALLS, FLOORS AND CEILINGS ARE
TIMBER, PLYWOOD AND FIBRE CEMENT
PANELS, WITH JOINTS EXPRESSED BY
SHADOW GAPS AND COVER STRIPS.
EXTERIOR LOUVRES CONTROL PRIVACY
AND SUN. GROUND FLOOR PLAN TOP.
PHOTO MICHAEL NICHOLSON.

ABOVE AND TOP LEFT
KRONENBERG HOUSE, ALEXANDER
TZANNES, KILLCARE, NEW SOUTH
WALES, 1997
TO ENTER THIS BEACH HOUSE ON A
STEEP SITE NORTH OF SYDNEY, VISITORS
CLIMB UP FROM THE STREET TO A BACK
ENTRANCE THAT OPENS DRAMATICALLY TO
THE OCEAN AHEAD. THE ARCHITECTURAL
IDEA IS A VERANDAH HOVERING OFF THE
SLOPE. SLIDING GLASS DOORS AND
LOUVRES OPEN TO ADMIT SEA BREEZES.
HIGH WINDOWS CONDUCT DAYLIGHT
FROM ALL DIRECTIONS. SLEEPING AND
UTILITY AREAS ARE AT THE NORTH AND
SOUTH ENDS OF THE LIVING ZONE.
PHOTOS BART MAIORANA.

ABOVE RIGHT
CASHMAN/PICKLES HOUSE, LIPPMANN
ASSOCIATES, WOMBARRA, NEW SOUTH
WALES, 1995
APPROACHED FROM ABOVE AND ACROSS
A BRIDGE TO A CLEARING, THIS HOUSE
ON THE COAST SOUTH OF SYDNEY IS
A PREFABRICATED STEEL STRUCTURE
SHEATHED WITH MARINE-GRADE PLYWOOD
AND GLASS. AN OPEN LIVING ZONE AND
WIDE TIMBER DECK OCCUPY THE LOWER
FLOOR – WHICH MOSTLY HOVERS ABOVE
SLOPING LAND. THE CENTRAL STAIRCASE
LEADS TO A BEDROOM AND STUDY.
PHOTO FARSHID ASSASSI.

RUSTIC RETREATS

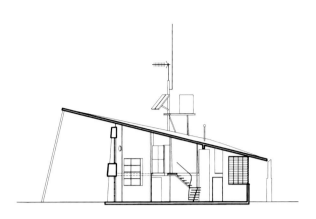

South of Sydney (and even in the Blue Mountains to its west), temperatures sink below freezing in winter and isolated houses are sometimes exposed to frosts and mists in the morning and to icy afternoon winds blowing up from the Antarctic. The architecture for these weather conditions is naturally defensive.

Classic plans for houses near the lower coasts of the continent are often adapted from the letters C, E, H, U, V or Y. These formats allow rooms to be arranged in wings which 'embrace' sundecks and courtyards to shelter them from strong winds.

One technique – exemplified by Clinton Murray's hilltop house at Merimbula, on the NSW south coast (1996) – is to build a house around a central court so the space is wind-protected but still sunny – and then to project a sundeck off the living room to allow Pacific Ocean views to be savoured on benign days. In this project, Murray also cantilevered another sundeck from an upstairs bedroom suite.

Near Apollo Bay, Victoria, a bush weekender by Melbourne architect Kerstin Thompson has been composed in plan as a boomerang of sequential bedrooms and bathrooms which have small windows facing west. To the east, a large living room is given prospects to the south, east and north, with a deck catching northern sun all day.

On a clifftop site at Burraworrin, on Melbourne's Mornington Peninsula, Greg Burgess has also developed a house to block winds from the ocean – with two curved arms protecting a central open

ABOVE
NIGEL LEVINGS HOUSE, GROSE BRADLEY, CAREY GULLY, SOUTH AUSTRALIA, 1996
THIS HOUSE IN THE ADELAIDE HILLS IS A DOMESTIC EXEMPLAR – SYMBOLICALLY AND PRACTICALLY – OF AUSTRALIAN CONCERNS TO PRESERVE THE PLANET'S ECOLOGY. KEY STRATEGIES OF THERMAL EFFICIENCY, SOLAR POWER, RAINWATER RETENTION AND WASTE RECYCLING ARE INCORPORATED IN A MUD-BRICK PAVILION WITH A STEEL SERVICES TOWER THAT IS REMINISCENT OF FARM WINDMILLS.
PHOTO TOM BALFOUR.

RIGHT
JEAN SOLOMON HOUSE, LARCOMBE & SOLOMON, LEURA, NEW SOUTH WALES, 1995
INSPIRED BY AN IDEA OF TENUOUS DWELLING ON THE EDGE, THIS CLIFFTOP HOUSE IN SYDNEY'S BLUE MOUNTAINS HAS BEEN BUILT IN TWO PARTS. ONE IS 'THE BLOCK': A TWO-STOREY TIMBER BOX ON A CONCRETE SLAB, CONTAINING THE BEDROOMS, BATHROOMS AND KITCHEN. THE OTHER IS 'THE CANOPY', A FLOATING AND IRREGULAR STRUCTURE OF STEEL AND GLASS, CONTAINING THE OPEN LIVING SPACE AND DECK BENEATH A ROOF OF THREE DESCENDING LEAVES OF METAL.
PHOTO ERIC SIERINS.

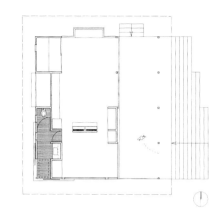

ABOVE AND RIGHT
KANGAROO VALLEY HOUSE,
STUTCHBURY & PAPE, NEW SOUTH
WALES, 1999
A SQUARE SHED, HALF OPEN AND HALF
WALLED, IS TOPPED BY A STEEL SKILLION
ROOF WHICH IS FOLDED UP SHARPLY TO
THE NORTH AND HELD WITH A SEQUENCE
OF V STRUTS TO ALLOW ALL-DAY
SUNLIGHT INSIDE. THIS ONE-BEDROOM
HOUSE IS FRAMED IN BLACKBUTT AND
FINISHED WITH TURPENTINE AND
CORRUGATED STEEL. LIVING SPACES
LOOK EAST TO A GLADE OF PINE TREES.
FLOOR PLAN TOP. PHOTOS PATRICK
BINGHAM-HALL.

ABOVE AND TOP RIGHT
'TANGLEWOOD', METIER 3, THREDBO,
NEW SOUTH WALES, 1997
A 24-METRE ROCK WALL ALIGNS NORTH-
WEST/SOUTH-EAST TO ANCHOR THIS
HOUSE IN THE NSW SNOWY MOUNTAINS.
CAR AND PEDESTRIAN ENTRY BRIDGES
LEAD FROM THE STREET TO THE GARAGE
AND ADJACENT FRONT DOOR. INSIDE,
TWO 'HABITATION PODS' – ONE FOR
AMENITIES AND THE OTHER FOR LIVING –
FACE NORTH-EAST AND ARE CONNECTED
BY A GROUND FLOOR CORRIDOR AND
FIRST FLOOR BRIDGE. PHOTOS TIM
GRIFFITH.

131

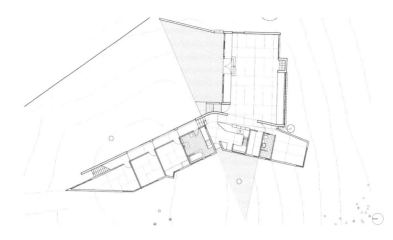

space. This house is orchestrated to look like an organic cluster of pods, but the internal rooms are linked as they would be in a homogenous building. This Burraworrin house is strongly reminiscent of Burgess' Hackford house at Taralgon, Victoria (1981).

Visually, all three of the above houses represent an interesting theme in recent Australian domestic architecture: the use of wood to express a monolithic quality that is normally associated with masonry constructions.

At Merimbula, Murray has used massive lengths of hardwood – recycled from obsolete bridges and wharves – to construct the kind of basic post-and-beam structure that inspired Classical Greek temples. The frame is filled in with glass panels and horizontal boards of yellow stringybark – producing a strongly monumental aesthetic.

The Victorian houses by Thompson and Burgess both conceal their frames behind claddings of boards fixed vertically and punctured with white-framed windows. A similar strategy was used by Queensland architect Gerard Murtagh for another monolithic residence at Sunshine Beach, near Noosa, built in 1996.

In Sydney's Blue Mountains, Caroline Larcombe and Nicholas Solomon have built a schismatic clifftop house (1995) in which a two-storey timber-sheathed pavilion – a defensive container for private rooms – anchors a single-storey, glass-walled living zone hovering above the ground.

Another house of contradictory character is a house in the NSW Snowy Mountains by Melbourne

ABOVE AND RIGHT
WEST COAST HOUSE, KERSTIN THOMPSON, VICTORIA, 1999
A TIMBER-SHEATHED BLADE KINKS AROUND A COASTAL SPUR, BROADENS TO HOLD ROOMS AND PASSAGES, THEN OPENS TO A WIDE DECK. THIS 'OCCUPIED WALL' IS DIVIDED BETWEEN ITS TIMBER-CLAD, SMALL-WINDOWED, NIGHT ZONE AND A DAY-LIVING REALM OF CONCRETE AND GLASS, WHICH OPENS TO SEA AND MOUNTAIN VIEWS. THE IDEA OF A HOUSE WEAVING ACROSS ITS SITE IS A NOVEL COMMENT ON POPULAR AUSTRALIAN IMAGES OF SHEDS ISOLATED IN RURAL LANDSCAPES. PLAN TOP. PHOTOS JOHN GOLLINGS.

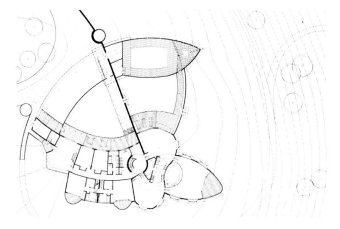

ABOVE
BURRAWORRIN, GREGORY BURGESS,
FLINDERS, VICTORIA, 1999
A HOLIDAY COMPOUND FOR FOUR
FAMILIES RAMBLES ACROSS THE CREST
OF A CLIFF EXPOSED TO CAPRICIOUS,
SUB-ANTARCTIC WEATHER. FROM THE
ENTRY VESTIBULE, CURVED TIMBER
PODS RADIATE AROUND NORTH-FACING
OUTDOOR AREAS, SHIELDING THESE
SANCTUMS FROM ANTARCTIC SOUTH-
WESTERLIES. INTERNAL SPACES HAVE
RESTRICTED VIEWS UP AND DOWN THE
COASTLINE, WHILE THE FROND-TOPPED
LOOKOUT POST OFFERS A FULL-CIRCLE
PANORAMA. GROUND FLOOR PLAN TOP.
PHOTO TREVOR MEIN.

BEACH HOUSE, CLINTON MURRAY, MERIMBULA, NEW SOUTH WALES, 1996
MASSIVE HARDWOOD COLUMNS AND BEAMS, RECYCLED FROM OBSOLETE BRIDGES AND WHARVES, ESTABLISH THE STRUCTURE OF A COASTAL RESIDENCE WHICH WRAPS AROUND A POOL COURT (OPPOSITE) TO SHELTER IT FROM COASTAL WINDS. THE FRAME IS FILLED IN WITH YELLOW STRINGYBARK BOARDS AND EXTENSIVE GLAZING. FROM THE BALD TIMBER STREETFRONT (TOP RIGHT), A GLAZED HALLWAY (TOP LEFT) LEADS TO A TWO STOREY FAMILY REALM AT THE REAR, OVERLOOKING THE OCEAN. PHOTOS ALISON TAYLOR.

architects Metier 3. Here, a stone wall runs north-west/south-east to anchor two timber boxes which contain the living areas.

When houses are built on flat bush sites which do not directly command a distant prospect, the architectural response is often a small hut or pavilion built on a clearing of land. The exact circumference of unwooded space around the house is often regulated by local councils concerned about the dangers of summer bush fires that can be rapidly fanned by north-westerly winds from the desert.

While the architecture of monolithic houses is an expression of the strength of the wall, the architecture of the hut is the celebration of the roof. Like the famous Australian Akubra, it is designed as a wide-brimmed hat which blocks sun and rain, and delivers a kind of crowning distinction to the body beneath.

At Kangaroo Valley, a farming area south of Sydney, Stutchbury & Pape have built a simple, square pavilion of timber which has half its floor space open to the elements as a deck. Both this area and the indoor zone are roofed with a steel skillion which dramatically tilts up towards the north to exploit the trajectory of the sun.

In the hills of Adelaide, Sydney architects Grose Bradley pointed an arrowhead-shaped skillion beyond the earth walls of a circular hut equipped with ecology-sensitive energy and waste systems. There is another gesture of thrust in an external steel tower which carries solar panels and reminds observers of Australia's pioneer tradition of windmills irrigating farm pastures.

OPEN HOUSES

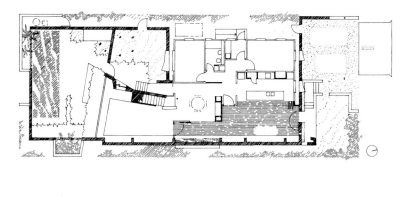

ABOVE
Q HOUSE RENOVATION, DONOVAN HILL, BRISBANE, 1998
IN MAJOR RENOVATIONS TO A SMALL BUNGALOW, A NEW DOUBLE-HEIGHT COOKING/DINING ZONE OPENS TO GARDEN BEDS AND FISHPONDS VIA SLIDING WALLS AND SCREENS. ALTHOUGH PERMANENTLY ROOFED, THE SPACE ACTS MUCH LIKE AN OUTDOOR COURT. IT CATCHES AND CHANNELS BREEZES, WINTER SUN, SUMMER SHADE AND REFLECTED LIGHT TO OTHER PARTS OF THE HOUSE. UPSTAIRS IS THE BIRD'S NEST BALCONY OF THE MAIN BEDROOM. FLOOR PLAN TOP RIGHT. PHOTO JON LINKINS.

Australians like to relax in outdoor rooms which offer shade but are also open to the subtlest airs of scorching Januaries.

While most colonial houses were baldly Georgian, they were soon elaborated with sun-reactive verandahs, pergolas and porte cochères. Updates of India's Bengali bungalows (interpreted via the English and United States crafts movements) have been popular since the late 19th century.

Although the verandah is usually recognised as Australia's vital vernacular theme, another strategy is now common: the idea of a house turning away from the street (with a blank facade) so that living areas flow to a central or rear courtyard (and/or upstairs deck).

Since the 1970s, Australians have substantially revised many of the nation's older houses to install bedrooms and studies near the street entry (usurping the formal drawing room) – and to establish direct links to the back garden by demolishing fragile 'fibro' lean-tos containing laundries, bathrooms and kitchens. These are replaced with multi-use 'family rooms' that include open kitchens.

Dark terrace houses are often centrally punctured on their sunny sides with compact garden courts that also conduct daylight indoors.

Where space allows, new courtyard houses with alphabetic floor plans are highly desired. Styling inspirations include Balinese compounds, the mid-century ranches of Mexico's Luis Barragán, traditional Spanish-Mediterranean villas, Santa Fe adobe dwellings and the low, white, modern boxes of 1950s California and Florida.

THIEL HOUSE, TROPPO, DARWIN, 1999
SEE CAPTION OPPOSITE. PHOTO PATRICK BINGHAM-HALL.

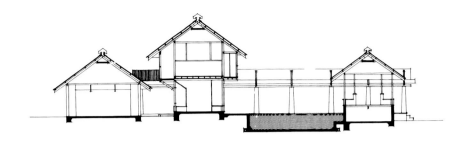

THIEL HOUSE, TROPPO, DARWIN, 1999
INSPIRED BY COURTYARD COMPOUNDS
IN BALI AND SRI LANKA, THIS BAYFRONT
RESIDENCE HAS LIVING PAVILIONS AND
OUTDOOR ZONES AROUND A SWIMMING
POOL. TO ADAPT TO TROPICAL WEATHER
SHIFTS, THESE AREAS HAVE FOLDING
DOORS, LOUVRES, SLATTED SCREENS
AND SHUTTERS. A PATH LEADS FROM A
DEFENSIVE STREET WALL, PAST PONDS
AND PLANTS, TOWARDS A MARINA AND
BAY. ROBUST MATERIALS – RENDERED
CONCRETE, TIMBERS AND STEEL – WERE
CHOSEN TO SUIT THE NORTHERN
TERRITORY'S INFORMAL CULTURE AND
HARSH CLIMATE. CROSS-SECTION TOP.
PHOTOS PATRICK BINGHAM-HALL.

OOI HOUSE, KERRY HILL, MARGARET RIVER, WESTERN AUSTRALIA, 1998
A HOVERING STRUCTURE OF STEEL AND GLASS IS ANCHORED TO A GENTLE SLOPE BY A STABILISED EARTH WALL (COMMON IN THIS DISTRICT). ALONG THE NORTH (UPPER) SIDE OF THE HOUSE, A GABLED ROOF SHELTERS A SEQUENCE OF SERENE BEDROOMS AND BATHROOMS. THE OPEN, FULLY GLAZED LIVING ZONE FACES SOUTH BENEATH A SKILLION ROOF AND OPENS NORTHWARD TO A SHELTERED DECK WITH A BLACK POND. FLOOR PLAN THIS PAGE. EAST/WEST SECTION OPPOSITE TOP. PHOTOS MARTIN FARQUHARSON.

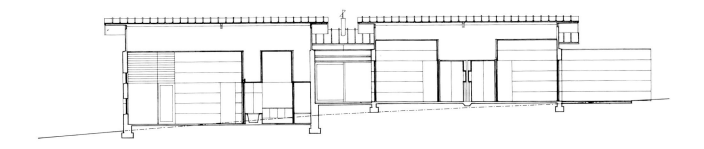

SUBURBAN SWERVES

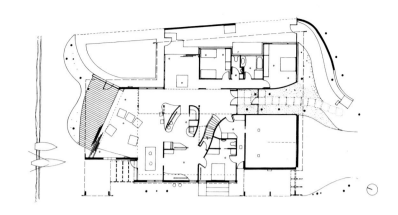

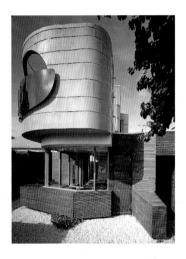

In the Macquarie Dictionary, 'swerve' is defined as a deviation from the straight course. Boisterous expressions of this impulse can occasionally be found in otherwise ordinary suburbs.

Architects like John Mainwaring in Noosa and various small offices in Melbourne regularly produce irregularly bendy and kinky houses that are self-consciously out-of-character with their angular, symmetrical neighbours.

Many of these domestic statements are intended either to radically interrupt the repetition of historic streets or to metaphorically raise a finger to the nostalgic European styling of mass-built tile-roof villas – popularly described as 'sprawling brick venereals'.

Although the 1950s and 1960s produced some modernist houses with circular elements, and there were creative experiments with triangular geometries in the 1970s, the current tendency towards overtly eccentric form-making did not really become a notable strand of activity until the 1980s. In that decade of vigorous reactions against modernism, some Melburnians, including Robinson Chen and Bilt Moderne (both firms now disbanded), Ivan Rijavec and NeoMetro began to design houses with either extraordinarily irregular and monolithic qualities (often contrasted by glazed north walls) or with facades fragmented into disparate elements in different colours and textures.

Melbourne now is a hotbed of non-conforming house designers and Perth has several architects who conceive (and sometimes build) disorderly structures.

ABOVE LEFT
PORT MELBOURNE HOUSE ADDITION, SHANE WILLIAMS, VICTORIA, 1997
A THREE-LEVEL 'ESCAPE CAPSULE' IS PLUGGED ONTO THE BACK OF A 19TH CENTURY HOUSE – PROVIDING A NEW KITCHEN ON GROUND, A FIRST FLOOR LIVING ROOM AND A ROOF DECK WHICH IS SHELTERED FROM SEA WINDS BY A WRAP-AROUND WALL OF WEATHERED ZINC. PHOTO NAOMI KUMAR.

ABOVE
GOH RESIDENCE, ODDEN RODRIGUES, DALKEITH, WESTERN AUSTRALIA, 1998
A STEEL PERGOLA AND A GLAZED GALLERY (CONTAINING LIVING AND DINING ROOMS AND A STUDY) HAVE BEEN ADDED TO THE NORTH SIDE OF A 1963 HOUSE ORIGINALLY DESIGNED BY GEOFFREY SUMMERHAYES, THEN ALTERED BY COLIN MOORE. PHOTO MARTIN FARQUHARSON.

TOP AND OPPOSITE
CANAL HOUSE, JOHN MAINWARING, NOOSA, QUEENSLAND, 1994
SURROUNDED BY BRICK AND TILE VILLAS IN A SUBTROPICAL CANAL SUBDIVISION, THE MAINWARING HOUSE UPDATES THE AREA'S EARLIEST BEACH SHACKS WITH A CASUALLY BOISTEROUS 'LARRIKIN' STYLE. THE ARCHITECTURE OF SLOT WINDOWS, SLIDING SCREENS AND LOUVRES ALLOWS SUBTLE MANIPULATION OF SUN AND BREEZES. SEVERAL WALLS OF PINK MASONRY ANCHOR LIGHT WALLS AND ROOFS OF PLYWOOD BOARDS AND CORRUGATED STEEL. GROUND FLOOR PLAN TOP. PHOTOS MICHAEL NICHOLSON.

WAREHOUSES

The loft conversions of lower Manhattan have sparked a 25-year trend (mainly in Sydney and Melbourne) to transform obsolete brick industrial buildings into modern residences.

Although photographers and artists have always shacked up in large old buildings, expensive commercial conversions did not begin until the late 1970s, with a batch of developments near central Sydney. The display units were furnished with sleek Italian seating, Persian rugs and Asian artefacts, as foils to the blackened hardwood roof trusses and walls of rough brickwork. Buyers were mainly prosperous bachelors and urbane couples – often enticed by pictorial features in local interiors journals.

In the mid-1980s, after a few sporadic fitouts in Melbourne, warehouse recycling became a dynamic mainstream strand of the property industry. Many talented young architects were sought out by entrepreneurs to conceive trendy transformations. Leading warehouse specialists of that decade were Robinson Chen, Nonda Katsalidis, Ivan Rijavec, NeoMetro Design and Bilt Moderne – many of whom continue with larger projects in the 1990s. As experimental designers, they appreciated the potential of lofty and austere 'character' spaces to showcase daring 'sculptural insertions' – walls and cabinets in singular shapes and finished with exotic materials.

Warehouse conversions continued in both Sydney and Melbourne during the 1990s, and there were a few developments in Hobart, Brisbane, Adelaide and Perth. In Darwin, industrial tin sheds are sometimes furnished with tables and cabinets creatively recycled from the hulls of boats captured with cargoes of illegal immigrants.

Sydney's most notable recent warehouse conversions include Kerridge Wallace's mansard-roofed house/office (1995), a Surry Hills residence by Jahn Associates (1999), the Darlinghurst atelier of Sam Marshall (1999), two multi-apartment refits by Dale Jones-Evans (1996 and 1999), the Grace apartments in Camperdown by Bonus Architects (1999), and refurbishments of large waterfront buildings at Balmain (Julius Bokor, 1999) and Pyrmont Point (Daryl Jackson-Robin Dyke, 2000).

Memorable industrial rescues in Melbourne include Ivan Rijavec's Freeland house (1994), Anthony Styant-Browne's 'shed-in-shed' (1994), Stephen Varady's Slobham/Parham residence (1995), Kerstin Thompson's Fitzroy renovation (1996), the Hotel Lindrum by Swaney Draper with Terry Fripp (1999) and several 1999 projects by Wood Marsh. Other projects were completed by Peter Zellner, McBride Charles Ryan, McGauran Soon, Brearley Middleton and Tom Kovac.

The most vivid aesthetic gesture from this decade's crop of industrial domiciles is Wood Marsh's skeletal roof truss, black courtyard and blood-red pool at the Taylor residence (1999). On a dark and stormy night, this macabre scene can arrest an unacquainted eye and make the subconscious squirm with faint horrors from movie homicides. The antidote for that mood? A swim.

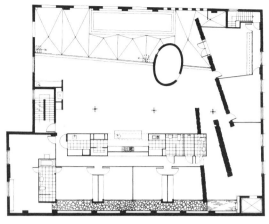

EXOTIC AUSTRALIA
THE LINE AND THE PLACE

CHRIS JOHNSON

1 PETER BRIDGES AND LENORE COLTHEART OUTLINED MANY AUSTRALIAN EFFECTS OF ENLIGHTENMENT PRINCIPLES IN THEIR UNPUBLISHED 1998 PAPER 'THE ELEPHANT'S BED? SCOTTISH ENLIGHTENMENT IDEAS AND THE FOUNDATION OF NEW SOUTH WALES.'

2 SEE ARTHUR PHILLIP, 'THE VOYAGE OF GOVERNOR PHILLIP TO BOTANY BAY; WITH AN ACCOUNT OF THE ESTABLISHMENT OF THE COLONIES OF PORT JACKSON AND NORFOLK ISLAND; COMPILED FROM AUTHENTIC PAPERS WHICH HAVE BEEN OBTAINED FROM THE SEVERAL DEPARTMENTS, TO WHICH ARE ADDED THE JOURNALS OF LIEUTS. SHORTLAND, WATTS, BALL AND CAPT. MARSHALL, WITH AN ACCOUNT OF THEIR NEW DISCOVERIES.' FACSIMILE OF THE 1789 EDITION, ADVERTISER PRINTING OFFICE, P.123.

3 BARRIE SHELTON HIGHLIGHTS A SIMILAR DIVISION IN 'LEARNING FROM THE JAPANESE CITY: WEST MEETS EAST IN URBAN DESIGN,' 1999. HE HIGHLIGHTS CONTRASTING WAYS OF READING SPACE: IN THE EAST AS AN OPEN PLATFORM (RELATING TO 'AREA') AND IN THE WEST AS AN ENCLOSURE (ARISING FROM THE 'LINE' OF THE WALL). AUSTRALIA DISPLAYS THE EASTERN APPROACH MORE OFTEN THAN EUROPE.

Two opposing concepts guided Australian architecture towards the end of the twentieth century. One led to structures which stand upon and hover above the ground to show separation and superiority. The other generated buildings which come from and merge with their contexts. Both approaches continue the eternal struggle between humans and the land.

The first idea leads to architecture that, like a bridge, touches the earth lightly and displays clean, modern technology in simple and mostly rectangular forms oriented to the sun. The second is represented by buildings that remould the earth in flowing forms, displaying the craftsmanship of local materials. In contemporary circumstances, the former could be related to the Sydney architecture of Glenn Murcutt and the latter to the buildings of Greg Burgess from Melbourne. Or the two approaches could be considered historically, to link to the traditions of the Classical and the Romantic.

Australia was founded upon this duality. Recent research by historians Peter Bridges and Lenore Coltheart[1] shows intriguing oppositions of values among the colonial Governors and builders of New South Wales during the late eighteenth and early nineteenth centuries – and many of these reflect the different Enlightenment cultures which developed in England and Scotland. The English attitude was to dominate Nature, while the Scottish tended to relate to the environment.

The first patterns of order on the landscape were laid by Governor Arthur Phillip after his arrival in 1788. According to an account published the following year, Phillip said 'there can be few things more pleasing than the contemplation of order and useful management arising gradually out of tumult and confusion ... by degrees, large spaces are opened, lands formed, *lines* marked, and a prospect at least of future regularity is clearly discerned.'[2] These observations suggest that Phillip applied an English Enlightenment approach: to lay improvements upon the ground and subsume the land, almost arrogantly, to the needs of the new population. Phillip's main achievements were setting out the main streets and building the first Government House and wooden barracks for soldiers and convicts.

In 1810, Governor Lachlan Macquarie arrived in Sydney with his wife, Elizabeth: both bringing the softer values of the Scottish Enlightenment. Mrs Macquarie especially viewed the significance of public works as nutrients of progress rather than signifiers of cultural dominance. The Macquaries developed Australia's first Gothic works of architecture and a sequence of picturesque landscapes. They created Sydney's first public garden, Hyde Park, and the appropriately named Macquarie Place.

One of Macquarie's first developments was the Sydney Hospital, constructed as three buildings along the city's eastern ridge and providing accommodation far in excess of the colony's needs. More than its practical role of caring for the sick, it was a symbol of the administration's commitment to the health of the settlement.

The Macquarie lighthouse at South Head (designed by Francis Greenway as the first Civil Architect) also combined practicality with symbolism. The tower shone beams of light to guide ships into the port and, just as importantly, was a visible landmark on the horizon of the town, conveying its connection to the rest of the world. Even the forts which Greenway designed for Macquarie were either carefully tucked into the landscape (at Dawes Point), or were raised from sandstone platforms (at Bennelong Point).

Looking back on those origins of Australian settlement, I relate Phillip to the Classical tradition of the line and the Macquaries to Romantic notions of place.[3]

I assume the line to represent universal order – the pen strokes that generated the convict-built roads between the early towns of Sydney and Parramatta, or the grids of survey pegs which mapped the boundaries of free settlers' farms across the ridges and valleys of the east coast. The line regulates an English colonial system of axes and symmetry – and when applied in the landscape, it often has been open-ended in a way which contradicts the enclosed European square. It is about space that flows onwards.

Since Arthur Phillip, the line has been repeated in the planning of country towns with long main streets, and cities with post-war arrays of high-rise; and in the architectures of the shed, the verandah and the skyscraper. Today it can be seen as horizontal streaks by Murcutt, Grose Bradley, Hassell and Stutchbury & Pape, and in the Olympic Boulevard which created a coherent order for the Sydney 2000 venues at Homebush. It can also be seen soaring upwards in towers by Denton Corker Marshall, Harry Seidler and Nonda Katsalidis.

Set against the line, I think of place as a more organic and evolving idea about architecture which comes from the land rather than being imposed from above. Australia's most renowned organic forms are the giant boulders of Uluru-Kata Tjuta (Ayers Rock-the Olgas) in the desert of the Northern Territory. Beside those monoliths, Greg Burgess has designed an Aboriginal cultural centre which seems to crawl out of and wriggle along the red ground. Here, the formality and symmetry of Classical architecture are ignored in favour of an informal design program of multiple entries and meandering movement between indoor caves and outdoor campsites. This is exploration without a destination.

Less obviously naturalistic but equally organic and irregular are the works of architecture in Melbourne by Ashton Raggatt McDougall, Ivan Rijavec and LAB Architecture Studio, which show the powers of the computer to organise fantastic three-dimensional structures.

Australia was perceived by its European colonists as a blank canvas – an attitude still persisting in the legal principle of *terra nullius* – for development and mineral excavation. While this belief lingers in white consciousness and land laws, it is a barrier to reconciling the violent history and continuing tensions between the Caucasian and indigenous populations. In architecture though, there have been some recent gestures of mutual recognition in the design of small centres celebrating Aboriginal culture and sacred lands. Among those designed by white men, Burgess' Uluru centre is about place, while the Bowali centre in the Northern Territory's Kakadu National Park, by Glenn Murcutt and Troppo, reads from the air as a streak of silver metal across the earth, and at ground level as a monumental verandah linking a series of tin huts. Both complexes are approached obliquely, according to Aboriginal custom: Uluru from 'round the back' and Kakadu diagonally.

The two notions of the straight line and the wandering place also seem to merge in the Girrawaa Creative Work Centre at Bathurst, NSW, the first Australian building designed by a university-qualified Aboriginal architect. This scheme, by Dillon Kombummerie, manager of the Merrima unit in the NSW Department of Public Works and Services, curves the line and kinks the place to form a habitable figure of a goanna lizard with a long tail. Here, the sacred totem of the local Wiradjuri people is transformed into the outline of a place. The Merrima group is continuing to develop a zoomorphic style, using eels and fish as well as land creatures, as an appropriate contemporary basis for Australian architecture related to the land.

This book reveals many other interesting variations and syntheses of the line and the place.

For instance, the reading realm of Nield and Mainwaring's Sunshine Coast University Library is a place which interprets Louis Kahn's theory of linking contemplative silence with the light of knowledge. However, it is anchored by a grand verandah which powerfully confirms the ceremonial axis of the campus.

4 BLURRED EDGES ARE ALSO SEEN IN RENZO PIANO'S SYDNEY ARCHITECTURE. HIS AURORA PLACE TOWERS ARE CLOAKED WITH FAN-SHAPED BLADES OF GLASS: A RESPONSE FROM AN INTERNATIONAL ARCHITECT TO SYDNEY'S CLIMATE AND OPEN CHARACTER.

5 IN HIS 1998 BOYER LECTURES, AUTHOR DAVID MALOUF REFERRED TO THE AMALGAMATION OF BOTH LOCAL AND UNIVERSAL QUALITIES AS PART OF THE RICHNESS OF AUSTRALIAN CULTURE.

6 IT TOOK EIGHT YEARS BEFORE GOVERNMENT TURNED FROM DEMANDING THE REMOVAL OF BARNET'S CARVINGS TO SEEING THEM AS LEADING THE WORLD AND AS THE BEGINNING OF ART IN AUSTRALIA.

In Melbourne, Sean Godsell's rusty metal domestic cage thrusts out aggressively from its suburban ridge; yet this residence is grounded to sundecks and gardens which are intimately associated with the indoor living space.

Sydney's Olympic Games venues, at Homebush and smaller sites scattered further west, display both architectural approaches. Some venues – including the archery facility by Stutchbury & Pape, the shooting centre by Group GSA and the whitewater rafting venue by Grose Bradley – are light, long and open-ended structures framed in steel. Others – like Bligh Lobb's Stadium Australia, the Aquatic Centre by Cox Richardson with Peddle Thorp, the Velodrome by Ryder SJPH and the Equestrian Centre by Equus 2000 – are enclosed and inward-looking places, some relying on heavy elements built of masonry.

Other Olympic works blur the distinctions between the line and the place – particularly the major water and art installations by George Hargreaves, Paul Carter, Ruark Lewis, Janet Laurence, James Carpenter and Ari Purhonen. In different ways, all of these works rely on strongly linear structures, which are then subverted by disorderly intrusions of ephemeral substances.

A powerful example of the fusions and discrepancies is seen at the south end of the Olympic Boulevard, where Janet Laurence's fogs emanate vaguely from tall wands embedded in a meandering creek. These can be viewed from three footbridges designed by Denton Corker Marshall, which cross the creek as straight structures installed on oblique angles. They lead to Bligh Voller Nield's tennis complex: a place of small pavilions and courts around a circular stadium which symbolically terminates the Olympic axis.

One of the most important buildings at Homebush – the Olympic Park Rail Station by Hassell – powerfully expresses the symbolism of the line with its subterranean tracks, banks of escalators, glass-walled lifts and long steel roof. The canopy is constructed of hyperbolic paraboloid segments that have been compared to gum leaves. These roof profiles build the line into a rhythm which gives a rippling effect across the landscape and blurs the edges of the building against the sky.

The idea of rhythmic repetition of a linear building across the landscape also appears at Gabriel Poole's house at Lake Weyba, Queensland, at Peter Elliott's glasshouse at the Ballarat Botanic Gardens in Victoria and the Brisbane Convention Centre by Cox Rayner.

There is another blurring of boundaries in the repeating timber battens of Andresen & O'Gorman and Alice Hampson in Brisbane, and in the translucent materials chosen by Sydney architects Lawrence Nield, Richard Francis-Jones and Lahz Nimmo to orchestrate sunlight at the edges of their structures.

I see this tendency to blur distinctions as an emerging characteristic of Australian architecture that does not come from a state of confusion but from a new concern for subtlety and comfortable, informal relationships between buildings and their settings.[4]

Another kind of ambiguity between the line and the place can be seen in Brisbane, where Donovan Hill's C House sets up a complex sequence of artificial landscape plates which hover above, and are separate from, the steep site. These are resting places in a meandering navigation of the entire topography, involving sixteen flights of stairs climbing to a roof which looks back to the city. Here, the line meanders between isolated places stacked in layers. It becomes a narrative journey, as well as a network of connections.

Both of these developments – one private and the other public – manipulate the line to seemingly relate to a change of Australian consciousness: a growing political commitment to the ideas of cultural diversity, international free exchange and travel, and communications by networks rather than hierarchies.

All of these ideas have been gradually developing in Australia since the colony was founded in the last twelve years of the eighteenth century. At that time, Britain was beginning to translate the proprieties of English Anglicans and Methodists and Scottish Presbyterians to the harsh circumstances of an isolated prison camp also populated by many Irish Catholics.

As the new colonists spread out to secondary prisons on Norfolk Island and Tasmania, and then to new farm settlements west, north and south of Sydney, some administrators began to make decisions independent of the exploitative policies of the British Home Office. In particular, Governor Macquarie embarked on a program of ambitious building which brought him into serious disputes with his superiors back in London. Although his term, from 1810 to 1822, produced many important works designed by his Civil Architect, Francis Greenway, Macquarie returned to London in disgrace, leaving his further plans to be abandoned.

Australia's diverse climates and vegetation patterns – from the tropical north to cold Tasmania – required the settlers to modify old-world methods of construction and adapt kitsets and pattern book designs shipped out from England. Most of the early huts were built of hand-split timbers, often with bark roofs. But the palette expanded to include bluestone and granite in Victoria and Tasmania, sandstone or sandstock bricks in Sydney and limestone in Perth. In the semi-tropical north-east of the continent, timber, corrugated tin and canvas were the most common materials. All around the country, ventilation and shade were key concerns. From the 1820s onward, verandahs and pergolas were regularly added to bald Georgian facades.[5]

The first compelling signal of an Australian impulse to separate from Britain was the 1854 Eureka rebellion at Ballarat in Victoria, where several hundred goldminers barricaded themselves on top of a hill to protest against the harsh costs and conditions of their mining licences. As a gesture of secession, they raised a new flag of Australia: a gold Christian cross and the four stars of the Southern Cross constellation on a navy ground. Soldiers quickly quelled the riot in a massacre of thirty miners inside the stockade, but the flag has remained a powerful symbol of white Australian independence.

In 1888, Australia's most influential magazine, *The Bulletin*, opposed celebrations for the centenary of British settlement and called for the Eureka incident to be commemorated instead as the defining moment of Australia's history. This stance reflected escalating nationalism among the intellectuals who were the magazine's contributors and constituency. Poet Henry Lawson wrote 'A Song of the Republic' and recorded daily rural life with witty tales like 'The Drover's Wife' and 'The Loaded Dog'. In the 1880s and 1890s, artists of Victoria's Heidelberg School depicted the Australian landscape with an informal style of painting that captured the extraordinary clarity of antipodean sunlight. Key works of this period were 'Shearing the Rams' by Tom Roberts and 'Golden Summer' by Arthur Streeton.

In architecture, too, new signs of Australian informality began emerging in the 1880s. A significant example was Colonial Architect James Barnet's controversial designs for sandstone plaques around the colonnade of the General Post Office. His freestyle carvings commemorated the daily work of shearers, postmen and other ordinary Australians, instead of the distinguished faces of civic notables. With government approval for Barnet to continue, Europe's tradition of symmetrical formality was rejected in favour of an informal realism that better reflected the emerging culture.[6]

These late nineteenth-century displays of independence coincided with early testing of the telegraph: a technology, like today's Internet, with enormous ramifications for Australia. As telegraphic communications

7 WALTER BURLEY GRIFFIN AND HIS WIFE MARION HAD WON THE INTERNATIONAL COMPETITION FOR THE DESIGN OF CANBERRA, THE NATIONAL CAPITAL CITY, IN 1912. WHILE IN AUSTRALIA, THEY ALSO PLANNED THE SYDNEY SUBURB OF CASTLECRAG, WHERE HOUSES AND BUSH GARDENS ARE STRONGLY INTEGRATED ALONG CIRCUITOUS STREETS.

gradually increased, and steamships replaced sailing ships as conveyors of mail and supplies, Australia's acute sense of isolation from the northern hemisphere began to diminish.

During the twentieth century, Australian architecture has continued to change and mature, always in response to local climates and cultures. Before and after the Federation of States in 1901, the English Arts and Crafts and Queen Anne Revival styles were being interpreted in the larger cities as 'Federation' villas surrounded by verandahs and dressed with wooden fretwork. In the local translations, timberwork and decorative objects often included motifs inspired by Australian leaves and flowers. In Melbourne, a leading Federation-style architect was Harold Desbrowe-Annear. His Sydney counterparts were Howard Joseland and B.J. Waterhouse, with Government Architect Walter Liberty Vernon responsible for many civic monuments of the period. In Queensland, Robin Dods was developing houses, known as Queenslanders, which were lifted above the ground by lattice-skirted stilts to respond to the sub-tropical heat, humidity and insect plagues. Less ornamental stilted houses, with shutters and screens to manipulate sun, rain and breezes, were being built around Darwin by Beni Burnett.

In 1918, Leslie Wilkinson arrived from London to become Australia's first professor of architecture at Sydney University. He brought with him an enthusiasm for Spanish Mediterranean monasteries and houses, which captured the support of Sydney society clients. In 1912, two protegés of Frank Lloyd Wright in Chicago – Walter Burley Griffin and Marion Mahony Griffin – brought concepts updated from South American and Japanese architecture, as well as new town planning agendas to create garden cities. Like Wright, they were particularly concerned to blend architecture and Nature.[7]

In the mid-1930s, Australia began to build its first pure modernist buildings – some in the streamlined 'P&O liner' style inspired by Erich Mendelsohn's Schocken department store in Germany (1928), and others in the cubist manner proposed by Le Corbusier, the Bauhaus School and the Dutch De Stijl movement. Although the streamlining style did not last beyond the outbreak of the Second World War in 1939, cubic modernism has been a constant force in Australian architecture since the 1950s.

After the war ended in 1945, Australia received large numbers of refugees from central Europe – who have since transformed the cultures of Melbourne and Sydney with sophisticated tastes in the arts and hospitality. They were the principal patrons for architects and artisans proposing progressive concepts.

Austrian architect Harry Seidler, who trained with Bauhaus founders Walter Gropius and Marcel Breuer in America, has been an extraordinarily influential force on Australian architecture since he built the Rose Seidler House, a home for his mother, in Killara, Sydney, in 1950. This monumental box of white concrete is elevated above its garden like Le Corbusier's 1929 Villa Savoie outside Paris. It was one of Australia's first abstract modern buildings to be philosophically intended to surmount the landscape by separation. Since then, Seidler has produced many significant houses, as well as more than a dozen of the nation's most elegant skyscrapers.

While Seidler was leading the International Style in Sydney from the 1950s to the 1970s, his approach was being contradicted by architects of the Sydney School – initially including Peter Muller, Neville Gruzman and Bruce Rickard – proposing more organic houses influenced by Frank Lloyd Wright and Japanese provincial traditions. Many of their points of dispute were fused together by Danish architect Jørn Utzon's design for the Sydney Opera House. His scheme, drawn for an international competition in 1957 and internally completed by other architects in 1973, combined industrial materials (concrete, glass, steel, plywood), futuristic construction technologies and primally satisfying forms (segments of a sphere) finished with a traditional, earthy product, ceramic tiles.

During the same period, Melbourne was a hotbed of intellectual inquiry and debate, led by Robin Boyd (who wrote Australia's first important architectural histories) and his partners Roy Grounds and Frederick Romberg.

Since the 1980s, there have been vigorous contests in all the main Australian cities between pure modernism and dynamic, hybrid styles which express postmodern theories of deconstruction and, in Robert Venturi's phrase, 'complexity and contradiction.' This has broadened the variety of building approaches.

All of these tensions and debates have contributed to a contemporary Australian architectural situation that is healthily variegated. This diversity has developed from initial injections of ideas from around the world – and it is making Australian architecture increasingly interesting.

Since Governors Phillip and Macquarie set up their English and Scottish Enlightenment orders for European settlement, the continent's development has been progressively influenced by two centuries of illustrated documentation flowing from Europe and America. The Macquaries arrived from Scotland with books on building styles; Australian architects of the late nineteenth century subscribed to sea mail copies of *The Builder* magazine from London. More recently, the post-Second World War housing boom was aesthetically influenced by California modernist prototypes shown in the 1950s Los Angeles journal *Arts + Architecture*. During the last twenty years, Australian architects have enthusiastically consumed international design books and magazines. Now, in a reversal, many foreign publications regularly highlight Australian projects – and there is much potential for further cultural cross-fertilisation.

But foreign photographers and publishers show their readers a blinkered vision of Australian architecture – images of immaculate domestic objects isolated in wide pastoral landscapes, huts captured by tropical jungles or living rooms looking out to dazzling water. The architecture of Australian cities is less interesting to foreign observers because it is more familiar, and not necessarily tidy to frame in the lens.

When scholar Edward Said identified Europe's fascination with 'the other' in his 1978 book *Orientalism*, he was writing about Victorian adventurers discovering the Middle East. Today, Australia is another attractive destination for travellers seeking exotic curiosities. And in a world marketplace which thrives upon images and commodities, Australian architecture can be whatever the observer wants to see.

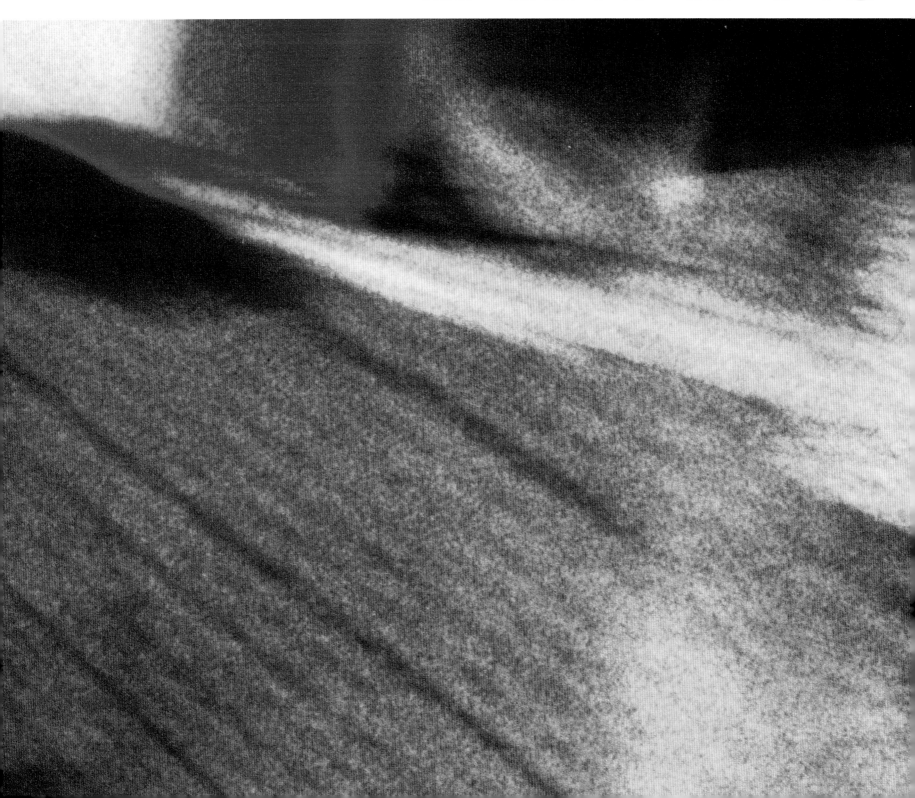

EXEMPLARS

CIVIC SYMBOLS
ARCHERY PAVILION

STUTCHBURY & PAPE, 1999
ARCHERY 2000, NEWINGTON, NEW SOUTH WALES

Beyond the mangroves from Sydney's Olympic sports precinct, the archery pavilion streaks across a grass field at supercharged velocity. In response to the physics of an arrow in flight, its huge steel awning is precisely calibrated to soar, hover and twist along its 100 metre trajectory from east to west.

Tilted up to the north sun, the roof falls low to the south and extends to shade archers facing targets set up against the green mangroves and golden grasses along Haslam's Creek. In the morning and late afternoon, the sun slips under the blade to glisten on the corrugations of the metal and cast lattices of long shadows off its sub-structure.

In terms of functions and cost, this landscaped amenities block is one of the humblest Olympic Games facilities. Architecturally, however, it is a poetic fusion of mathematics and metaphor. As well as dramatising the deadly physical forces of the graceful art of archery, it captures a primal paradox which characterises Australia: the need to shelter from the sun while desiring to revel in it. This quandary generated the verandah within thirty years of English settlement. It was another version of the bark awnings and rock overhangs already used by Aborigines for 40,000 years.

The archery pavilion's hovering roof is tethered to the ground on the south side by triangular concrete stanchions with plate steel pin connections and, on the north, by an angled, sequentially twisted array of red poles. The latter are detailed to emulate the bowstring notches, tail feathers and tip caps seen in a quiver of arrows. This

support system allows the roof to sway in high winds.

The building itself is a sequence of nine six-metre-square cubicles of galvanised steel frames and walls of either recycled timber or metal-clad reverse brick veneer. The capsules establish a syncopated rhythm of 3, 2, 4 along a ground grid of 14 bays.

Because the site was formerly a rubbish dump and the new soil is still subsiding, the cubes sit on independent concrete slabs connected by ventilation links. The entire structure is planned to be unboltable and demountable for reassembly elsewhere, if required.

With security a strong concern for this isolated site, the service cubes are robustly built and do not have windows. Instead, they are skylit by translucent roof panels secured by mesh grilles.

Remarkable companions to the pavilion are two battalions of hardwood telegraph poles which are precisely regimented on both sides of the shooting field and descend in height towards the targets. These denuded Sherwood Forests add vertical, staccato counterpoints to the building's horizontal sweep. They are part of a new landscape of native grasses, casuarinas, mounds and residual water channelled across the site.

Architect Peter Stutchbury and landscape architect Phoebe Pape generally seek synergies between modern architecture and natural environments. Their mid-career practice continues to explore the brutal-humane and organic-tectonic antitheses which have occupied members of the Sydney School since the late 1950s.

TOP LEFT DETAIL OF THE NORTH FACADE, LOOKING EAST.

ABOVE LOOKING SOUTH-WEST ACROSS STUTCHBURY & PAPE'S LANDSCAPE OF RECYCLED TELEGRAPH POLES.

OPPOSITE LOOKING SOUTH WEST, WITH OLYMPICS VENUES SEEN BEYOND THE ARCHERY FIELD AND MANGROVES.

ALL PHOTOS PATRICK BINGHAM-HALL.

ABOVE NORTH SIDE OF THE ARCHERY PAVILION, LOOKING ACROSS THE NEWINGTON SITE AND MANGROVES ALONG HASLAM'S CREEK. ROOFS OF THE SYDNEY SHOWGROUNDS EXHIBITION CENTRE ARE BEYOND THE MANGROVES AT LEFT, WITH OLYMPIC STADIA AT RIGHT.

WEST ELEVATION

EAST ELEVATION

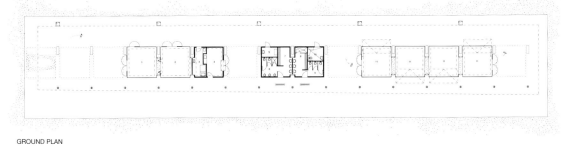

GROUND PLAN

ABORIGINAL PLACE

GREGORY BURGESS, 1995
ULURU-KATA TJUTA ABORIGINAL CULTURAL CENTRE
ULURU (AYERS ROCK), NORTHERN TERRITORY

LEFT AERIAL VIEW NORTH TO ULURU (AYERS ROCK) WITH THE CULTURAL CENTRE IN THE FOREGROUND.

ALL PHOTOS JOHN GOLLINGS.

The only building allowed close to Uluru, the sacred monolith marking the centre of Australia, is a visitor centre which explains how the local Anangu people and their traditional Tjukurpa (law) relate to the natural systems of their ancient homeland.

Although Uluru is seen by some tourists simply as an extraordinary mountain (it is the world's largest unvegetated rock), the custodians honour it as a home of mythical creatures and a source of legends. Anangu elders point up the rock to dark bands and caves known as tracks and eggs left by giant serpents from the Dreamtime.

The Uluru-Kata Tjuta Aboriginal Cultural Centre also blurs time and reality by physically recreating two legendary snakes, Liru and Kuniya, who circle each other as they glide across the sand and spinifex. Just as spinifex grasses grow around open patches of ground, the centre sinuously wraps about a clearing scattered with mulga trees and dominated by the gnarled skeleton of a dead desert oak. In myth, this clearing is the ancient battleground of the snakes. It opens to the north-east, allowing the heads of the two creeping bodies to frame the blazing monument beyond.

Melbourne architect Gregory Burgess worked with the Mutijulu community and the Australian Nature Conservation Agency to develop the serpentine design. Using fingers to draw furrows in the sand, the joint managers and their architect planned a winding and narratively rich journey for the tourists who arrive daily in campervans and buses to climb the rock or watch its transitions of colours as the sun rises and sets.

From the carpark to the west of the centre, visitors walk around the outside of the south building before turning back to enter through its mouth at the eastern end of the clearing. The narrow and winding path never opens up to reveal a destination, or even the next phase of the journey. It is traditional for Aborigines to wander unobtrusively and arrive obliquely: they do not relate to the central, ceremonial axes of urbane societies.

In many other respects, the architecture avoids Western ways of doing things. Externally, it displays no iconic gestures of the kind favoured for postcard images by developers of most leisure attractions. Its form exaggerates the undulations of the surrounding dune country. And its palette of materials – bloodwood and copper roof shingles above a structure of preservative-treated cyprus trunks, blocks made from local sand and hand-split timber boards – comes directly from the Earth.

There is no conclusion or obvious way to walk through the facility: its layout encourages slow meandering around and between the indoor and outdoor spaces – and both realms are defined by red earth walls and ground. Inside, the atmosphere is elaborated by recorded songs and animal calls, wall paintings, artworks, tools, weapons and cloths. Outdoors, the sounds are likely to come from mirin mirin (crickets), kipara (bush turkeys) and tinka (goannas). Away from the site, Anangu hunt emus and red kangaroos. They feed on maku (grubs), ili (bush figs) and many kinds of seeds with distinctive tastes and properties.

TOP VIEW OF THE SOUTH BUILDING AND ENTRANCE FROM THE EAST.

ABOVE THE NORTH BUILDING, WITH THE UPPER-LEVEL CAFÉ AND SOUTH ARM BEHIND THE COURTYARD.

RIGHT NINTIRINGKUNPAI: THE MAIN PLACE FOR LEARNING ABOUT THE JOINT MANAGEMENT OF THE PARK.

OPPOSITE TOP SOUTH BUILDING, ENTRANCE TREE AND COURTYARD FROM THE EAST.

OPPOSITE BOTTOM EXHIBITION AND PERFORMANCE SPACE.

159

The centre's 'focus' is not a formal hall or spectacle, but the fluctuating vacuum of the clearing (used for gatherings and dances). This plan gives regular chances for sunny respite from the gloom of the indoors; opportunities not offered by the enfilades of chambers found in many classical museums.

Burgess also exploits the great Gothic theme of darkness pierced by dramatic shafts of sunlight. This contemplation-promoting strategy transfers surprisingly well from medieval cathedrals under the grey skies of Europe to his neo-primal mud caves in the scorching antipodean desert. He continues the Gothic inspiration of the forest with a tree-like structure in the centre of the main learning zone that filters skylight through fine timber fronds and branches.

Burgess' organic style continues the anti-modernist approaches developed by an older 'kindred spirit', Kevin Borland, a Melburnian prominent in the 1970s who has pursued socialist philosophies of communal humanism. Burgess also appears to be influenced by the Arts and Crafts and Art Nouveau movements of the early 20th century, by United States architects Frank Lloyd Wright and Bruce Goff, and by the Hungarian tradition of shingle-roofed buildings.

The centre's eccentric planning, earthy materials and bush carpentry together produce a harmonious composition which opposes the modern tendency to manufacture rural sheds from pre-milled sheets of steel and glass. It is a convincing expression of Australia's natural and native imaginations, and a valuable antidote to its 'civilised' mentalities.

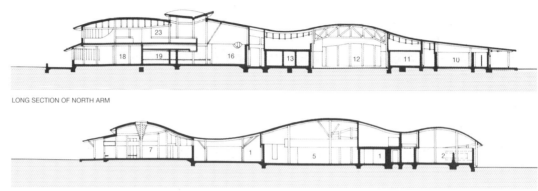

LONG SECTION OF NORTH ARM

LONG SECTION OF SOUTH ARM

KEY

1 Entry Courtyard
2 Entry
3 Tjukurpa
4 Store
5 Anangu Maruku Punu
6 Maruku Witja
7 Joint Management Display
8 Dead Desert Oak
9 Inma
10 Minyma
11 Watti
12 Multi-purpose
13 Toilets
14 Courtyard
15 Rainwater Tanks
16 Gumlake Shop
17 Kiosk
18 Café
19 Kitchen
20 Office
21 Cool Room
22 Store

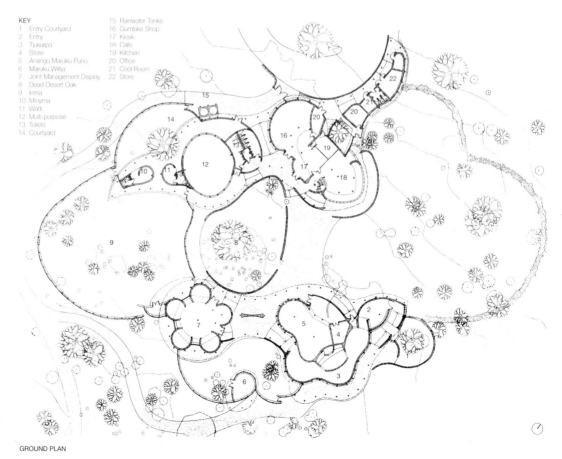

GROUND PLAN

BELOW LOOKING TOWARDS ULURU
FROM THE SOUTH-WEST.

OPPOSITE LEFT NORTH BUILDING,
SHOP AND UPPER LEVEL CAFÉ FROM
THE NORTH-WEST.

OPPOSITE FAR LEFT LOOKING ALONG
THE ROOF OF THE SOUTH BUILDING
TOWARDS ULURU.

TOWER COMPLEX

DENTON CORKER MARSHALL, 1994
GOVERNOR PHILLIP TOWER, GOVERNOR MACQUARIE TOWER
AND THE MUSEUM OF SYDNEY ON THE SITE OF FIRST
GOVERNMENT HOUSE, SYDNEY

ABOVE DETAIL OF THE STAINLESS STEEL
CRATE TOPPING GOVERNOR PHILLIP TOWER.

RIGHT THE NORTH AND EAST FACADES OF
GOVERNOR PHILLIP TOWER AND THE
SANDSTONE WALL AND PROJECTING GLASS
VIEWING CUBE OF THE MUSEUM OF SYDNEY.
AT REAR LEFT IS CHIFLEY TOWER, BUILT
AROUND THE SAME TIME TO A DESIGN BY
KOHN PEDERSON FOX WITH TRAVIS
PARTNERS. PHOTO GAVIN OAKES.

OPPOSITE LEFT THE NORTH FACADE OF
GOVERNOR PHILLIP AND THE ENTRANCE TO
THE MUSEUM OF SYDNEY. AT RIGHT IS 'THE
EDGE OF THE TREES', AN INSTALLATION OF
WHISPERING POLES BY SYDNEY ARTISTS
JANET LAURENCE AND FIONA FOLEY.

OPPOSITE RIGHT FARRER PLACE, LOOKING
NORTH TO THE HISTORIC EDUCATION
BUILDING, WITH THE LOWER WEST FACADE
OF THE BUILDINGS AT RIGHT.

PHOTOS BY JOHN GOLLINGS.

Sydney's 1900s office building boom concluded six years after the stock market crash of 1987 and at the tail of a consequent recession. The last high-rise project to be completed in that cycle is a 227m-high complex which adds two restrained grey pillars to the city's north-east skyline and relates sympathetically, at ground, to three courts edged by Victorian terraces. Most particularly, it stands clear of the buried ruins of Sydney's first formal house, built for Governor Arthur Phillip after his arrival with the First Fleet in 1788.

This development by Denton Corker Marshall is a bundle of significant components. Towards the south of the site, Governor Macquarie Tower (GMT) and its northern neighbour, Governor Phillip Tower (GPT), share a monumental loggia and courtyard as well as a plaza, Farrer Place, to their west.

On the north side of GPT, the Museum of Sydney occupies three floors of the building. Its entrance, café and bookshop open to First Government House Place, which leaves the original house plumbing and foundations under a pavement inlaid with the floor plan and a glass window revealing the ruins.

Along the west edge of the museum's forecourt, a glade of poles blurs the path of arrival. This interactive sculpture, *The Edge of the Trees* by Janet Laurence and Fiona Foley (white and Aboriginal artists), whispers mysterious, discontinuous messages from early English colonists and local Eora natives. The metal columns and recycled telegraph trunks are set into a crunchy ground of gravel and are embellished by stains, oxide

powders and gooey substances behind glass fascias. Scraps of archaic writing, taken from State archives, overlay some surfaces.

Like that artwork, some displays inside the museum exemplify the postmodern ideal of palimpsest – layers of meaning and history – expressed as confused collages of diverse fragments.

The towers themselves display the logic of international corporate modernism – but also allude subtly to the stripped Classicism of late 19th century high-rises in Chicago by Louis Sullivan and Dankmar Adler. Other Sydney developments built around the same time – especially nearby Chifley Tower by Kohn Pederson Fox with Travis Partners (1993) – were instead inspired by the more elaborate Moderne style of New York skyscrapers in the 1920s and '30s.

Of the two Governors Towers, Phillip is the most accomplished work of architecture – despite its difficult site dilemmas – while the shorter (150m) Macquarie is planned as a deferential building.

Aesthetically, GPT updates (by ruthless abstraction) the Classical Greek tripartite proportioning system of a substantial base with a plain or regularly patterned 'torso' and a flamboyant crown. Its top is a sparkling stainless steel crate which cleanly intersects a rooftop plant box of black glass and repeats the 12m square and 4m by 1.35m facade patterns.

Meanwhile, Macquarie displays modernism's rejection of podia and hats – a strategy less successful than that of its companion, despite similarly tartan facade treatments. GMT's south face is marked by a

stack of curved balconies and stepped setbacks from the street.

In practical terms, the Phillip design solves many basic issues of scale and civic manners which were ignored in most notorious towers of the International Style.

Its north (museum) forecourt is defined by a monumental wall of sandstone which relates to the backs of Young Street terraces (west) and the front of the Colonial Secretary's Building (east across Phillip Street). It works with them to establish a comfortable, three-sided embrace for human activity.

The wall gradually ascends through five face textures (rough to smooth) and conceals a balcony used for outdoor performances.

Projecting from the wall is a glass 'viewing cube' which thrusts diagonally towards the site's north-west corner. Internally, it concludes the route through the museum – and offers a sudden outlook to observers who, ironically, are themselves displayed to spectators outside on the forecourt.

To the east, GPT stands back behind another historic row of terraces along Phillip Street – allowing a sunny and sheltered yard set with café tables. Here, an 8m cantilever is supported by load-transfer beams dropping beneath the first level of offices 40m up.

Internally, the towers are joined by a cross of public spaces: two loggias off a shared foyer which replaces long-vanished lanes across the site. All three of these polished stone chambers are sublimely lofty – lending the splendid atmosphere of Gothic cathedrals to contemporary halls of commerce and government.

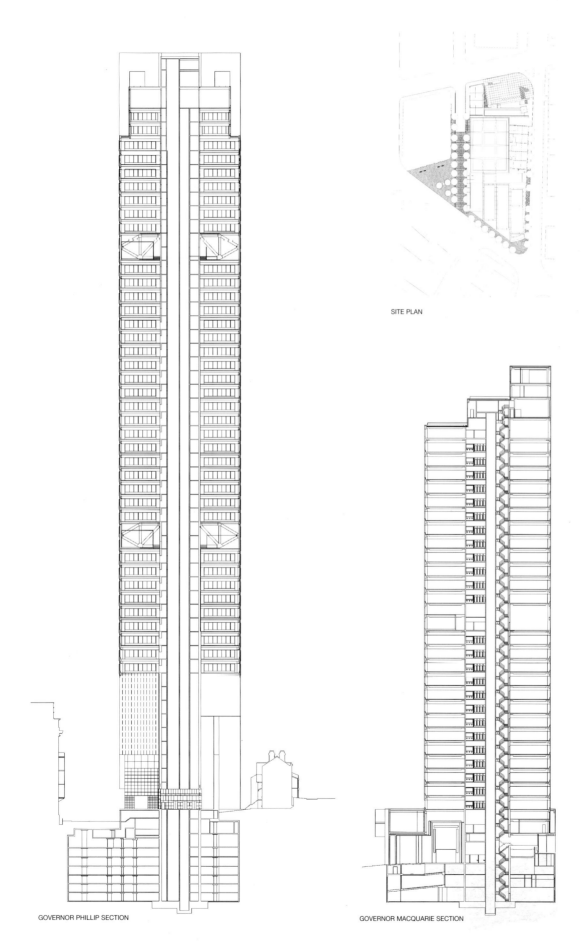

SITE PLAN

GOVERNOR PHILLIP SECTION

GOVERNOR MACQUARIE SECTION

OPPOSITE AERIAL VIEW OF THE SITE, LOOKING NORTH TO THE SYDNEY OPERA HOUSE AND HARBOUR, WITH CIRCULAR QUAY AT LEFT. GOVERNOR PHILLIP TOWER HAS THE ROOF CRATE AND GOVERNOR MACQUARIE TOWER HAS CURVED BALCONIES AT RIGHT. BEHIND THEM, IN THE GARDENS, IS THE CURRENT GOVERNMENT HOUSE, WITH ITS FORMER STABLES (NOW THE CONSERVATORIUM OF MUSIC) AT RIGHT. PHOTO JOHN GOLLINGS.

ACADEMIC LIBRARY

LAWRENCE NIELD & PARTNERS AUSTRALIA WITH
JOHN MAINWARING & ASSOCIATES, 1997
UNIVERSITY OF THE SUNSHINE COAST LIBRARY
SIPPY DOWNS, QUEENSLAND

What should an Australian library look like? An adventurous answer to that question is discovered 90 minutes north of Brisbane, in a paddock (once a sugar cane field) which is being developed as the University of the Sunshine Coast.

On a plain still populated by kangaroos, but with new housing estates creeping over the horizon, the three-storey library designed by Lawrence Nield (Sydney) and John Mainwaring (Noosa) is already the focus of an embryonic village devoted to tertiary education. Other buildings accommodate university administration, a ceremonial hall, the science and arts faculties, and a sports club.

Despite its symbolic centrality on the campus, the library displays an insouciant energy which contradicts the tone of gravitas anticipated in a 1995 masterplan by Mitchell/Giurgola & Thorp of Canberra with Geoffrey Pie from Brisbane.

MGT and Pie imposed on their maps of Sippy Downs a grid comparable to Thomas Jefferson's French Classical layout for the University of Virginia at Charlottesville, USA (1817). In their scheme, new buildings will face each other along east-west avenues on both sides of the library. Between and parallel to these, a prime axis has been ruled down the main entrance drive, through a formal lawn and the library, to conclude at a small lake which holds and cleans groundwater for seepage into a neighbouring national park.

Although the library was to be built across this central axis – symmetrically interrupting the vistas up and down – Nield's and Mainwaring's design instead moves the building sideways and frames the axis with a 'grand verandah' or 'breezeway'.

This long, lofty, batten-screened space is elevated to match the library's first floor reading hall, so its staircases at both ends block the prospects for observers at ground level. But an optimistic sense of onwardness is maintained by the visibility of sky at both ends of the space – perhaps to be interpreted as light beyond the tunnel of study.

In the houses of semi-tropical Queensland, verandahs are often treated as outdoor living rooms – cool transition spaces between the interior and outdoors – while breezeways are used as airy thoroughfares. At the library, both functions are delivered on a civic scale, producing an Australian version of Europe's medieval monastery cloisters and Britain's Oxbridge colonnades.

As well as offering ceremonial elevation (via the staircases) up to the realm of wisdom, the verandah is a sociable place. Barbeques are popular with students and a bench runs along the north screen wall to allow them to sit and read or eat; perhaps turning to watch games on an adjacent field. The screen's timber slats filter the sun's glare and allow breezes to circulate. Even inside the air-conditioned reading rooms, the outdoor atmosphere of the verandah is subliminally felt.

All of the library's five facades – walls and sawtooth roof – are vigorously animated by irregular layers of structure that unfold from the south in diverse materials – steel, plywood, timber slats. Sunlight slips through intermediate

ABOVE LOOKING EAST ALONG THE PRIME AXIS OF THE SUNSHINE COAST CAMPUS.

THIS PAGE RIGHT THE GRAND VERANDAH.

OPPOSITE TOP THE EAST SIDE.

OPPOSITE BOTTOM WEST FACADE, ELABORATED BY PERFORATED METAL SUNSCREEN BLADES.

NEXT PAGES THE GRAND VERANDAH ON THE NORTH SIDE OF THE LIBRARY.

ALL PHOTOS ANTHONY BROWELL.

ABOVE SOUTH SIDE, SHOWING 'WOOF' (WALL-ROOF) TREATMENTS.

ABOVE RIGHT THE GRAND VERANDAH.

OPPOSITE THE NORTH-WEST CORNER.

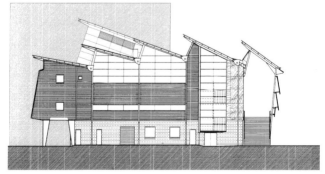

EAST ELEVATION

zones of glass to illuminate the ground floor offices and upstairs reading areas.

The library is Australia's best (and arguably first) multi-storey public building in the 'Sunshine Coast Style' which a coterie of architects have been applying to houses and small pavilions since the 1970s.

The Coast approach updates and refines Queensland's history of rustic sheds and huts. Traditionally, these were knocked together by amateur builders using plentiful materials like corrugated tin, sheets of asbestos cement and plywood, louvred windows and local timbers.

Mainwaring's contributions to the genre include novel elements called 'woofs' – roofs which fold down one or more sides of a building and often serve as sunscreens. Both his office and Nield's (which had not previously collaborated) are disposed to conceive buildings as dynamic collages which test the divisions and tensions between cohesion and chaos.

With this project, they aimed to contradict the conventional planning of libraries as bunkers – by blasting open the building to allow daylight to flood the interior. Reading booths are placed beside the windows, with book shelves in the darker centres of the halls. Yet the interior is comparable to massive brick woolstores built in Sydney and Brisbane in the late 19th century – with bale storage and processing on lower levels and skylit upper floors for examining the wool. The library's atmosphere also reflects Louis Kahn's poetic ideas about silence and light – and confirms the library as a place of contemplation and enlightenment.

GROUND FLOOR PLAN

FIRST FLOOR PLAN

SECOND FLOOR PLAN

RESURRECTION CITY

ASHTON RAGGATT MCDOUGALL, 1995
STOREY HALL, RMIT UNIVERSITY, MELBOURNE

ABOVE FOUR FACADES ALONG SWANSTON STREET: FROM LEFT, THE POLYCHROMATIC BUILDING 8, THE VICTORIAN STOREY HALL, THE NEW ANNEXE AND SINGER HALL.

OPPOSITE FACADE AND ENTRY GROTTO.

NEXT PAGES THE AUDITORIUM.

ALL PHOTOS JOHN GOLLINGS.

Science's explanations for erratic behaviour across all scales of the universe are inspiring some audacious digital concepts on the screens of progressive architects. Only a few have so far been built.

In 1995, Melbourne's Ashton Raggatt McDougall completed one of the first computer-modelled examples of the conceptual theme which British writer Charles Jencks has called 'the architecture of the jumping universe.' Jencks' book of that title was published in the same year as RMIT University unveiled ARM's refurbishment of historic Storey Hall as a conference centre – incorporating a new annexe and interior displaying kaleidoscopic geometries in shocking colours.

Tucked between two 19th century edifices, the annexe seems to fracture and recompose the classical facades of its neighbours.

Jencks' book and ARM's building are bold moves to usurp the symmetry of classicism and the gridded regularity of 20th century modernism; using digital systems for drawing structures. These allow fresh interpretations of architecture's eternal problem: how to represent the meanings of human life and the systems of the cosmos.

It's significant that Storey Hall's annexe is discreetly marked by a plaque labelled 'Resurrection City.' Obviously announcing that a neglected heritage monument has sprung back to life, these words also acknowledge the constant transitions of metropolitan culture. The renovation displays a host of artistic allusions to the universal human themes of birth, the body, temptation, sex, violence, shame, enlightenment, death and life after

death – as interpreted by romantics since the Middle Ages.

To explain their scheme, the architects refer to medieval notions of resurrection as 'bringing the body parts together.' They also allude to 'Dante-esque themes' of divine love, dark sexuality and death which have pervaded European culture since Dante Alighieri, a 13th century citizen of Florence, told a dream of Beatrice, subject of his passion, being poisoned by a Cupid-Jesus figure who then ascended with her to a higher world.

Storey Hall also resurrects ideas from the Romantic period of the early Enlightenment – a period, like now, of immense scientific and cultural upheaval. In the early 1800s, English poet William Blake was inspired by Dante's visions of ascension and both writers have influenced ARM, partly through their discussions with another Venturi-inspired Melbourne expressionist and Blake fan, Peter Corrigan.

There are strong similarities between Storey Hall and adjacent Building 8, designed by Corrigan and completed 18 months earlier. Both facades are like richly coloured, irregularly patterned and deeply textured tapestries. Both buildings emphasise non-Euclidean geometries and propose, most explicitly at Storey Hall, a millennial ascension from the bondage of 'rational' abstraction.

The upper facade of Storey Hall's annexe is appliquéd with a dynamic frieze of textured tiles and metal frames: exploiting Roger Penrose's aperiodic patterning system, which requires two templates (in this case diamonds) to generate an infinitely non-repetitive arrangement. The

architects describe this layered part of the facade as 'shrouded in veil and drapery, folded sash, delicious lace and strong rope lines.'

The lower facade is dominated by a fractally irregular entrance 'grotto' outlined in lurid green and purple. Both these colours and the romantic concept of the grotto as a dark, dangerous 'mousehole' have powerful religious and cultural connotations; some relating to the past uses of the old building, formerly called Hibernian Hall, as a meeting place for women's liberationists and Irish Catholics.

The interior is navigated via serpentine paths winding erratically up and around an elaborate and colourful auditorium occupying two floors at the heart of the building. Beginning in the grotto foyer of grass green concrete, formed like the inside of an irregularly faceted diamond, the observer discovers various astonishing chambers designed to challenge the eye with uncommon colours, pixillated patterns and erratically folded forms. Normally straight lines of sight are distorted to produce impressions of spaces blurred together in disturbing combinations.

Storey Hall is steeped with visual allusions to current shifts of culture. Some structural features revive memories of lost or threatened Melbourne landmarks. Also the garish, kinky styling seems more representative of erotic imagination than the dignity of empirical logic and learning. Certainly, ARM's architecture highlights the chaos of transforming scholarly institutions into commercial sellers of new packages of knowledge to international customers.

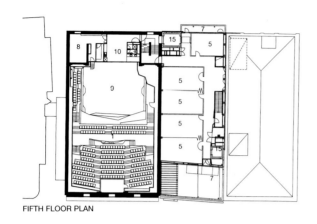

FIFTH FLOOR PLAN

WEST (SWANSTON STREET) ELEVATION

Building 8   Storey Hall   Annexe   Singer Building

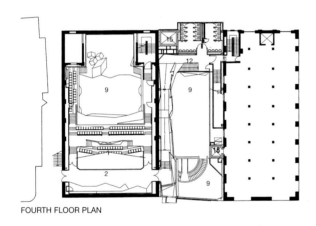

FOURTH FLOOR PLAN

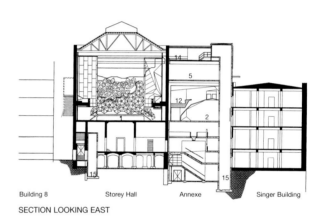

SECTION LOOKING EAST

Building 8   Storey Hall   Annexe   Singer Building

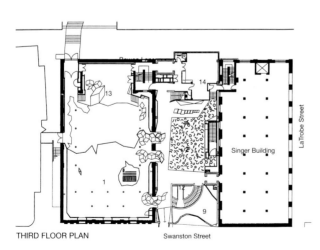

THIRD FLOOR PLAN

Swanston Street

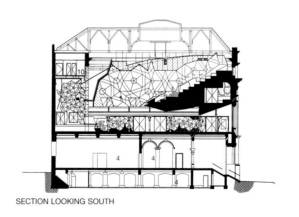

SECTION LOOKING SOUTH

KEY
1 Auditorium   9   Void
2 Foyer   10 Dressing Room
3 Reception   11 Bridge
4 Gallery   12 Balcony
5 Seminar   13 Stage
6 Office   14 Kitchen
7 Terrace   15 Lift
8 Store   16 Café

RIGHT LOOKING DOWN TO THE AUDITORIUM
FOYER FROM ITS BALCONY.

BELOW THE AUDITORIUM FROM THE STAGE.

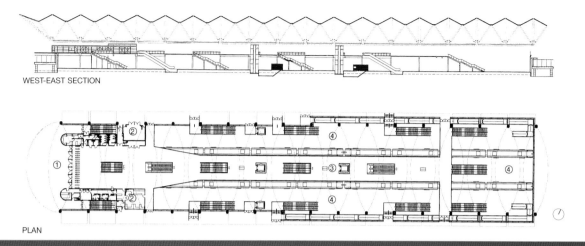

WEST-EAST SECTION

PLAN

RAIL TERMINAL

HASSELL, 1998
OLYMPIC PARK RAILWAY STATION
HOMEBUSH BAY, SYDNEY

OPPOSITE LOOKING SOUTH-EAST TO THE MAIN ENTRANCE, ACROSS STATION SQUARE. PHOTO MICHAEL NICHOLSON.

ABOVE WEST ENTRANCE FROM STATION SQUARE. PHOTO GAVIN OAKES.

ABOVE RIGHT THE RAILWAY HALL AND PLATFORMS. PHOTO PETER HYATT.

RIGHT THE HALL, SHOWING VIERENDEEL ROOF TRUSSES SHAPED LIKE GUM LEAVES. PHOTO MICHAEL NICHOLSON.

NEXT PAGES THE SOUTH FACADE. PHOTO JOHN GOLLINGS.

Sydney's Olympic Park Station updates Europe's 19th century equivalent of the Gothic cathedral - the train terminal. Its design distills this industrial age type to one prime element – a vaulted roof of metal and glass, spanning across the tracks and platforms to shelter passengers and luggage.

With that gesture of reduction, the architects, Hassell, abandoned the dominant element of most railway stations – their monumental masonry edifices. Since the first terminals opened at Liverpool and Manchester in 1830 (for George Stephenson's *Rocket*), they have been designed as important public icons, with formal facades and lofty foyers incorporating ticket booths, refreshment kiosks and waiting rooms. To signal building function, the facade might incorporate one or two large lunette windows: semi-circular to echo the roofline of the train shed concealed behind.

This Australian station, designed in the 'tectonically rational' style of British modernist Norman Foster, has lost all obvious ornament – but traces of symbolism remain. The east and west entrances of the 220 metre-long structure are arched in the manner of the old vaults and lunettes. And there is a kind of facade gesture: an exaggerated peak flipped up at the west end of the roof, a device recalling baseball caps worn by insouciant youths around the world. Of course, youth, sport and global sharing are prime aspirations of the Olympic Games 'family' – and they are strong themes, too, in Australian culture.

The architectural drama of the Olympic Park station is created by its low, repetitive, exaggerated length, accentuated by sunlight dancing along the silver zincalume and glass-ridged roof. This was formed with 18 mirror-pairs of Vierendeel trusses (producing veined segments that are often compared to gum leaves when seen from below). It streaks across the site with the cyclical power and dynamics of a track athlete.

The canopy was modelled in paper during the design phase and its external appearance recalls the crisp folds of origami. The trusses spring from and span between thick columns of concrete evenly spaced along the north and south edges of the building.

Because Sydney's climate is hotter than that of the European cities where rail stations were first built, the roof is not glazed as extensively as some predecessors. Yet the hall has a remarkable sense of transparency and brightness. Its long walls are glazed at ground level and the roof ridges are formed as skylights (avoiding the steel reinforcing that would be assumed in conventional engineering).

Certain practical choices have also generated the station's style. Its low exterior profile stems from a decision to install subterranean railway tracks to avoid roads across the Olympic site. After excavation, the platforms now sit 6.5 metres below ground, open to the roof and surrounded by glass-balustraded galleries on ground level. This open, two-tier format generates a mood of excited anticipation and camaraderie when crowds pour out of the trains (up to 50,000 people per hour) and surge up the banks of escalators towards the stadia spectacles beyond.

UNIVERSITY ENSEMBLE

WOOD MARSH WITH PELS INNES NEILSON KOSLOFF, 1996, 1998
BUILDINGS C–G, DEAKIN UNIVERSITY, BURWOOD, VICTORIA

Australian universities spent the 1990s in a losing battle against savage cuts to their government subsidies – a situation which continues to transform Academia from a public service to a semi-commercial industry. Administrators reluctantly recognise that their role now is to sell business-tailored packages and qualifications to worldwide buyers – while appearing to maintain the Oxbridge tradition of coaching, testing and grading students selected for their high intellectual calibre.

Ironically, these contractions have boosted architecture, producing several dozen notable buildings on campuses around the country. Many are intended to broadcast subliminal impressions of the commissioning institution's quality and progressive aspirations.

Victorian universities and architects have produced most of the innovative recent facilities. One example is at Deakin University's suburban Burwood campus: a 'pinwheel' ensemble of five blocks flung around a spiral staircase of concrete. Designed by Wood Marsh with Pels Innes Neilson Kosloff (PINK), this suite is prosaically named Buildings C, D, E, F and G.

Three buildings (D–F) are long, narrow and sombre blocks clad with grey and black versions of modernist steel and glass curtain walls from the 1950s.

They are subservient to Building C, a seven-storey landmark in a graphically gestural style influenced by 1960s American minimalist sculpture. Housing the Vice Chancellor's offices on the top floor, it has a seductively ovoid profile clad with polished white precast panels. The facades are highlighted by rows of narrow vertical windows like the arrow slots of ancient forts. It is sited for visibility around the campus and has a high-level sign announcing the university's name to drivers on the nearby highway. Because Deakin is headquarted in Geelong, Victoria's second largest city, this out-of-town advertising is important.

These four buildings (C–F) are linked to the central staircase by stacks of bridges extending from their internal corridors. Standing separately, but adding visual emphasis to the group, is three-storey Building G, which links two existing blocks which have their backs turned to this configuration. It has an austere facade of precast panels punctured by square windows – but its severity collapses into concertina folds above the ground floor café, bookshop and colonnade of *pilotis*.

Why twirl buildings around a pivotal staircase? Radial planning is often thought to stem from the late 18th-century proposals by British brothers Jeremy and Sir Samuel Bentham for a Panopticon prison of cell blocks arrayed around a central inspection house. But the pinwheel model used at Deakin is more like a hospital prototype drawn by French architect Antoine Desgodets in the late 1600s. His pivotal element was a domed atrium which could draw together the hospital community and ventilate 'unhealthy' air through roof gaps.

Deakin's outdoor staircase also offers fresh air and a place for accidental meetings among users of the subsidiary structures. The bridges also allow wheelchairs to

PREVIOUS PAGES BUILDING C AT LEFT AND BUILDING F AT RIGHT, BOTH LINKED TO THE SPIRAL STAIR. PHOTO JOHN GOLLINGS.

TOP DETAIL OF THE SPIRAL STAIRCASE LINKING BUILDINGS C, D, E AND F. PHOTO TIM GRIFFITH.

ABOVE LOOKING ACROSS THE SPILL PONDS AND GRASS TERRACES BESIDE THE NORTH LAWN. PHOTO JOHN GOLLINGS

MAIN PICTURE BUILDING G AT LEFT AND THE NORTH FACADE OF BUILDING C, WITH BUILDING F IN THE BACKGROUND AT RIGHT. PHOTO TIM GRIFFITH.

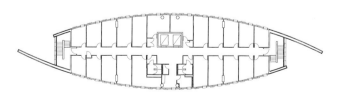

BUILDING C TYPICAL FLOOR PLAN

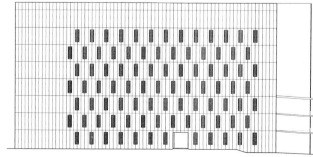

BUILDING C WEST ELEVATION

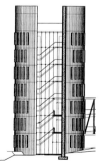

BUILDING C SOUTH ELEVATION

cross between the buildings after first using one of the ensemble's two lifts to reach a chosen floor.

Internally, all five buildings have offices, classrooms and service areas arranged on both sides of central halls. Partitions allow room shapes to be readily altered.

In education buildings, expensive air conditioning is usually avoided where possible, so there is an architectural agenda to plan natural systems of climate control. Common strategies are wall and roof insulation, turning primary glass facades to the north, fitting exterior sunscreens on glass facing west or north and, in cold zones like Melbourne, installing double glazing. Here, hot water heating has also been provided.

According to a campus master plan prepared earlier by Wood Marsh and PINK, Buildings C-G stand at the south end of the prime pedestrian avenue, which can be used for informal performances. When seen from cars in the turning circle beginning the boulevard, the architecture reads as an imposing composition – an effect emphasised by a monumental flight of steps leading up to the blank south-west wall of Building F.

Landscaping, designed by Tract, contradicts the cool modernism of the architecture with a complex and irregular scheme of concrete paths (marking expected pedestrian desire lines) criss-crossing lawns which slope six metres to the east. To the north, grass terraces are interrupted by a water feature of descending spill ponds – a kind of civic embellishment rarely seen on Australian campuses during the late 20th century.

OPPOSITE PHOTO JOI IN GOLLINGS.

ABOVE AERIAL PHOTO JOHN GOLLINGS.

189

EXHIBITION HALL

DENTON CORKER MARSHALL, 1996
MELBOURNE EXHIBITION CENTRE, MELBOURNE

ABOVE LOOKING SOUTH ALONG THE FOYER ALIGNED WEST OF THE EXHIBITION HALLS.

OPPOSITE ENTRANCE CORNER ACROSS SPENCER STREET, WITH BLADE CANOPY.

BOTH IMAGES JOHN GOLLINGS.

Australia's three largest cities, and others across Asia, now compete to host trade events likely to attract swarms of business delegates. In this context, the architecture of an exhibition hall can help to boost one city's recognition and revenue against another's.

Modern exhibition centres of steel and glass began with Joseph Paxton's gigantic Crystal Palace, built in Greenwich for Britain's Great Exhibition of 1851 – yet they share similarities with ancient market halls and souks built of stone and timber. All these venues for trade require a roof expansive enough to shelter at least one hall of stalls ranked on both sides of walkways. Australia's prime example of this still-evolving type is the Melbourne Exhibition Centre by Denton Corker Marshall.

The MEC's obvious advantage is the spectacle of its entrance on the north-west corner of the riverfront site. Here, an energetic ensemble of intersecting and tilted planes in steel and green glass transforms the abandoned concrete shell of a museum designed by Daryl Jackson in the late 1980s. Soaring skywards from the corner is a monumental metal blade skewered by a pair of fine yellow rods. Despite their improbable stability at 20 degrees off vertical, they rescue the blade's gravity-defying cantilever. Although this canopy clearly fails to give shelter from rain, it is a valuable signal of the centre's location in the city, and it answers the need for iconic images in marketing brochures.

When visitors step inside the glass doors of the two-storey entry pavilion, their eyes immediately lock to the 450-metre southward vista of the concourse – framed on its east side by the aluminium-clad wall of the exhibition hall and, to the west, by a raked facade of glass. Interrupting this lofty avenue are mezzanine balconies projecting at upward angles into the airspace; off-kilter panels of graphic signage, and a haphazard scatter of raw concrete seats. Although the hall itself is conventionally cubic, right angles have been rejected for most other elements of the architecture.

East of the concourse, the daylight-excluding exhibition hall provides 30,000 sq m of floor area. It can be split into 3000 sq m slices by sliding and folding walls fitted beneath roof trusses installed at 18 metre intervals. Delivery vans can drive inside through roller-shuttered openings off the rear yard. Tacked onto the outside wall are crates containing the refreshment kiosk, kitchen and other services.

Upstairs, on the first floor of the entry pavilion and extending along a mezzanine platform separating the double-height hall and concourse, there are meeting and function rooms. Some have large windows overlooking the exhibitions.

Unlike other Australian exhibition centres with expressive roofs of repeating paraboloid shells or with canopies draped beneath sky-thrusting columns, the Melbourne venue has a simple birdwing roof sweeping 84 metres across the building. This drops to the lower canopy of the west colonnade – which serves both as a path and a verandah formally fronting a lawn leading down to the Yarra.

Propping up the colonnade's roof is a battalion of tilted yellow sticks, arranged to form a double allée

ABOVE WEST FACADE FROM ACROSS THE YARRA RIVER. PHOTO TIM GRIFFITH.

OPPOSITE RIGHT SOUTH END OF THE FOYER, WITH THE BACKS OF PROJECTING SIGNS OVERHEAD. PHOTO JOHN GOLLINGS.

OPPOSITE FAR RIGHT BENCH SEATING IN ONE OF THE LOBBIES. PHOTO TIM GRIFFITH.

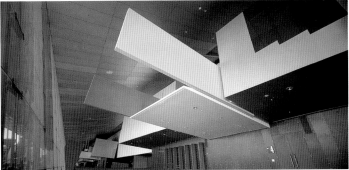

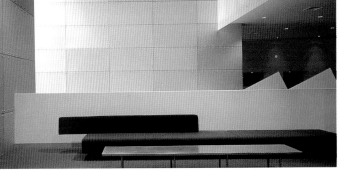

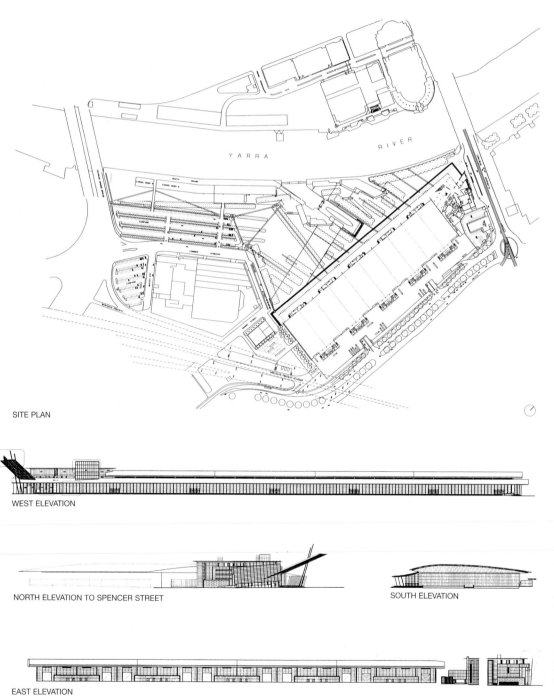

SITE PLAN

WEST ELEVATION

NORTH ELEVATION TO SPENCER STREET

SOUTH ELEVATION

EAST ELEVATION

along the building. It provides shelter for pedestrians who want to walk between the exhibition centre's waterfront neighbours: a maritime museum to the south and a casino/leisure complex across Spencer Street to the north. But it is not often used because the venues are usually reached by car. Also security staff regularly close the MEC's western doors to avoid unauthorised entry and to contain trade show delegates in the vicinity of the displays. (The doors unlock automatically if sensors detect fire.)

It's a notable characteristic of MEC and other modern civic buildings with enclosed cores (casinos to opera houses) that the architecture often incorporates long swathes of glass bringing panoramas of the outside world into the public foyers like giant cinema screens.

When central Melbourne is seen from the air, the broad silver sweep of its exhibition centre roof stands out from the cityscape more dominantly than the highest office towers or even the adjacent, larger, casino complex. But the idea of the birdwing hovering lightly above the building is not obvious at eye level.

The best clue to this aspect of the architecture is the edge of the colonnade canopy, where a thin skin of perforated metal clings to a line of steel ribs. This aerodynamic treatment, which disperses wind, later influenced another Melbourne architect, Peter Elliott, in his design for the Spencer Street Footbridge, 1999. His glassy passage, added to an existing vehicular bridge, crosses the Yarra from the city to land neatly next to the centre's astonishing porch on Southbank.

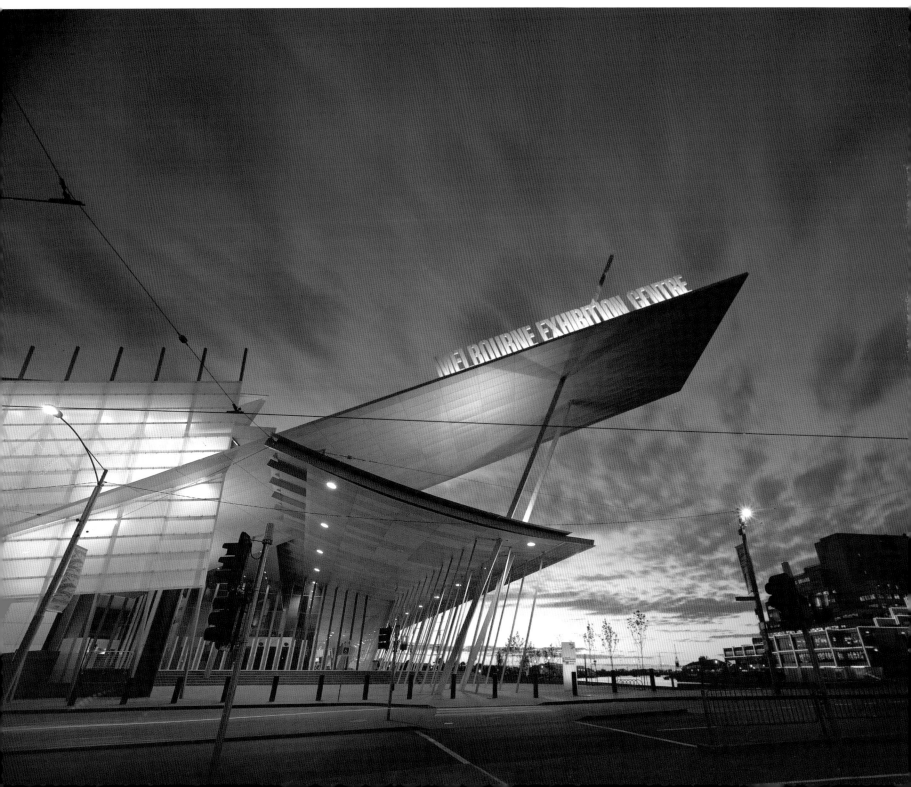

VISITOR CENTRE

GLENN MURCUTT WITH TROPPO, 1994
BOWALI VISITOR INFORMATION CENTRE AND HEADQUARTERS,
KAKADU NATIONAL PARK, NORTHERN TERRITORY

Kakadu National Park is one of the planet's most extreme terrains. Its volatile climate fluctuates between thunderstorms, torrents, fierce sun and debilitating humidity. The land reacts like a chameleon to these tropical weather shifts, but its character – whether lush green or arid red; flooded or parched – remains profoundly earthy. Slothful crocodiles remind wanderers and swimmers that they have entered one of the oldest realms on Earth.

Many travellers schedule Kakadu as an antipodean must-see, and the park's administrators – the Australian Nature Conservation Agency with the Mirarr Gundjeihmi people – have been upgrading its facilities since the 1980s.

The architectural centrepiece is a visitor education and administration centre called Bowali; the Aboriginal name for a local creek which drains wet season rains. Opened in 1994, it is one of several visitor centres designed by Glenn Murcutt of Sydney – this time working with Troppo, a Darwin studio directed by two of his younger admirers, Adrian Welke and Phil Harris. Their Bowali collaboration includes design advances for both practices.

Murcutt is the father of a 'modern Australian vernacular' or 'tin shed' style of Miesian steel-and-glass pavilions topped by languidly rolling roofs of corrugated zincalume. From the late 1970s to the early 1990s, he and a national coterie of followers built many houses and small buildings topped by sparkling steel aerofoils, bird wings, waves and shallow-arced vaults. These were likened by his biographer, Philip Drew, to the curling lengths of tree bark which shaded Aboriginal

humpy shelters in the outback, but curved roof profiles had rarely been used previously by Australian architects. These aeronautical hats also supported a popular idea of Murcutt's buildings 'touching the earth lightly' on delicate steel feet – although a significant number of his structures sit on concrete slabs.

After extensive international publicity of Murcutt's charismatic 'regional' architecture, he appears to be moving on from key strategies and myths which have explained his mid-career output. Some of his new buildings (which he has not allowed us to publish here) employ timber sun baffles (projecting in dramatic vertical arrays from horizontal sequences of windows) instead of his familiar system of sensor-responsive metal louvres draped outside glass walls. In contrast to his earlier modernist commitment to sunlit 'universal' space, he now sometimes designs dark chambers as narrative preludes to rooms flooded with brilliant sub-Capricornian sunlight. And he regularly builds walls of rammed earth or concrete: tough gestures of landscape domination instead of the 'respectful separation' of structure from nature claimed for his hovering pavilions.

Bowali displays some of these fin-de-siècle transitions. While it includes the rolling roofs, raised floors and primitive hut styling which Murcutt and Troppo had both produced previously, it also offers novel responses to three special qualities of the site: its exposure to monsoon downpours, the culture of the native people and the profound atmosphere of the land and sky.

The main building is a sequence

ABOVE THE HEADQUARTERS BUILDING, WITH THE VERANDAH OF THE VISITOR CENTRE AT RIGHT.

OPPOSITE TOP AERIAL VIEW OF THE COMPLEX, LOOKING NORTH.

OPPOSITE LOOKING NORTH TOWARDS THE SCREENED VERANDAH.

NEXT PAGES SOUTH ELEVATION OF THE VISITOR CENTRE, SEEN FROM OUTSIDE THE MEETING ROOM OF THE HQ BUILDING.

ALL PHOTOS JOHN GOLLINGS.

BELOW LEFT LOOKING NORTH ALONG THE
MAIN VERANDAH WITH BILLABONG AND
ENTRY AT LEFT AND CORNER CAFÉ.

OPPOSITE TOP LEFT LOOKING SOUTH
ALONG THE VERANDAH.

OPPOSITE BOTTOM LEFT DETAIL OF THE
FOLDING SLATTED SCREEN AT THE NORTH
END OF THE VISITOR CENTRE.

OPPOSITE RIGHT LOOKING SOUTH ALONG
THE VERANDAH TO THE ADMINISTRATION
HEADQUARTERS HUTS.

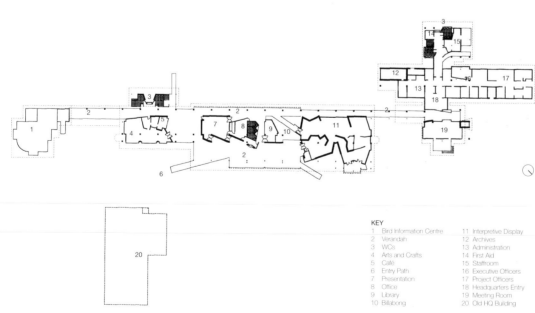

KEY
1 Bird Information Centre
2 Verandah
3 WCs
4 Arts and Crafts
5 Café
6 Entry Path
7 Presentation
8 Office
9 Library
10 Billabong
11 Interpretive Display
12 Archives
13 Administration
14 First Aid
15 Staffroom
16 Executive Officers
17 Project Officers
18 Headquarters Entry
19 Meeting Room
20 Old HQ Building

of irregular interiors (including a library, café and display rooms) contained by rammed earth and glass walls and strung along a verandah leading from an existing bird information centre to the new park headquarters (which contains conventionally rectangular offices).

In sympathy with Aboriginal patterns of informal movement, the planning requires visitors to arrive obliquely instead of frontally: sidling up to an inconspicuous entrance via a ramp from the car park. In the public zone, tourists meander between dim display rooms, bright gathering spaces and the ironbark-planked deck, which is raised above the ground and spatially ordered by thick tree trunks paced along the its edge.

Compared to local rock shelters and reminiscent of Louis Kahn's 'room and garden' at the Kimbell Art Museum, the deck is protected by what may be one of Murcutt's and Troppo's last curved roofs: an expanse interrupted by a giant dish gutter ('the creek') before kicking up sharply to the south-west. Suspended beneath the roof's fine, corrugated edge is a kinked screen of timber battens which casts delightful light and shadow effects across the deck, cuts glare and intensifies the outlook to frame a narrow panorama of land and sky.

The centre's reaction to rains is unforgettable. The roofs, lacking edge gutters, capture occupants within veils of wet percussion, magnified by waterfalls plunging from the dish gutter to a billabong and creek flowing along the building. It's an awesome assault on the ears, eyes and nostrils.

APARTMENT BLOCK

NONDA KATSALIDIS, 1994
MELBOURNE TERRACE, MELBOURNE

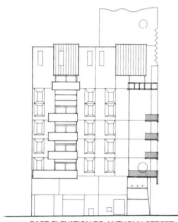

EAST ELEVATION TO ANTHONY STREET

OPPOSITE GENERAL VIEW OF MELBOURNE TERRACE FROM ITS PRINCIPAL CORNER ON FRANKLIN AND QUEEN STREETS. PHOTO JOHN GOLLINGS.

Public antipathy to bald blocks of high rise housing is supporting a tendency to design apartment buildings as collages of contrasting colours, materials and fragments. This approach opposes some fundamental tenets of modernism, particularly the idea that a building's structural system should be explicit. For this reason, the style is reviled by architects of the skeletal school, yet it's proving popular with affluent Australian property buyers.

The collage theme emerged in Melbourne during the 1970s in support of Robert Venturi's theories on the dissonance of cities. Like Europe's Art Nouveau movement a century ago, it expresses a desire (in the words of German writer Walter Benjamin, 1892–1940) to 'escape from an ivory tower beseiged by technology.' When post-medieval societies have been pressured by the ruthless march of mechanisation, there often have been contrary flowerings of ornament in the arts.

As a city of vigorous creativity, 1990s Melbourne certainly recalls Paris, Barcelona and Vienna in the 1890s. A seminal example of its fin de siècle mood is Melbourne Terrace, an eight-storey apartment block designed by Nonda Katsalidis before he joined new partners as Nation Fender Katsalidis.

Built in 1994 in a then-shabby area around Queen Victoria Markets and Flagstaff Gardens (several blocks north-west of the city centre), this elaborate stack of 65 dwellings above a car park attracted a full house of urbane residents (including the architect's family and friends). Their arrival in turn triggered a renaissance of the

neighbourhood, with new shops and cafés and more housing.

Melbourne Terrace updates the European tradition of building to the edges of sites and creating lively streetscapes. When designed, the city council was promoting its 'Postcode 3000' program of incentives to reactivate neglected precincts. Also, Victorian planners were finally stemming the spread of fringe subdivisions and encouraging housing conversions of existing industrial and commercial buildings.

When unveiled, the Terrace was controversial among architects because its design is ornate and polychromatic rather than reduced and severe. It is clearly intended to seduce observers with its palette of sensuous materials and colours.

The facades are energetic arrays of vertical and horizontal elements, projecting and receding, and there are dynamic plays of solid forms – concrete and copper-wrapped – against the transparency of glass windows and balcony balustrades. Even the concrete walls of the car park are given textured trims and oxide treatments in charcoal and coppery green.

The block was completed in two phases. First, a north-facing row of three attached buildings – named Equus, Roma and Mondo – was developed along Franklin Street from Anthony Street (a lane leading to the car park entrances). Then a taller, cubic, copper-helmeted building, called Fortuna, was added, facing west to Queen Street and wrapping around the corner to Franklin. It includes a café and shops on ground level as well as a first floor office.

All four entrances to these

TOP SUB-PENTHOUSE LIVING ROOM FROM THE MEZZANINE BEDROOM; DESIGN BY NIK KARALIS. PHOTO TREVOR MEIN.

ABOVE SUB-PENTHOUSE DESIGNED BY NIK KARALIS. PHOTO TREVOR MEIN.

RIGHT PENTHOUSES AND ONE OF THREE SERRATED ROOF ELEMENTS WHICH SIGNIFY BUILDING ENTRANCES ALONG FRANKLIN STREET. PHOTO JOHN GOLLINGS.

buildings are guarded by Greek and Roman figures created by local sculptor Peter Corlette. Katsalidis regularly commissions symbolic artworks for his projects.

Standing above the copper-clad mansard roofline along Franklin Street are three pairs of concrete blades with serrated edges reminiscent of Egyptian and Mayan stepped pyramids. These are skyline signals for building entrances at ground level. Cavities between each pair of blades are filled, Art Deco-style, with recessed panels of rippled green copper; stripes which continue down the facade to the doorways.

Internally, Melbourne Terrace is cleverly planned with two and three bedroom apartments in various single-level, mezzanine and two-storey penthouse configurations. They are grouped in isolated buildings to improve security, access and privacy, yet promote a sense of community among the residents. To reduce sound transference, most are stacked on the opposite sides of central stair and lift wells, with concrete party walls dividing the buildings.

In several respects, the space planning and styling were innovative for their time. For example, all the units have galley kitchens installed as part of large living/dining zones which open to generous balconies. This now-common arrangement updates the tradition of concealing kitchens from guests – and reflects a new tendency by Australians to cook quick meals, entertain informally and eat out regularly. Katsalidis was one of the first architects to recognise these shifts in city living and provide for them.

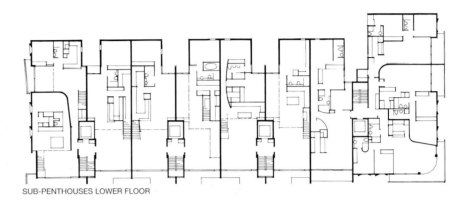

SUB-PENTHOUSES LOWER FLOOR

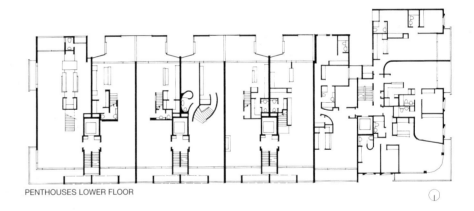

PENTHOUSES LOWER FLOOR

NORTH ELEVATION

205

HOUSES
TEMPLE OF BREEZES

BRIT ANDRESEN AND PETER O'GORMAN, 1999
MOOLOOMBA HOUSE, NORTH STRADBROKE, QUEENSLAND

ABOVE LOOKING SOUTH, UP FROM THE
ROAD TO THE PROJECTING BIRD'S NEST AT
THE NORTH-EAST END OF THE HOUSE.
PHOTO JOHN GOLLINGS.

RIGHT SOUTH-EAST SIDE OF THE HOUSE,
SEEN FROM THE TOP OF THE ENTRY STEPS.
PHOTO JOHN GOLLINGS.

OPPOSITE SCREENS FILTER INTENSE
NORTH-WEST SUNLIGHT IN THE DINING
AREA. PHOTO PATRICK BINGHAM-HALL.

Two of architecture's primal ideals are the hut and the temple – first invented to protect the body and comfort the psyche, on different scales to contain either a private household or a congregation. In diagram, both structures comprise a box and a triangular roof – the universal symbol of shelter. A contemporary fusion of these archetypes is found on a sand island off Australia's east coast.

North Stradbroke, reached by car ferry from the mainland, is a favourite semi-tropical retreat for Brisbane's arts community. Among its old fibro shacks and new brick villas are more than a dozen imaginative timber houses built on prime hill sites with ocean views.

Perched on a ridge called Point Lookout is the most marvellous of these weekenders: a meticulous assembly of indoor and outdoor living spaces invented by architect-teachers Brit Andresen and Peter O'Gorman. They built this residence for themselves beside another timber house which Andresen renovated with Timothy Hill for a client in 1986.

Andresen and O'Gorman's two-storey, three-bedroom residence borders a clump of banksia trees shading a sprawling blanket of long grass and fishbone ferns. When visitors surmount the steps from the street, they discover a symphonic composition of sticks, slats, steps, louvres and floating decks – orchestrated in native hardwoods, cypress and plywood and topped by a long, projecting gable roof of corrugated fibre cement. Beyond the elaborate craftsmanship, the essential gestures of the frame and the gable remain absolutely legible.

In various ways, the planning of this residence is unconventional for Australia. First, the architects have made minimum use of the site's ocean prospect. Instead of building a wide house with windows facing the water, they developed a long, narrow format which denies or masks sea views until arrival at the bird's nest belvedere projecting northwards on the upper level. This balcony culminates a journey through many different places to rest – some roofed but unwalled, some intimately contained, others open platforms. Atmospheres vary with the weather and time of day.

Another singular aspect of the site plan is the way the house and its complementary structures – a breezeway passage framed with vine-supporting lattice screens and a series of floating sundecks – are pushed to the back and sides of the property, to wrap around the central garden.

The whole ensemble – the framed path opening to the viewing decks and finally to the unfolding passages and spaces of the house – recalls Japan's Zen temples and stroll gardens of the 16th and 17th centuries. Like montages by today's film-makers, stroll gardens unrolled a landscape as a series of views, observed from structures winding around the periphery.

In construction, too, the house recalls the carpentry of 16th century Japanese 'tea architecture' – immaculate and sensuously austere buildings inspired by the Zen rituals of serving sublime tea.

Like Zen temples, the house has a complex yet logical hierarchy of primary and subsidiary structures, columns, beams, cross-bracing,

ABOVE THE DINING AREA, LOOKING SOUTH-WEST FROM THE STAIRS TO THE BIRD'S NEST. PHOTO PATRICK BINGHAM-HALL.

RIGHT LOOKING NORTH ALONG THE UPSTAIRS PASSAGE, WITH THE DINING AREA AND CENTRAL COURT BELOW. PHOTO PATRICK BINGHAM-HALL.

FAR RIGHT THE ARCHITECTS AT HOME. PHOTO JOHN GOLLINGS.

OPPOSITE THE FENCE AND PASSAGE MARKING THE SIDE BOUNDARY OF THE SITE AND SOUTH-EAST SIDE OF THE GARDEN. PHOTO BRIT ANDRESEN.

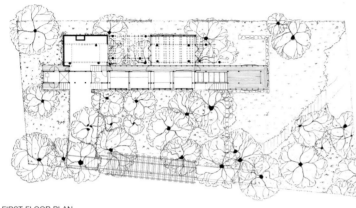

FIRST FLOOR PLAN

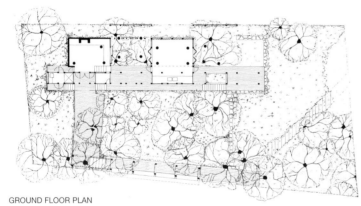

GROUND FLOOR PLAN

AERIAL PERSPECTIVE LOOKING WEST

OPPOSITE LOOKING NORTH ALONG THE SOUTH-EAST SIDE OF THE HOUSE FROM THE REAR DECK. PHOTO PATRICK BINGHAM-HALL.

roof trusses and claddings: all scaled and placed with respect for the modular proportions which promote visual harmony. Andresen and O'Gorman also talk of the Greek concept of *harmonica*: a structure so perfect that the removal of one component would cause the whole to collapse.

At Point Lookout, two north-south arms stretch out in parallel and are fused together by major and minor framing systems related to the 1200mm standard width of plywood sheets.

Along the west site boundary, one arm has garden courts alternating between a sunny, studio/kitchen and a darker 'winter' room with a fireplace. Here, the primary columns are 13 cypress trunks sunk deep into the sand. Inside the house, they are stripped of bark; outside, the bark is retained to evoke 'reciprocity' between nature's irregularity and the refinements of civilisation.

The other arm, addressing the garden, has square posts of dressed hardwood arranged in pairs at intervals of 600, 1200 and 2400mm. To tame warping, the members are paired to oppose the twists of their grains and bolted around plywood fills or wall panels.

Above a lower level of floating hardwood decks, upstairs sleeping and study cubicles are strung along a narrow passage overlooking the western courtyard and studio. This space, like a ship's gangway, opens out to the ultimate episode of the architectural narrative – the twilight denouement of drinks and conversation in the belvedere, watching the lorikeets swoop and the waves subside.

THE PUBLIC HOME

SEAN GODSELL, 1998
HOUSE AT KEW, VICTORIA

Deciphering architecture's wonders entails something like a Buddhist journey towards enlightenment. Lesson 1 teaches the value of discovering subtleties beyond first impressions. A useful case study of this principle is the house designed by Sean Godsell for himself and wife Annemarie Kiely.

Built in a peaceful suburban street leading down to Melbourne's Yarra River, this residence takes an aggressive posture in relation to neighbouring bungalows and villas of brick and tile. Thrusting out with a 5.5 metre cantilever from the top of a ridge above the road – underside clearly visible – it looms over the footpath with an unmistakeable aura of menace. There is no doubt that Godsell's glass box, armoured with rusty steel grilles, is opposing conventions about the appearance of domestic buildings.

Obviously the house is missing the universal symbol of human shelter – a gable roof. And its transparency contradicts the 'normal' notion of the house as a secure enclosure for private behaviour. While many people appreciate their homes as places where they can relax without clothes free from the eyes of the world, the Godsell residence blurs common understandings of private and public life. In the living room and main bedroom facing the street, people standing up are automatically performing on a public stage. This aspect of the architecture represents a daring assault on the assumptions of privacy commonly held by middle-class parents living in prosperous garden suburbs. Yet like all acts of in-your-face cultural provocation –

especially acts which may involve human nakedness – it forces the offended to answer a question: why is this really dangerous?

Part of Godsell's architectural concept – the hovering glass box – stems from the modernist prototype of Ludwig Mies van der Rohe's Farnsworth house (1950), built on a private pastoral property in Plano, Illinois. After glass facades began to be applied to city apartment blocks in the 1950s, the idea of displaying private lives to the street was parodied by director Jacques Tati in his classic film, Mon Oncle (1958).

Since the late 1970s, there have been various attempts by architects to modify glazed buildings with metal sunscreens. The notable Australian examples are Sydney architect Glenn Murcutt's houses from the late 1970s to the early 1990s – often draped with blinds of aluminium louvres controlled by sun-detecting sensors. With his house at Kew, Godsell has avoided Murcutt's charismatic roofs and appears influenced instead by the lattice sunscreening of Paris architect Jean Nouvel, especially his hotel set in Bordeaux vineyards (1989). In that project, Nouvel's amazing gesture was to shroud the glazed facades of a flat-roofed building with external grilles of rusted steel louvres which, like Murcutt's, can be adjusted.

Godsell's grilles, installed on the north and west facades of his 18 by 9 metre double cube, are not formed of sensor-controlled louvres but can be raised and lowered as shutters. In normal use, they are the standard sheets of rusty steel gridwork employed as platforms on industrial sites. The horizontal slats

ABOVE LEFT EXTERIOR DETAIL.

ABOVE FRONT ENTRANCE CLOSED.

OPPOSITE LOOKING SOUTH-EAST TO THE FRONT OF THE HOUSE, FROM THE ENTRY STEPS LEADING UP FROM THE STREET.

OPPOSITE TOP CONCEPT SKETCH.

PHOTOS EARL CARTER.

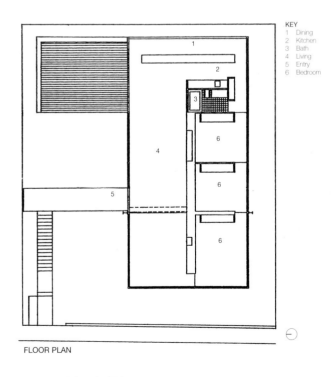

FLOOR PLAN

KEY
1 Dining
2 Kitchen
3 Bath
4 Living
5 Entry
6 Bedroom

block light when the sun is high or low in the sky. They also alter the density/transparency of the house when it is seen from different viewing points. These subtle shifts of surface effect are reminiscent of delicate moiré cloths and the timber screens of Japanese buildings.

As artistic statements, Nouvel's hotel and Godsell's house can be interpreted as the revenge of nature upon the perfect modernist object or as a 20th-century update of classical ruins in the landscape (a fashionable 18th-century idea).

Another metaphor is the cage. Are these buildings securing their occupants for protection (against the violence of the modern world) or to imprison them? In relation to a house, there also are connotations about the inevitable bonds of family domesticity.

All preconceptions dissolve as soon as visitors cross the threshold under the entry shutter – raised in a reverse mechanism to the drawbridge of a medieval castle. Inside the living zone, facing west to the street, the grilles fade to a state which Mies called 'almost nothing': the same diaphanous immateriality as a veil of gauze. Also, the interior is much cooler than expected, thanks to a thoroughly insulated roof and sprinklers under the house which water the garden of native grasses and cool air rising through the floorboards. And finally, the issue of privacy seems much less pressing: most areas of the house and its back sundeck avoid the glances of neighbours.

All these gradual realisations lead the disciple of architecture to a state of enlightenment where conclusions negate initial instincts.

TOP LEFT NORTH FACADE FROM THE ENTRY PATH, WITH THE FRONT SHUTTER OPEN. PHOTO PETER HYATT.

ABOVE LIVING ROOM LOOKING WEST. PHOTO EARL CARTER.

LEFT LOOKING ALONG THE NORTH GLAZING OF THE LIVING ROOM. PHOTO EARL CARTER.

RURAL RUIN

GARY AND JILL MARINKO, INCOMPLETE
POLL HOUSE, MARGARET RIVER, WESTERN AUSTRALIA

When Australian architects design houses for rural sites, many tend to follow the idea that their building should seem delicately separate from its natural context – like an alien spaceship shimmering down to earth. Sometimes, however, a convincing case is made for the opposite idea: of lodging a heavy building into the ground so it reads as a permanent part of the place. At Margaret River, Western Australia's winemaking and holiday region, the latter strategy has almost come together on a cleared site wrapped by a state forest.

One month before expected completion several years ago, a building dispute stopped work on a weekend farmhouse designed by Perth architects Gary and Jill Marinko – and it now seems unlikely to be completed to their original vision. But the structure and interior cabinetry were finished well enough to confirm the intelligence of their architecture.

Visits involve a southward car journey of several hours from Perth, ultimately driving through a gap in a wall of trees to follow an uphill track which swings around a patch of lavender bushes to conclude at tin sheds behind the house.

Here, visitors shake off the ennui of the road while admiring a vast downhill prospect over the roof of the house, across the pastures of the district. Soon they descend a ceremonial staircase (recalling the shallow cobbled steps of Italian hill towns) to the enclosed south courtyard and modest back door.

Arriving behind the building has four advantages. First, motorists are teased by their anticipation, then frustration, as they approach the prime facade and are then diverted around the back of the building. Halting uphill gives an instant picture of all the key 'fragments' on site: the single-storey house sweeping wide across the slope, the two-storey guest tower offset to the east, two major gum trees, the lavender beds, the marri trees, the tool shed and the water tank. On the way down, visitors can be shown to overnight accommodation in the guest pavilion beside the entry court. Finally, parking at the rear prevents cars from interrupting the magnificent vistas to be appreciated from the living zones, bedroom and northern terrace.

Inside the house, there is no foyer: merely a passage between the laundry and a study with a daybed, continuing the courtyard staircase towards the 'front' door to the north terrace above a bunker wine cellar with a tiny courtyard for tastings. This hall also intersects the prime east-west walkway across the house. At that junction, occupants need to decide which part of the interior to visit: a choice helped by a logical space layout. In this and other strategies, the Marinkos were influenced by 20th century rationalist Louis Kahn, who thought of the floor plan as 'a society of rooms.'

Minor utility chambers (Kahn's 'servant spaces') are lined in a row along the south side of the house, while the spacious living/dining and sleeping zones open north to the sun and panorama. Public areas occupy the eastern two-thirds of the house; the private bedroom and ensuite are at the west end.

The Marinkos' quartile plan of east-west/north-south division is

OPPOSITE THE NORTH FACADE OPENS TO A SUN COURT WITH A BROAD VALLEY PROSPECT. YELLOW PLYWOOD BIFOLD SCREENS CAN BE ADJUSTED FOR DIFFERENT SUN CONDITIONS. AT RIGHT IS A WINE CELLAR.

ABOVE DETAIL OF THE PLYWOOD SCREENS, STAINED YELLOW.

ALL PHOTOS JACQUELINE STEVENSON.

emphasised by monumental walls of stabilised earth (a Margaret River tradition). The recipe includes granite 'grit' (to turn the pink tone of the earth to grey) and extra cement for smoother surfaces.

In the living areas, there is a typically Kahnian atmosphere of both spaciousness and enclosure: an open floor plan contained by massive columns and walls. Kahn's architecture was largely inspired by Greek and Egyptian ruins, which he thought would guide intuitive observers to 'realisation' of the timeless ordering of the universe. In the Marinkos' scheme, columns and walls frame openings devised to reveal choice vistas of landscape to occupants in a protected place.

Shelter usually is symbolised by roofs – here seen in corrugated zincalume as a low-pitched plane, kinked and subtly twisted. Inside the house, a gracefully swooping ceiling of plywood continues externally as eaves which thicken the roof edge in sympathy with the massive walls.

Set against the raw, weighty structure are a chain of adornments (cabinets, wall linings, window shutters) made of plywood stained with tones of grey and acidic tints of yellow, blue and red. These sensual treatments are displayed most effectively inside the dark, cubic guest tower. Here, a confined yet high living chamber is overlooked by a gallery off the first floor bedroom. In the lofty space, ground floor gloom is penetrated by a shaft of skylighting, and by opening window shutters if desired. This interior exemplifies Louis Kahn's notions about the 'treasury of the shadow.'

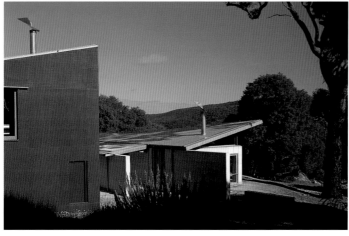

TOP ENTRY STAIRCASE TO THE SOUTH COURTYARD.

ABOVE LOOKING NORTH-WEST FROM THE DRIVEWAY, WITH GUEST PAVILION AT LEFT.

RIGHT DOUBLE-HEIGHT LIVING AREA IN THE GUEST PAVILION, WITH WALLS AND WINDOW SHUTTERS OF STAINED PLYWOOD.

OPPOSITE THE MAIN LIVING ROOM, LOOKING NORTH.

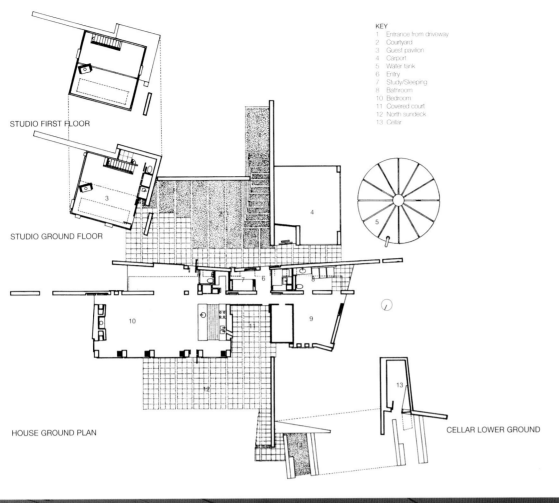

STUDIO FIRST FLOOR

STUDIO GROUND FLOOR

HOUSE GROUND PLAN

CELLAR LOWER GROUND

AMBIGUOUS ZONES

DONOVAN HILL, 1999
C HOUSE, BRISBANE

When people yearn for a dream house, are they wanting a cottage or a castle? This question has been debated in literature for at least six centuries – and was analysed intensively by French writer Gaston Bachelard in *The Poetics of Space* (1958). Seeking to synthesise opposite concepts, he suggested that the ideal house would answer both the eternal human need for shelter and containment and man's primal urge to take control of the outside world. 'The dream house,' he wrote, 'must possess every virtue. However spacious, it must also be a cottage, a dovecote, a nest, a chrysalis.'

Another metaphor, proposed in the 15th century by Italian humanist Leon Battista Alberti, compared the house to a miniature city. In Book V of his manual *On the Art of Building*, he claimed that a house 'should offer every facility and every convenience to contribute to a peaceful, tranquil and refined life.'

In young, egalitarian Australia, it is unusual to see architect-designed houses which could theoretically be interpreted as lyrical fusions of the cottage and the castle. The prime contemporary example is Donovan Hill's C House in Brisbane, a new-age citadel designed in 1991 and completed in 1999 for a bachelor considering a future household.

Occupying a suburban hillside with a distant prospect to the skyline of Queensland's capital city, this villa is experienced much like an Italian hill town. Sixteen flights of steps conduct occupants up and down a convoluted journey around a three-storey stack of chambers, corridors, courtyards, nooks, pools, gardens, pergolas and balconies.

Along the way, the architecture is gradually revealed as a sophisticated fusion of many stylistic influences.

The concept – embellishing a monumental structure of raw concrete with layers of intricate elements in fine woods, luxury metals, glass, ceramic tiles and water – owes much to the mid-20th century works of Italian sensualist Carlo Scarpa and to Chicago architect Frank Lloyd Wright's schemes of the 1910s. The meticulous timberwork is reminiscent of Zen temples and lanterns in Japan.

The architectural narrative begins with a steep right-of-way off a busy main road. Because the house cannot be seen from the street, its imposing size and aesthetic complexity are encountered as a surprise foreground to a hillside array of neighbouring houses in two-storey brick and tile.

For pedestrians, there is a choice of two approaches to the house, using parallel staircases designed in the European hill town tradition of shallow risers and broad treads.

The direct path to the entrance takes the west steps, under a vine-entangled pergola, to a landing and gate on the second of three main floor 'plates' (the house also has many minor shifts of level). A less usual way up is via the front lawn (an outdoor 'room' contained by low walls and raised plant beds), and the east steps.

Beside the lobby, several small chambers can be used as home-offices and storage rooms. A formal staircase is mounted to the general living level, where halls, rooms, terraces and alcoves wrap around

ABOVE LEFT THE PROJECTING 'BIRDS NEST' SUNDECK ON THE NORTH CORNER.

ABOVE RIGHT ENTRANCE AND PART OF THE NORTH-WEST FACADE, WITH STAIRS LEADING FROM THE LANDSCAPE PLATE TO THE LIVING PLATE.

OPPOSITE LOOKING WEST ACROSS THE SWIMMING POOL TO A SLATTED SITTING ENCLOSURE DESIGNED TO BE SHROUDED WITH VINES LIKE A 'WALK-IN BUSH.'

NEXT PAGES LOOKING NORTH ACROSS THE COURTYARD TO THE WALK-IN BUSH AND DECK. FIRE AT RIGHT, KITCHEN AT LEFT.

ALL PHOTOS ANTHONY BROWELL.

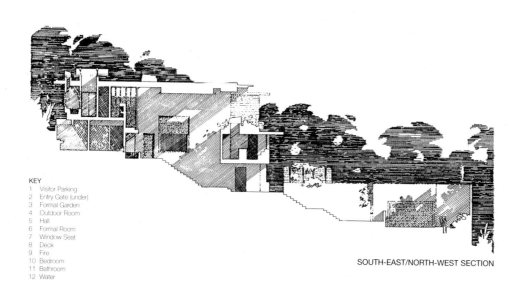

KEY
1 Visitor Parking
2 Entry Gate (under)
3 Formal Garden
4 Outdoor Room
5 Hall
6 Formal Room
7 Window Seat
8 Deck
9 Fire
10 Bedroom
11 Bathroom
12 Water
13 Laundry
14 Pool

SOUTH-EAST/NORTH-WEST SECTION

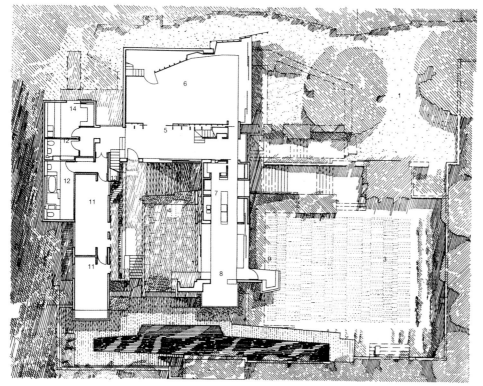

LIVING PLATE PLAN

a courtyard that serves as a meeting place, like a town plaza

At the top of these stairs, visitors are greeted by a pond and a rustic-style front door which opens to a sandstone-paved hall and a large living/dining zone and kitchen.

This lofty 'Formal Room' recalls the stone banqueting halls of medieval castles – and is even equipped with a gallery for the minstrels. Walls of smooth, warm white concrete bounce sunlight around the space and are partly lined with kauri panelling. Floors are rock maple boards.

Off the entry hall, a staircase rises to a third-floor retreat (bedroom, dressing room and ensuite) on the south-east side of the courtyard, above a floor of two small rooms which could be bedrooms or office cells. All rooms look towards the courtyard and view, with timber louvres on their back walls for cross-ventilation.

Wrapping around the courtyard's north and west sides are the four artistic highlights of Donovan Hill's village. A low pavilion, containing the kitchen and informal living areas, has a rooftop pebble garden (a fifth facade to be seen from higher levels). Nearby, a lattice-walled tower, to be cloaked with vines, encloses a reading alcove – and lights up like a lantern at night. Along the site boundary, a lap pool thrusts out from a ridge to hover above the front lawn.

Nearby, marking the north corner of the residence, is another seemingly precarious projection: a square timber balcony, designed in the manner of a bird's nest. When you sit in this intimate aerial nook, you feel like you rule the world.

ABOVE LOOKING NORTH-WEST FROM THE TOP FLOOR MAIN BEDROOM, ACROSS THE ROOF GARDEN OF THE KITCHEN WING, WITH THE BRISBANE SKYLINE BEYOND.

LEFT STAIRCASE TO THE MAIN ENTRANCE.

BELOW LEFT MAIN BEDROOM, WITH A STAIRCASE TO THE ROOF.

BEACH CABIN

JOHN WARDLE, 1997
ISAACSON-DAVIS HOUSE
BALNARRING, VICTORIA

In 1962, French performance artist Yves Klein produced a photo-montage of himself in suit and tie, jumping off a mansard roof. His 'leap into the void' lingers as one of the 20th century's classic images.

That picture of Klein's seemingly kamikaze art gesture has fascinated Melbourne architect John Wardle since he first saw it in his early years at the Royal Melbourne Institute of Technology. To him, it represents a heroic ideal of modernism: the urge to perform astonishing acts of bravery, even if they perversely contradict sensible human behaviour.

Like most of the 20th century's artistically ambitious architects, Wardle also has a Kleinian desire to perform amazing feats, but he cannot act alone. His profession requires him to serve clients and work in building teams, often with tight budgets, and his artworks need to be enjoyable to occupy.

With the Isaacson-Davis holiday house at Balnarring on Victoria's Mornington Peninsula, he appears to deliver modern architecture's equivalent of Klein's leap. At the front of the house, the living room lurches forward to confront startled visitors, projecting 5 metres westward at a height which seems to defy gravity and allows a car to be parked beneath.

It is not instantly noticed that the cantilevered box of cedar and glass is propped by a thin steel pole at its south-west corner. Technically, this is like Klein wearing a safety cable – it discounts the act of bravery – but it allowed Wardle to provide his clients with a desirable breakfast alcove off their kitchen. Designed 'like a caricature' of dining nooks in

caravans parked at the nearby camping ground, this zone projects as a box from the south wall, prematurely terminating a beam under the living room.

When architects plan buildings, they usually begin their thought processes with doodles that sketch the prime artistic ideas. Sometimes these are elaborated or altered as the design process goes on.

Wardle's Balnarring house began with the simple concept of a long, raw timber box hovering on one side of a flat coastal bush site, with the cantilevered living room as the astonishing gesture. However, this architect is one of Australia's most elaborate and detail-obsessed modernists: it is not in his nature to make plain buildings. He also is a humanist – seeking opportunities to exploit climate and site conditions to enhance emotional experiences. His designs appear influenced by 20th century sensualists Frank Lloyd Wright (US), Alvar Aalto (Finland) and Carlo Scarpa (Italy) – gurus currently followed more by architects in Queensland than by Wardle's peers in Melbourne.

All these artistic instincts led Wardle to a theory of the Balnarring house as 'a suitcase to be unpacked' for holidays. Although he retained the original idea of the box, he began to embellish it with a meticulous but irregular array of punctured windows, slatted sunscreens, projecting boxes, cutaway corners, sudden shifts of floor level, sliding screens of either timber or glass, and outdoor decks. Visitors drive up to the 50-metre-wide west frontage and walk along a central path with the house to their right along the site's south

ABOVE LEFT FRONT ENTRANCE AT THE WEST END OF THE HOUSE.

ABOVE THE SIDE ENTRY AND FRONT CANTILEVER, WITH CAR SPACE BENEATH.

RIGHT LOOKING ALONG THE NORTH DECK FROM STEPS BESIDE THE EAST BEDROOMS.

ALL PHOTOS TREVOR MEIN.

RIGHT CABINETRY DETAIL IN THE LOWER DINING AREA.

FAR RIGHT UPPER LIVING AREA AT THE WEST END, LOOKING BACK TO THE KITCHEN/DINING AREA AND ENTRY.

OPPOSITE BELOW CENTRAL DECK AND ENTRANCE ON THE NORTH SIDE.

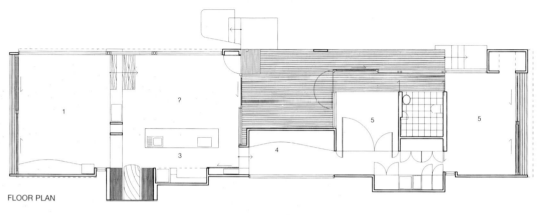

FLOOR PLAN

KEY
1 Living
2 Dining
3 Kitchen
4 Study
5 Bedroom

NORTH ELEVATION

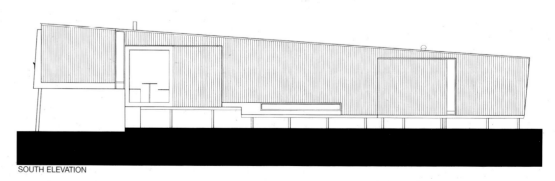

SOUTH ELEVATION

side. Past the cantilevered living room, they climb a protruding concrete block of four steps to an elevated sundeck which also serves as the porch. This unroofed area is contained by three walls of the house – one timber and two glass – and it opens north to the garden of tea-tree, banksias and native grasses.

To enter the house at this point requires turning 180 degrees to face back to the west. Here, a remarkably inconspicuous 'front' door is tucked in a niche beneath an overhanging corner of the building (forming a rain canopy). Guests step straight into the dining area and kitchen without being greeted in a foyer. This informal treatment of the threshold summons memories of old suburban Australia, when neighbours would visit each other via unlocked back doors to their eat-in kitchens.

Inside, a 'narrative journey' continues upstairs and around the living room, down through the kitchen, along a hallway that forms a dark and quiet study linking to bedrooms and bathrooms at the east end (capturing morning sun).

As occupants move around, they notice the unusual trick of floor-level strip windows – giving privacy while allowing glances to the ground outside. There also are many opportunities to admire unusually fine cabinetry; employing a palette of interesting veneers and acidic paint colours, sophisticated door hardware and flamboyant details.

With these elegant treatments, Wardle has transformed the supposedly humble beach shack into something akin to a jewel box.

SUBURBAN CITADEL

WOOD MARSH, 1994
GOTTLIEB RESIDENCE
CAULFIELD, VICTORIA

Australia's international reputation for lightweight, sun-seeking shed-houses is contradicted in the continent's sub-Antarctic latitudes by a genre of bunkers and fortresses with massive concrete walls artfully punctured by windows. The current leaders of this intimidatingly defensive style are Melbourne architects; mainly Denton Corker Marshall and a younger office, Wood Marsh. Both are influenced by 1960s abstract sculpture and brutalist architecture, 1980s Japanese minimalism and the visions of Soviet constructivists after the 1917 revolution.

Melbourne's most significant 1990s example of an urban fortress is Wood Marsh's Gottlieb house in Caulfield, a flat suburb developed since the 1950s. This two-storey, four-bedroom residence was designed as a protective enclosure for a growing family sensitive to the Holocaust experiences of European parents who came to Australia as war refugees.

Ironically, the owners asked Roger Wood and Randall Marsh to design their house at a time when these architects were internationally known for 1980s nightclub fitouts which incorporated prison camp imagery in chaotic sets sometimes labelled 'post-apocalypse-Baroque.' However, when Wood Marsh moved on from transitory interiors to permanent architecture, the practice switched its aesthetic agenda from desolate disorder to monolithic austerity. Both architects recognised that this shift would demand more elegant structural detailing and a palette of undecorated but sensuously textured materials: leading towards

Le Corbusier's poetic modernist vision of architecture as 'the correct and magnificent play of masses brought together in light.'

The Gottlieb house has been conceived as a monumental ensemble of arcane geometric shapes: most easily recognised in its floor plan of straight lines, squares, rectangles, ellipses and arcs; complicated by twisting some shapes on the drawing to clash with others at oblique angles. These gestures are subtle artistic reactions against the right angles and circles which are predictably used for modernist buildings.

In three dimensions, only two sides of the house are visible from a distance. Behind a front hedge and double carport (typical features of Australian suburbs), the west facade fronts the street with a belligerent attitude.

Projecting from the first floor of a windowless wall of raw concrete is a ribbed box faced with mirror-glass – creating a remote and mysterious aura, like someone wearing sunglasses. This object contains a bathroom and forms a canopy and marker for the entrance. The architects say it combines function and symbolism 'rather like the keystone of an arch.'

The other significant side of the Gottlieb house faces north to a lawn spanning between the front and back boundaries of the property. This long elevation has three main elements: a central colonnade (with concrete columns forming a verandah of much more monumental scale than is typical for Australian houses) framed by skewed 'bookends' finished in raw concrete and split-face black slate

OPPOSITE LEFT VIEW ALONG THE NORTH SIDE OF THE LIVING/ DINING ZONE, FROM OUTSIDE THE STACKED STONE KITCHEN POD AT LEFT.

RIGHT THE STONE-CLAD KITCHEN PROJECTING FROM THE NORTH FACADE.

BELOW FRONT (WEST) FACADE FROM ACROSS THE STREET.

ALL PHOTOS TIM GRIFFITH.

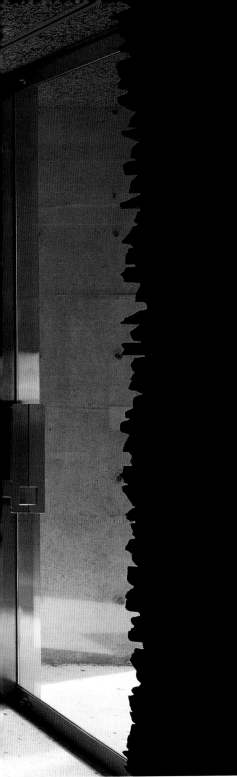

stacked in thin, rough-edged layers. The concrete bookend is part of an oval cylinder at the front of the house, which contains a ground-floor study and upstairs main bedroom, reached by a grand but austere concrete staircase. The black slate bookend, near the rear of the house, contains a ground-floor kitchen topped by the terrace off an upstairs study.

Between the front and back zones are a large living and dining room on the ground floor, opening to the colonnade/verandah and lawn, and three first-floor children's bedrooms, treated as individual cubes projecting from the north facade. There is also an informal family area at the back (east) end, overlooking a compact swimming pool in the garden.

After recovering from an initial sense of trepidation generated by the street facade, visitors to the house are likely to be impressed by its grand interior spaces and plays of sunlight and shadow across hard, bald walls and floors. To create a lively, bright atmosphere inside this bunker, Wood Marsh designed arrays of tall, narrow windows (a format drawn from classical rather than modernist architecture) which appear to either separate the building's monolithic forms or puncture its otherwise blank walls. In both cases, the idea is to contrast the transparency of the glass against the solidity of the stone and concrete. These juxtapositions are imaginatively orchestrated to establish dramatic visual rhythms throughout the building. It is a work which reveals some reasons why architecture is often compared to music.

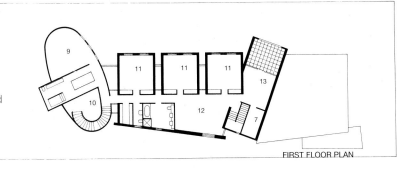

FIRST FLOOR PLAN

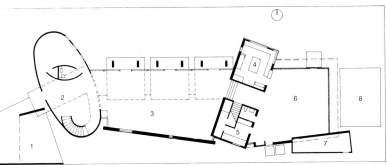

GROUND FLOOR PLAN

KEY
1 Carport
2 Foyer
3 Living/Dining
4 Kitchen
5 Laundry
6 Family
7 Plant
8 Swimming pool
9 Master bedroom
10 Void
11 Bedroom
12 Living
13 Study

PITCHING CAMP

GABRIEL POOLE, 1997
POOLE HOUSE 3, LAKE WEYBA
SUNSHINE COAST, QUEENSLAND

Gabriel Poole, an architect working on Queensland's sub-tropical Sunshine Coast, is the founder of a regional species of light, airy and informal houses which seem to crystallise the ideal Australian way of life. As a stereotypical scenario, this involves lightly dressed people drifting between sunny interiors and shady outdoor 'rooms', relaxing in deck chairs with little more serious to contemplate than whether to cook meat or fish for tonight's barbeque with the neighbours.

There is enough truth in this idyll for Queensland's tourist board to get away with hyping the state as 'beautiful one day, perfect the next.' But geographers know that hot situations tend to be tempestuous – and the potential for extreme weather conditions has to be answered in house designs.

Gabriel Poole's own current home, planned and shared with artist Elizabeth Frith, is a case study of clever, low-cost strategies for manipulating the sun, rain and wind to enjoy a comfortable life close to nature. Not surprisingly, the style of this residence – especially its materials and weather-reaction systems – is like a camp site.

Poole is the only well-known Australian architect who regularly produces houses like tents, with metal frames, roll-up walls of canvas, windows of sheet plastic and (particularly with his popular Tent House at Eumundi, 1990) bright-coloured canvas roofs with flying pennants; recalling nomad camps in the Middle East.

At Lake Weyba in the district of Doonan, Poole's latest house appears to be a more permanent camp than his earlier constructions.

It was built to a tight budget, but is designed to be the last home of a creative couple who had never settled for long in one place.

Poole's scheme divides the conventional idea of the house as a single building into a series of three steel-framed huts, clad with sheets of fibre cement and galvanised steel, linked by outdoor boardwalks and floating on steel feet above a ground cover of coastal scrub called wallum. Each pavilion is equipped with a rainwater tank.

The unusual site plan shows the three buildings descending in floor area from the northern pavilion of living zones to the southern cabin containing the bedroom. Between these is a structure containing some facilities found in camping park ablution blocks: a shower, a lavatory and a laundry. But its prime purpose is revealed by the central, ceremonial, spa bath sunk into the floor. It signifies the personal indulgences which Poole and Frith want to enjoy during their older years at their third shared house.

All the structures turn their backs to the south – Doonan's usual source of storms and cyclones. They open up to the sun and breezes with roller shutters, sliding screens and hinged plywood fins.

That basic climate response is clearly signalled by high-pitched skillion roofs of PVC sheet. These are tensioned by steel tubes at the top and bottom eaves and laced to the sides of each building with nylon ropes.

Beneath each PVC canopy is an inner roof/ceiling of twin-wall polycarbonate sheeting. The two layers, and their cavity of continually moving air, help to insulate and

FAR LEFT THE LIVING AREAS, OPENING TO THE FRONT DECK.

LEFT A SENSORY BATHROOM OCCUPIES THE CENTRE (AMENITIES) PAVILION.

BELOW THE NORTH-WEST FACADE FROM THE FRONT DRIVEWAY.

cool the interior. This twin roof system was inspired by the 'fly' tents used by the fettlers who laid Queensland's rail tracks.

When the trio of buildings is seen side-on, it is obvious that their north facades are double the heights of the back walls – and that Poole has horizontally divided the taller elevations into two halves equipped with different weather systems.

The upper halves are fitted with flyscreens (mosquitos often arrive around dusk) behind steel roller doors (to shut out rain and high summer sun, and for security). All The lower half of the largest building (the living pavilion at the front of the trio) is fitted with steel-framed screens of clear plastic (lighter and less costly than glass). Because they are fitted with counterweights, they easily slide up on tracks to the high zone of the facade (behind the roller doors), leaving the living spaces open to a wide sundeck.

Many of Poole's disciples consider this house to be the most elegant and masterful work of his chequered and prolific career – although he has built several other outstanding residences which included systems that were innovative for their time.

Poole's best architecture is not the adobe-style white terraced casas which many of his clients (from colder Australian cities) are currently demanding. The greater accomplishments are his dynamic and carefully crafted ensembles of everyday tin, plywood and fibro. His most wonderful structures perch on their sites in postures of both poise and tension; hinting that maybe they just might fly.

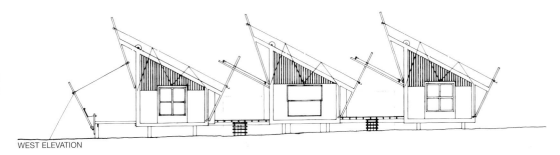

WEST ELEVATION

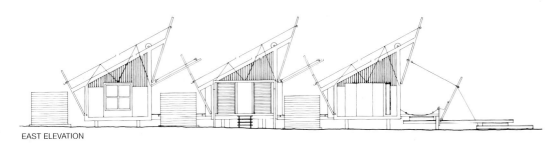

EAST ELEVATION

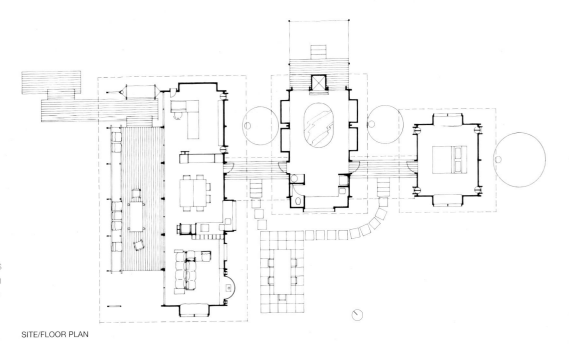

SITE/FLOOR PLAN

VOLUPTUOUS DOMESTICITY

IVAN RIJAVEC, 1996
CHEN RESIDENCE, KEW, VICTORIA

One of architecture's prime ironies is its reliance on fixed points of view and flat planes of paper to 'rationally' depict three-dimensional scenes which are really perceived by roving eyes and disorderly minds. In *The Origins of Perspective* (MIT Press, 1994 English translation), French scholar Hubert Damisch claimed that the systems of perspective drawing established in the Renaissance – using points, ruled lines and grids – reduce the viewer 'to a kind of cyclops.' The same problem of the sole and immobile eye also applies to architectural diagrams, which usually assume aerial viewpoints.

In the 1990s, however, the depiction of architecture began to be transformed by the powers of computer visualisation software and hand-held video cameras to roam around structures and through spaces; recording scenes from continuous perspectives. Architects are learning how to use these tools to generate buildings on screen in styles less limited by pens, rulers and axial vision.

In suburban Melbourne, a house by Ivan Rijavec graphically illustrates current tensions between linear and non-linear systems of design. The Chen residence is a white building (recalling the 1960s and 1970s ensembles of the New York Five) bursting with radial geometry. He describes it as a box compressing unruly curves which 'squish through the container to burst out at each end, finding expression on the front and rear facades.'

The house sits centrally on a flat block of land near the end of a typical mid-20th century suburban street. Its presence is signalled by

vertical scrolls projecting from the front (south) facade. These provide a canopy for the threshold outside the red front door and include the window of a first-floor observation lounge off the main bedroom.

Inside, formal rooms and a garage are placed towards the front, with family zones at the rear, opening northwards to a lawn. Upstairs, there are four bedrooms (three with balconies), a study and bathrooms.

Although Rijavec's design is revolutionary in 20th-century terms, it is tethered to a historical line of anti-Classical expression dating back to the Italian Baroque, with particular links to the optical games of Francesco Borromini (1599–1667), who sought to 'deceive the view of the passer-by.' Like Borromini and his later disciples, Rijavec aims to 'test the limits of cognition such that the perceiver becomes self-conscious about the relativity of spatial reality.'

Conceiving deceitful architecture has become seriously feasible with computer visualisation software like Rijavec's Autocad, 3D Studio Max and form.Z packages. These programs have helped him move on from his earlier penchant for grids, 'dumb boxes' and arcs to produce several dwellings which ostentatiously swirl, tilt and twist. Although these are not homes for conservative occupants, his clients can contemplate realistic pictures and advance fly-through tours of their potential environments.

Along with his neo-Baroque teases of the eye and cortex, Rijavec has been reapplying the white paint which characterised many heroic buildings of the 20th

OPPOSITE SOUTH FACADE WITH THE FRONT ENTRY AND DRIVEWAY.

THIS PAGE LEFT CENTRAL STAIRCASE FROM THE FRONT DOOR.

ABOVE FRONT ENTRANCE PORCH.

ALL IMAGES JOHN GOLLINGS.

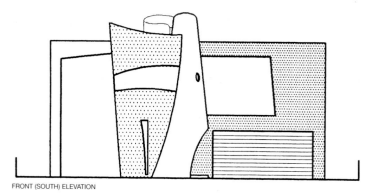

FRONT (SOUTH) ELEVATION

century. Le Corbusier and other pioneers of modernism thought of white as signifying the socialist ideal of disciplined refusal of sensual excesses. But Rijavec's Chen residence – as well as his Freeland stables conversion (1994) and Alessio house (1997) – infuses this pure and hygenic colour with erotic connotations.

Most obviously, the interiors of all three residences are centrally dominated by white staircases which ascend in contorted curves of a suggestively vulvic character. The Chen staircase is the focus of a two-storey circuit of irregularly shaped rooms, styled as a swirling dance illuminated by a circular skylight. At the climax of the spectacle, the plaster balustrades twist and flare out in opposite directions: a theatrical finale which leaves observers wondering how such a singular ensemble could technically be achieved.

One final question: why does Rijavec want to design buildings to disturb the minds of onlookers? He understands Carl Jung's early 20th century psychological theories (confirmed by recent scientific readings of volunteers' brainwaves) that most people feel pleasure when they see archetypes (objects in traditional shapes) and become tense when shown unfamiliar items or disorderly arrangements. But this architect has his own mental wiring: he belongs to a coterie of radicals who oppose common tastes and assumptions as a tactic towards inventing novel visions. Although unconventional architecture is not intended to be popular, it can be valued as one of the stimulants needed by exciting cultures.

KEY

1	Entry portico	12	Garage
2	Foyer/Hall	13	Void
3	Formal living	14	Study
4	Formal dining	15	Bedroom 2
5	Family living	16	Bedroom 3
6	Family dining	17	Bedroom 4
7	Kitchen	18	Bathroom
8	Laundry	19	Lavatory
9	Pantry	20	Ensuite
10	Powder room	21	Robe
11	Store	22	Main bedroom
		23	Observation lounge

ABOVE REAR LAWN AND NORTH FACADE.

OPPOSITE STAIRCASE/LIGHTWELL LOOKING SOUTH FROM THE FIRST FLOOR STUDY.

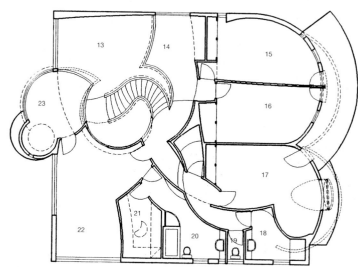

FIRST FLOOR PLAN

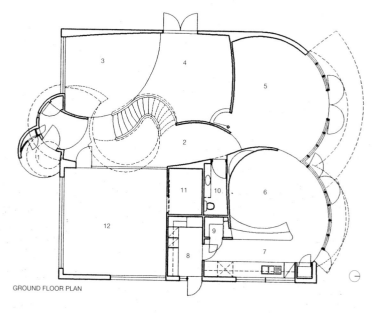

GROUND FLOOR PLAN

ON THE LEDGE

GROSE BRADLEY, 1995
NEWMAN/WOODHILL RESIDENCE
WOMBARRA, NEW SOUTH WALES

Australian architecture was born from an early 19th-century marriage between English Georgian buildings of bald masonry (offering scant protection from dazzling sun) and a weather-shielding structure thought to have been invented in medieval Spain: the verandah. In the two centuries since that amalgamation, verandahs have become the principal signifiers of 'authentic' Australian houses.

In the 1950s, and again in the 1980s, the verandah changed from its historical role as an added feature to become the conceptual basis for entire houses. This shift of thinking was triggered by the radical steel and glass residences built by German modernists in the United States in the late 1940s and '50s. Their floating glass boxes inspired Australian architects to glaze houses much more generously than was done before the Second World War – and to link interiors more closely to their external surroundings. The 'outdoor room' is now a pervasive ideal in antipodean housing – especially emphasised in latitudes north of Victoria.

However, there is a crucial difference between the early glass boxes of US modernists and the later 'tin shed' adaptations by Glenn Murcutt and his disciples. While the American models usually had flat (apparently absent) roofs, Australian examples are often distinguished by sweepingly gestural canopies of corrugated steel. Usually including wide eaves, they form emphatic yet pragmatic symbols of shelter.

A classic example of the modern Australian verandah residence has been built at Wombarra, near Wollongong, NSW, by Murcutt's

leading protegé in Sydney, James Grose, and his partner, Nicola Bradley. Their Newman/Woodhill residence, along with Murcutt's Simpson-Lee house at Mt Wilson (1993), represents a significant shift away from the 'touch the earth lightly' philosophy which helped to popularise the Murcutt style in the 1980s. Both are built upon concrete slabs laid across sloping sites which had been excavated.

While the Simpson-Lee house is free-standing in steel and glass, the Grose Bradley project is anchored by massive concrete walls cutting into and across the fall of the ground. Along with the concrete platform, these support and delineate (like the cup of a hand) two light and transparent pavilions. They also frame a dramatically converging entry tunnel – likened by the architects to a Queensland breezeway and covered by a floating canopy of metal – that leads from the street to the building entrances and courtyard.

The two pavilions are athletic-looking structures with galvanised steel bones and ribs, glass skins and zincalume-finished skillions hovering overhead.

The larger shed, containing the 'public' facilities of the living/dining area and kitchen, is placed to the west of the site, near the street. Private quarters – one bedroom, a study, a bathroom and dressing room – are in the smaller building, near a plantation of eucalypts to the west, at the base of the Illawarra escarpment. They are both oriented northwards – to take advantage of both the daily track of the sun and a dramatic downhill prospect towards the Pacific. The site is part

OPPOSITE TOP LOOKING EAST ALONG THE BREEZEWAY TO THE STREET.

OPPOSITE BOTTOM DETAIL OF THE NORTH FACADE OF THE MAIN PAVILION, WITH BEDROOM PAVILION AT REAR.

ABOVE EAST (ENTRY) ELEVATION.

ALL PHOTOS BART MAIORANA.

BELOW BEDROOM PAVILION, LOOKING WEST ACROSS THE COURTYARD.

BOTTOM DETAIL OF THE LIVING AREA, LOOKING WEST.

OPPOSITE LOOKING WEST FROM THE KITCHEN TO THE LIVING/DINING ZONES.

of a provincial steelworking city that spreads along a plateau captured between mountains and the ocean.

Over the past three decades, Australian architects have been thoroughly educated in the principles of 'passively' managing summer and winter sun to develop comfortable indoor temperatures without resort to air conditioning. Many offices, including Grose Bradley, also have employed banks of aluminium-framed glass louvres (a product originally favoured mainly for the windows of lavatories) to manipulate breezes. And they often install rooftop ventilators – some models looking like jaunty silver birds – to extract warm air rising from interior spaces. All of these strategies are classic treatments for houses of the style known as 'Australian vernacular.'

Another characteristic of modern Australian houses is their aura of open space and horizontality – both qualities associated with the continent's natural landscapes. In Grose Bradley's work, these sensibilities are strengthened by various recurring treatments that help to optically expand interiors: providing large, open rooms for general living, painting walls off-white (or leaving pale concrete unpainted), laying timber floors, fitting louvred windows and blinds and arranging structural members (particularly window mullions) in horizontal grids. Externally, horizontality is primarily emphasised by the sweep and tilt of expansive, fine-edged metal skillions. Flying rooflines are often the key gestures seen in Grose's early concept scribbles – and they are outstanding highlights of the house at Wombarra.

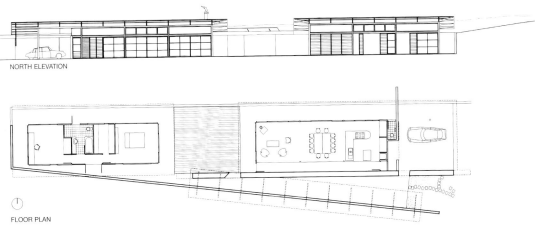

NORTH ELEVATION

FLOOR PLAN

BUSH CRAFT

REX ADDISON, 1999
HOUSE AND STUDIO, TARINGA, QUEENSLAND

Down an overgrown right of-way in Taringa, an old suburb of sub-tropical Brisbane, there is a tangled secret garden of native eucalypts, introduced cocos palms, vines and ferns. This wild and melancholy gully was the childhood home of architect Rex Addison – and he lives there again now, with wife Susan, in an eccentric tree house and detached art studio. He designed them as intimate places for solace, creativity and relaxation.

Both dwellings are elevated on stumps and are imaginatively and precisely built with common materials; mainly plywood, clear fibreglass sheets, corrugated steel, pine, hardwoods and river stones. To add sparks of sensually brilliant tropical colour – like parrots against the greenery – the timber stumps are stained red and the steel poles are wrapped with red rope. These treatments have been compared to Chinese architecture but Addison says he first used red on his early buildings in Papua New Guinea, as a strategy to deal with red spit from local people chewing betel nuts.

In the context of Australian architectural history, these buildings are sophisticated updates of the pioneering and 'alternative' tradition of hand-made (do-it-yourself) huts and sheds. The lineage of this type includes many single-skin buildings dating back at least to the 1860s (especially the Queensland works of R. G. Suter) and houses built by bush carpenters without architects.

The property is marked by various minor legacies of the DIY attitude which prevailed across Australia until the 1960s (when the first generation of pampered post-war baby-boomers became adults).

Over many years while Addison was a child, he watched his father and grandfather improve this site with small projects: a bridge across the water-course at the base of the gully, retaining walls terracing the slope, steps, paths and a barbeque shelter (now relocated) which the family claim looked better than the municipal structures found along state highways.

To protect this special landscape after his parents died, the Addisons subdivided and sold his childhood house, allowing them to build new dwellings in the thick of the jungle.

These timber-framed structures are elevated to allow cool air to flow underneath (and avoid ants). They were designed in close sympathy with the garden and to preserve established 'desire lines' of movement around the site.

The idea was to build a two-storey house on the gully's south slope, linked by the bridge to a printmaking and design studio near the foot of the north slope. The latter replaces the ruins of his first project as an architecture student – a studio-shed using the hexagonal geometry of Frank Lloyd Wright.

When Addison studied in the 1960s, the profession's leaders were interested in robust buildings planned with diagonal, triangular and hexagonal patterns. Addison's latest pavilions, along with many of his 1970s and 1980s works, still include diagonal arrangements.

They also confirm his skills at composing complex and irregular architectural collages, employing diverse materials, layers of structure and clean, weatherproof resolutions of technically tricky junctions.

Their crowning highlights –

ABOVE EAST ENTRANCE TO THE HOUSE, WITH THE LIVING ROOM AT RIGHT.

ABOVE LEFT ENTRY FACADE (SOUTH) TO THE STUDIO PAVILION, WITH SEATS ON BOTH SIDES OF AN EXISTING BRIDGE ACROSS THE BASE OF THE GULLY.

LEFT MID-LEVEL LIVING ROOM, WITH PALM FROND-FIGURED WOODEN PANELS ALONG THE GABLE.

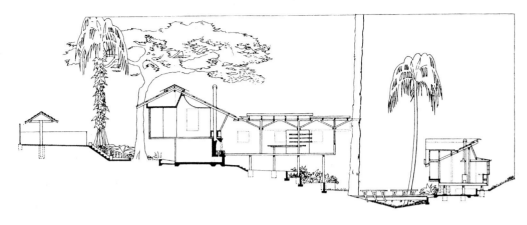

SECTION

flamboyant and dominating roofs –
also continue a prime theme of his
career; linking back to his early
observations of the *haus tambaran's*
(men's meeting houses) in PNG.

Externally, the Taringa roofs are
dynamic arrangements of ridges
and valleys – likened by Addison to
mountain ranges and including a
dramatic V inversion on the studio.
Internally, they vary the heights of
key rooms which conventionally
would have flat ceilings. They also
allow carefully placed windows to
snatch particular views or sunlight
filtering through the trees.

Ridgelines are ventilated by
raised strips of clear fibreglass
which allow hot air to escape under
their edges. The ridge of the living
area is internally lined by hinged
panels of plywood fretwork in leaf
patterns inspired by an overhanging
cabbage tree palm. These are
counterweighted with cords strung
with lead fishing sinkers and can be
flipped open on cloudy days to
gain more light.

Beneath those kinetic canopies,
both structures are timber-framed
with hardwood floors and wall
studs at 1200 mm intervals, clad
and braced with plywood sheets
and sashless, double-hung
windows. Upper zones are overlaid
with corrugated steel panels and
punctured with air vents.

The aerial highlight of this old
jungle compound is the timber sundeck projecting eastwards from the
living area – a skeletally slatted box
with collapsing corners and a lid
propped up to shade the platform.

In style and structure, it's another
nod from Brisbane to the
meticulously crafted huts which
have constantly inspired Addison.

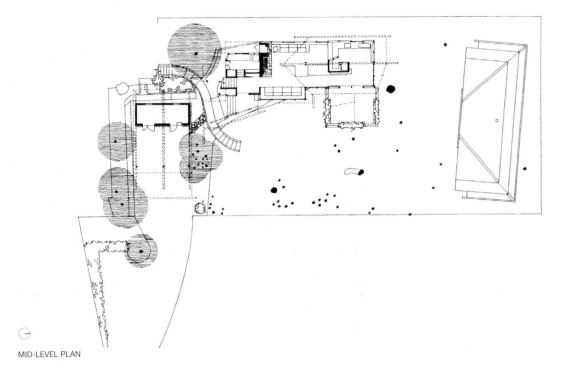

MID-LEVEL PLAN

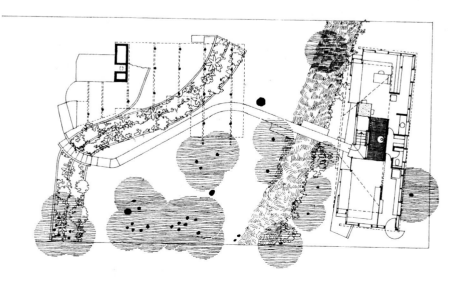

GROUND LEVEL PLAN

COURTYARD COMPOUND

ALEX POPOV, 1997
HOUSE AT MIDDLE COVE, NEW SOUTH WALES

ABOVE NIGHT VIEW OF THE MAIN COURT, LOOKING WEST.

OPPOSITE LOOKING UPHILL AT THE SOUTH-EAST FACADE OF THE LOWEST PAVILION, WITH THE MAIN BEDROOM ON THE TOP FLOOR.

ALL PHOTOS KRAIG CARLSTROM.

In traditional China, the family home was often a cluster of low pavilions built of rammed earth or bricks, sheltered by hipped roofs with wide eaves, arranged informally around a courtyard, and surrounded by substantial walls. Normally there would be only one penetration of the enclosure: an entrance fitted with wooden doors or a circular moon gate. The designs of these entries were important public displays of family style.

As a child in Shanghai, Alex Popov absorbed the idiosyncracies of many courtyard houses: learning, for example, the custom of moving off to one side after entering a compound – as a precaution to avoid the devil.

After Mao Ze-dong's Communist Party took power in 1949, Popov's Russian family was forced to leave China – and he grew up to be a globetrotter. He has since lived in Australia, Denmark and Spain, and travels regularly to Scandinavia and Europe.

That long background of close exposure to the crucibles of great architecture is evident in the mature and humane designs of his recent houses in Sydney. One evocative example is a residential complex of pavilions which 'dribble down' a sloping sandstone ridge to dramatically conclude at the edge of a harbourside cliff.

Although this is another of what Popov calls his 'big man's houses' – referring to eminent clients – the architecture avoids those European classical gestures – columns, pediments, monumentality – that are routinely exploited to signify status, wealth and conservatism.

Instead, it revives many aspects of the sociable Chinese housing of his youth – also seen in old villages of Bali, Sri Lanka and Japan.

As a particular inspiration, Popov acknowledges the sukiya-style Katsura palace in Kyoto, developed since the 17th century. It is a diagonal arrangement of pavilions connected by passages and covered by massive, hovering roofs of black thatch. Wide eaves allow windows and doors to remain open and balconies to be occupied during downpours; they also protect walls from weathering.

On arrival at the Sydney house, it seems to sink modestly behind a berm littered with decaying gum leaves. From the footpath, all that can be seen of the 800 sq metre hermitage is a pitched roofline of brown copper above a low, sand-tinted wall of rendered masonry – which is largely hidden in a trough, like a haha in an English field. There is a central entry porch and a steel-gated driveway.

As soon as the timber gate clicks and swings open, the stature of the complex is revealed – though not its extent. To the left and right of a descending staircase, garden terraces step down towards two cubic pavilions with copper roofs. These are linked by a roofed hall/foyer off the entry court – and by a first floor footbridge which dominates the prospect from the gate. It can be used as a stage for outdoor performances.

Inside the front door, the focus of the residence – a central lawn with an adjacent swimming pool – is revealed by a wall of glass.

Around that green blanket an assortment of structures are built in harmonious natural materials –

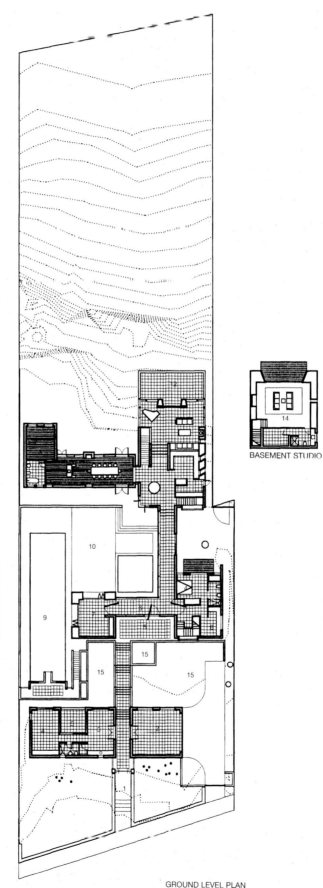

BASEMENT STUDIO

UPPER LEVEL PLAN

GROUND LEVEL PLAN

including a historic sandstone cottage which takes much of the site's harbour view. It was built in 1936 as a drafting office for staff of Walter and Marion Griffin, Chicago architects who began developing this bush locality after planning Canberra.

Now the Griffin cottage forms part of an informally luxurious domestic campus of colonnades, corridors, garden courts and cubic buildings with heavy masonry bases and glassy upper floors leading to balconies. These contain living areas, creative studios, playrooms and bedroom suites.

Externally, the architecture recalls an ancient fortified village, but inside, the atmosphere is sunny, modern and relaxed. Most rooms and corridors have good outlooks to at least one zone of the garden or the bush and harbour – but the whole situation is never revealed.

Navigating the complex is purposely indirect. Popov's floor plan includes a realignment of the prime walkway – a sudden shift to the right (as at Katsura) stops the devil rushing through – and this disjointed axis is intersected by many cross-paths. Numerous opportunities are also provided to 'dissolve' from the indoor spaces to spend time outside.

The irregular spatial layout is further complicated by the falling land – requiring frequent drops of floor level. On the other hand, Popov has 'expanded the cross-section' to create three storeys at the north-west end of the complex, thus rewarding those who arrive at these ultimate rooms with splendid views of a harbour bay beyond a curtain of gum trees.

ABOVE LEFT NORTH-WEST ELEVATION.

ABOVE FRONT ENTRANCE AND GALLERY, WITH MAIN COURTYARD AT RIGHT.

LEFT LOOKING FROM THE UPSTAIRS BEDROOM IN THE SOUTH CORNER OF THE HOUSE DIAGONALLY ACROSS THE MAIN COURTYARD.

PASTORAL HOMESTEAD

DENTON CORKER MARSHALL, 1998
SHEEP FARM HOUSE, KYNETON, VICTORIA

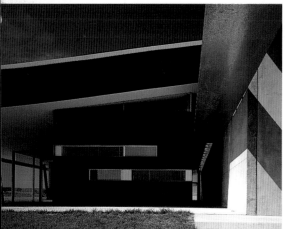

Foreign interpretations of Australian housing focus on light tin sheds and breezy verandahs isolated in picturesque landscapes in warm latitudes. But these models are opposed by some Melbourne architects who deal with coastal bush and rural highland sites that are frequently exposed to bitter south-westerlies off sub-Antarctic Bass Strait. Hostile weather requires bold resistance – buildings with walls oriented to break the wind and shelter living spaces.

Several Melbourne architects – Greg Burgess, Nonda Katsalidis and Kerstin Thompson – have built holiday houses which respond to rugged seaside sites with merchant navy allusions to tea chests, ship's prows and cargo containers.

Meanwhile, Denton Corker Marshall is building residences formed of concrete slabs, lodged firmly in excavated earth beside large, sparsely planted, walled courtyards. Ironically, these austere, cold-weather houses share many similarities with courtyard housing designed for hot Spanish and central American climates.

One recent example is a farm house at Kyneton, built on windy granite hills north-west of Melbourne. This bare countryside breeds sheep with ultra-fine wool.

When first seen from a ridge on the road, the house reads as a long, low streak of bald concrete tilt-up slabs (most are 4.6 metres high), in sombre tones. Although obviously a man-made structure, it offers no immediate signal that it might be a dwelling.

Arrival is by an avenue lined with aspen trees: a treatment which revives the tradition among colonial farmers to plant windbreaks of statuesque exotic species, proving more effective and elegant barriers than straggly native eucalypts.

The driveway ends with a cavity in one of the concrete walls, which allows entrance to a large gravel courtyard, relieved by a square grove of 16 olive trees and a line of Irish strawberry trees. The house is still not visible – it lies behind a doorway cut into a high black concrete slab which leans casually against the courtyard's east wall. It is another example of DCM's 1990s tendency to distinguish its buildings with tilted sticks, poles, blade canopies and wall planes. But it also has an important climate control function: to stand away from the house itself, isolated by an open passage (a 'breezeway') behind the courtyard, and thus to separately absorb much of the solar heat of high summer.

In terms of world architecture, the leaning black wall adds a novel idiosyncracy to a genre of austere and cubic courtyard residences which began with traditional Spanish-American pueblo dwellings and was updated by mid-century Mexican modernist Luis Barragán. The Kyneton house appears influenced generally by Barragán's style and by the raw concrete monuments of Tadao Ando in Japan; it also recalls (especially with its vertical wall slots) the classic Nuendorf house in Majorca (1989) by John Pawson and Claudio Silvestrin. As a local connection, University of Melbourne scholar Philip Goad links it to a farmhouse at Bouddi, north of Sydney, built by Barragán-influenced Melbourne architect

TOP LEFT LOOKING EAST ACROSS THE LANDSCAPE FROM THE NORTH VERANDAH.

BOTTOM LEFT LOOKING SOUTH-EAST TO THE LIVING ROOM FROM THE YARD, WITH THE MASTER BEDROOM AT RIGHT.

ABOVE LOOKING NORTH TO THE ENTRY FACADE FROM THE DRIVEWAY.

ALL PHOTOS TIM GRIFFITH.

EAST-WEST SECTION LOOKING SOUTH

EAST-WEST SECTION LOOKING NORTH

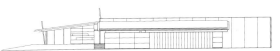
NORTH ELEVATION, MACHINE SHED

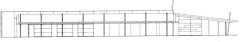
EAST ELEVATION, HOUSE

OPPOSITE TOP LEFT BREEZEWAY BETWEEN THE MAIN ENTRY WALL AND THE HOUSE, WITH ENTRANCE AT LEFT.

OPPOSITE TOP RIGHT LOOKING FROM THE LIVING ROOM THROUGH THE KITCHEN AND DINING AREA TO THE SOUTHERN TERRACE.

OPPOSITE BELOW LOOKING INTO THE ENTRY COURTYARD.

Guilford Bell (1912–92) for artist Russell Drysdale. Like DCM at Kyneton, Bell ignored Barragán's palette of sizzling ochres to instead employ cool whites and greys. Both projects also seem related to 1960s American land art.

But those aesthetic links rely only on the architecture of the courtyard. The house itself is a transparent structure under a massive mono-pitched roof – part of a hybrid composition like the Majorca office park by Alberto Campo Baeza and Luis Ignacio Aguerre (1995).

Built beyond the courtyard's leaning black slab (and entered through it), the house sits on a concrete platform at the edge of a knoll which commands a prospect across the farmlands downhill. It is a long pavilion (set across the ridge) of glass and metal. In winter, the interior is heated by an open fireplace and water coils in the floor slab; in summer, it is shaded by wide roof eaves.

When visitors slip through the slot in the black slab, into the mysterious beyond of the breezeway, they face yet another of the architecture's sequence of thresholds – this time, the ultimate door inside.

It opens into a lobby interrupting a north-south line of bedrooms, bathrooms and utility capsules – and the easterly outlook is initially restricted. Then the interior suddenly expands to the glassy living zone and the full rural panorama. This spectacle – where the sky is compressed under the hovering roof and the ground spreads out to the far horizon – contradicts the earlier confinements of the architectural journey.

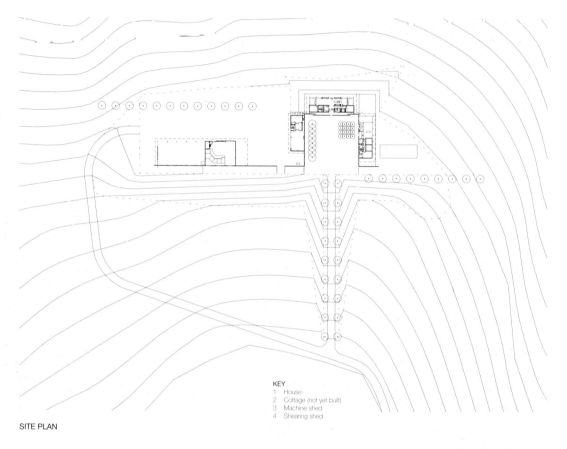

KEY
1 House
2 Cottage (not yet built)
3 Machine shed
4 Shearing shed

SITE PLAN

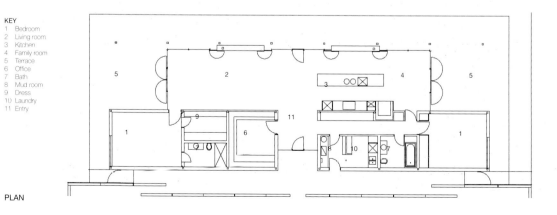

KEY
1 Bedroom
2 Living room
3 Kitchen
4 Family room
5 Terrace
6 Office
7 Bath
8 Mud room
9 Dress
10 Laundry
11 Entry

PLAN

EXEMPLARS CREDITS

ARCHERY 2000
Architecture and Landscape Stutchbury & Pape. **Developer** Olympic Co-ordination Authority. **Project Management** Keith O'Sullivan. **Engineering** Robert Herbertson, Ché Wall, Gary Seeto, Livio Chariot, Grant Potter. **Lighting Design** John Cully. **Environmental Advice** Ché Wall. **Construction** Cooinda Constructions.

ULURU-KATA TJUTA ABORIGINAL CULTURAL CENTRE
Architecture Gregory Burgess – Greg Burgess, Peter Ryan, Steve Duddy. **Engineering** PJ Yttrup & Associates, W.O. Ross & Associates. **Landscape Design** Taylor Cullity. **Construction** Sitzler Brothers.

GOVERNOR PHILLIP TOWER, GOVERNOR MACQUARIE TOWER AND THE MUSEUM OF SYDNEY ON THE SITE OF FIRST GOVERNMENT HOUSE
Architecture and Landscape Design Denton Corker Marshall (NSW) – Richard Johnson, Jeff Walker. **Developers** NSW State Superannuation with Comrealty, NSW Department of Planning, NSW Department of Public Works, City of Sydney Council, Historic Houses Trust of NSW, Friends of First Government House. **Project Management** Colin Ging & Partners, Peter Root & Associates. **Engineering** Ove Arup, TWA Consultants, Norman Disney Young, Ledingham Hensby & Oxley, Robert Fitzell Acoustics, Wilkinson Murray Griffiths. **Archaeology** Anne Bickford. **Conservation Research** Unisearch. **Artworks** Janet Laurence, Fiona Foley, Sidney Ball, Rodney Broad, Jan Senbergs. **Exhibition Development** Historic Houses Trust of NSW – Peter Watts, Peter Emmett. **Construction** Grocon, Concrete Constructions.

SUNSHINE COAST UNIVERSITY LIBRARY
Architecture Lawrence Nield & Partners Australia with John Mainwaring & Associates – Lawrence Nield, Neil Hanson, John Mainwaring, Annabel Lahz, Joanne Case. **Developer** Sunshine Coast University. **Library Consultant** David Jones. **Engineering** Taylor Thomson Whitting, McWilliams Consulting Engineers, Lincolne Scott, Steve Paul & Partners. **Landscape Design** John Mongard. **Interior Design** AHA Design. **Construction** Evans Harch.

STOREY HALL
New Architecture Ashton Raggatt McDougall – Howard Raggatt, Stephen Ashton. **Developer** RMIT University. **Engineering** John McMullen & Partners, Irwin Johnston & Partners, Watson Moss Growcott. **Conservation Advice** Allom Lovell & Associates. **Construction** Hansen & Yuncken.

OLYMPIC PARK RAIL STATION
Architecture and Landscape Design Hassell – Ken Maher, Rodney Uren. **Developer** Olympic Co-ordination Authority. **Project Management** Gutteridge Haskin & Davey. **Engineering** Tierney & Partners, Connell Wagner, RFA Acoustic Design. **Signage Design** Emery Vincent Associates. **Construction** Leighton Contractors.

DEAKIN UNIVERSITY BUILDINGS C-G
Architecture Wood Marsh (design) with Pels Innes Neilson Kosloff. **Developer** Deakin University. **Engineering** Meinhardt, Rimmington & Associates, Bassett Consulting Engineers, Carr Marshall Day. **Landscape Design** Tract. **Construction** Baulderstone Hornibrook.

MELBOURNE EXHIBITION CENTRE
Architecture Denton Corker Marshall. **Developer** Victorian Department of Business and Employment. **Construction Authority** Office of Major Projects. **Engineering** Ove Arup, Connell Wagner. **Construction** Baulderstone Hornibrook.

BOWALI VISITOR INFORMATION CENTRE AND PARK HEADQUARTERS
Architecture Glenn Murcutt & Associates with Troppo Architects. **Developer** Australian Nature Conservation Agency. **Engineering** Meinhardt (NT). **Landscape Design** Clouston. **Exhibition Design** Simons Lancashire Design. **Construction** PW Baxter.

MELBOURNE TERRACE
Architecture Katsalidis Architects – Nonda Katsalidis, Bill Krotiris, Holger Frese, Geoff Cosier, Dean Cass, Zvonko Orsanic, Nigel Fitton, Colin Sakinofsky, Kathie Hall, Jacqui Wagner. **Developer** Melbourne Terrace. **Engineering** Richard Eckhaus & Partners, Simpson Kotzman, Case Consulting Engineers. **Construction** Construction Engineering.

MOOLOOMBA HOUSE
Architecture Peter O'Gorman, Brit Andresen. **Engineering** John Batterham. **Leadlight** Peter Nelson. **Construction** Peter O'Gorman, Graham Mellor.

KEW HOUSE
Architecture Sean Godsell. **Engineering** John Mullen & Partners. **Landscape Design** Gordon Ford. **Construction** RD McGowan, AE Vickery.

POLL HOUSE
Architecture Gary Marinko Architects – Jill Marinko, Gary Marinko. **Engineering** Bruechle Gilchrist & Evans. **Construction** Name declined.

C HOUSE
Architecture Donovan Hill – Brian Donovan, Timothy Hill, Fedor Medek, Michael Hogg. **Engineering** Matthew Porl Nagy. **Landscape Design** Donovan Hill, Butler & Webb.

BALNARRING HOUSE
Architecture John Wardle. **Engineering** Street Moorehouse. **Construction** Kane Constructions (Vic), Mal McQueen.

GOTTLIEB HOUSE
Architecture Wood Marsh. **Engineering** John Garner & Associates. **Landscape Design** Gordon Ford. **Construction** HBC Building.

POOLE HOUSE 3
Architecture Gabriel and Elizabeth Poole. **Engineering** Bligh Tanner. **Construction** Barry Hamlet, Bill Smith.

ADDISON HOUSE AND STUDIO
Architecture Rex Addison. **Engineering** Mani Salmon. **Construction** Lon Murphy, Ian Campbell.

CHEN HOUSE
Architecture Rijavec Architects – Ivan Rijavec, Emma Young. **Engineering** Demelis Felicetti. **Construction** Bo Curtis.

NEWMAN/WOODHILL HOUSE
Architecture Grose Bradley – James Grose, Jon Florence, Nicola Bradley. **Engineering** PWG Patterson, Kaybond. **Developers and Construction** Rob Newman, Felicity Woodhill.

MIDDLE COVE HOUSE
Architecture Alex Popov. **Engineering** Bond James Norrie. **Construction** The Construction Connection.

SHEEP FARM HOUSE
Architecture Denton Corker Marshall. **Developers** Lyndsay and Noel Henderson. **Engineering** Bonacci Winwood. **Construction** Richard Buckley.

SELECTED READING

Apperly, Richard; Robert Irving, Peter Reynolds. *A Pictorial Guide to Identifying Australian Architecture: Styles and Terms from 1788 to the Present*. Sydney: Angus & Robertson, 1989.

Beck, Haig and Jackie Cooper. *Rule Playing and the Ratbag Element*. Basle: Birkhauser, 2000.

Bingham-Hall, Patrick. *Austral Eden: 200 Years of Australian Architecture*. Sydney: The Watermark Press, 1999.

Bingham-Hall, Patrick (ed.). *Olympic Architecture: Building Sydney 2000*. Sydney: The Watermark Press, 1999.

Birmingham, John. *Leviathan: The Unauthorised Biography of Sydney*. Sydney: Knopf/Random House, 1999.

Burns, Jenna Reed. *Australian Beach Houses: Living by the Sea*. Sydney: Lansdowne Press, 1999.

Carter, Paul. *The Lie of the Land*. London: Faber & Faber, 1996.

Cox, Philip. *Cox Architects: Selected and Current Works*. Master Architect Series I. Mulgrave: Images Publishing, 1994.

Drew, Philip. *The Coast Dwellers: Australians Living on the Edge*. Melbourne: Penguin Books, 1994.

Drew, Philip. *The Masterpiece: Jørn Utzon, A Secret Life*. Melbourne: Hardie Grant, 1999.

Drew, Philip. *Touch This Earth Lightly: Glenn Murcutt In His Own Words*. Melbourne: Duffy & Snellgrove, 1999.

Droege, Peter (ed.) *Intelligent Environments: Spatial Aspects of the Information Revolution*. Amsterdam: North-Holland/Elsevier, 1997.

Evans, Doug. *Aardvark: A Guide to Contemporary Melbourne Architecture* (with CD). Melbourne: RMIT, 1998.

Goad, Philip. *Troppo: Towards an Architecture for the Top End*. Sydney: Pesaro Architectural Monographs, 1999.

Goad, Philip. *Melbourne Architecture*. Sydney: The Watermark Press, 1999.

Gruzman, Neville. *Architecture Into Millennium 3*. Sydney: Lend Lease Corporation, 1993.

Hamann, Conrad. *Cities of Hope: Australian Architecture and Design by Edmond & Corrigan 1962–1992*. Melbourne: Oxford, 1993.

Hansen, Gilbert (ed.) *Imaginary Australia – B 52/53*. Århus: Arkitekturdsskrift B, 1995.

Howells, Trevor and Colleen Morris. *Terrace Houses in Australia*. Sydney: Lansdowne Press, 1999.

Irving, Robert (ed.) *The History & Design of the Australian House*. Melbourne: Oxford University Press, 1985.

Jackson Daryl. *Daryl Jackson: Selected & Current Works*. Master Architect Series II. Mulgrave: Images Publishing, 1996.

Jackson, Davina and Leon van Schaik. *40 UP: Australian Architecture's Next Generation*. Sydney: Lend Lease Corporation, 1999.

Jahn, Graham. *Contemporary Australian Architecture*. Sydney: Craftsman House/Gordon & Breach Arts International, 1994.

Jahn, Graham. *Sydney Architecture*. Sydney: The Watermark Press, 1997.

Johnson, Chris. *Shaping Sydney: Public Architecture and Civic Decorum*. Sydney: Hale & Iremonger, 1999.

Johnson, Paul-Alan. *The Theory of Architecture: Concepts, Themes & Practices*. New York: Van Nostrand Reinhold, 1994.

Judd, Bruce. *Designed for Urban Living: Recent Medium-Density Group Housing in Australia*. Canberra: Royal Australian Institute of Architects, 1993.

Keniger, Michael. *Australian Architects: Rex Addison, Lindsay Clare and Russell Hall*. Canberra: Royal Australian Institute of Architects, 1990.

Luscombe, Desley and Anne Peden. *Picturing Architecture: Graphic Presentation Techniques in Australian Architectural Practice*. Sydney: Craftsman House, 1992.

Margalit, Harry and Philip Goad. *Durbach Block: The Luminous Space of Abstraction*. Sydney: Pesaro Architectural Monographs, 1999.

McLeod, Ross (ed.). *Interior Cities*. Melbourne: RMIT, 1999.

Metcalf, Andrew. *Architecture in Transition: The Sulman Award 1932–1996*. Sydney: Historic Houses Trust of NSW, 1997.

Michell, George. *New Australia Style*. London: Thames & Hudson, 1999.

Moore, R. John and Michael Ostwald (eds.). *Hidden Newcastle: Urban Memories and Architectural Imaginaries*. Sydney: Gadfly Media, 1997.

Morrison, Francesca. *Sydney: A Guide to Recent Architecture*. London: Ellipsis, 1997.

Murphy, Peter and Sophie Watson (eds.). *Surface City: Sydney At the Millennium*. Sydney: Pluto Press, 1997.

Quarry, Neville. *Award-Winning Australian Architecture*. Sydney: Craftsman House, 1997.

Pickett, Charles. *The Fibro Frontier: A Different History of Australian Architecture*. Sydney: Powerhouse Publishing/Transworld, 1997.

Rollo, Joe. *Contemporary Melbourne Architecture*. Sydney: UNSW Press, 1999.

Seidler, Harry. *Harry Seidler: Selected and Current Works*. Master Architect Series III. Mulgrave, Vic: Images Publishing and Sydney: Craftsman House, 1997.

Spearritt, Peter. *Sydney's Century: A History*. Sydney: UNSW Press, 1999.

Stapleton, Maisy and Ian Stapleton. *Australian House Styles*. Mullumbimby, NSW: The Flannel Flower Press, 1997.

Stevens, Garry. *The Favored Circle: The Social Foundations of Architectural Distinction*. The MIT Press, 1999.

Taylor, Jennifer. *Australian Architecture Since 1960*. Canberra: The Royal Australian Institute of Architects, 1990.

Turnbull, Lucy Hughes. *Sydney: Biography of a City*. Sydney: Random House, 1999.

Van Schaik, Leon (ed.). *Tom Kovac*. London: Academy Editions, 1998.

Van Schaik, Leon (ed.). *Building 8: Edmond & Corrigan at RMIT* (3 vols.). Melbourne: Schwartz Transition Monographs, 1996.

Van Schaik, Leon (ed.). *Bell: The Life Work of Guilford Bell Architect 1912–1992*. Melbourne: Bookman Transition, 1999.

Van Schaik, Leon (ed.). *Transfiguring the Ordinary*. Melbourne: Printed Books, 1995.

Van Schaik, Leon (ed.). *Fin de Siècle?: And the 21st Century*. Melbourne: RMIT, 1993.

Vitta, Maurizio (ed.). *Grose Bradley: The Poetics of Materiality*. Milan: L'Arca Edizioni, 1998.

Walker, Bruce. *Gabriel Poole: Space in Which the Soul Can Play*. Noosa, Queensland: Visionary Press, 1998.

Wark, McKenzie. *The Virtual Republic: Australia's Culture Wars of the 1990s*. Sydney: Allen & Unwin, 1997.

Woolley, Ken. *Ken Woolley and Ancher Mortlock & Woolley: Selected and Current Projects*. Master Architect Series IV. Mulgrave, Vic: Images Publishing, 1999.

Zellner, Peter. *Pacific Edge: Contemporary Architecture on the Pacific Rim*. London: Thames & Hudson, 1998.

INDEX

INDEX

INDEX